THE IRISH MISSIONARY MOVEMENT
A Historical Survey, 1830–1980

GW00778073

EDMUND M. HOGAN

The
Irish Missionary
Movement

A Historical Survey
1830–1980

GILL AND MACMILLAN

Published in Ireland by
Gill and Macmillan Ltd
Goldenbridge
Dublin 8
with associated companies in
Auckland, Budapest, Gaborone, Hamburg, Harare, Hong Kong,
Kampala, Kuala Lumpur, Lagos, London, Madras,
Manzini, Melbourne, Mexico City, Nairobi,
New York, Singapore, Sydney, Tokyo, Windhoek
© Edmund M. Hogan 1990, 1992
First published in hardback 1990
This paperback edition published 1992
Print origination by
Seton Music Graphics Ltd, Bantry, Co. Cork
Printed by Colour Books Ltd, Dublin

British Library Cataloguing in Publication Data
Hogan, Edmund M.
The Irish missionary movement:
A historical survey 1830–1980
I. Title
266
ISBN 0-7171-1965-3

Contents

Acknowledgments

I AM especially grateful to Professor Oliver MacDonagh (Director of the Research School of Social Sciences at the Australian National University) for supervising my first excursion into the study of mission history. Some of the fruit of work conducted under Professor MacDonagh appears for the first time in this book. I am also indebted to Dr John O'Brien (Department of Modern History, University College, Cork) for guiding my second excursion, which resulted in a field study of missions in West Africa. In undertaking the present study, I wish to acknowledge the support and encouragement of my Provincial, Fr Con Murphy, S.M.A., who afforded me ample time and opportunity and took a keen interest in the project at all stages. I wish also to thank my colleagues in the Society of African Missions who bore with me patiently during the past two years and instinctively offered encouragement in those moments when I most needed it. To my own family, and especially my mother, Mrs Mary Hogan, I owe a deep debt of gratitude.

I thank the staffs of St Patrick's College Library, Maynooth, University College Library, Cork, the British Library, the Central Catholic Library, Dublin, and the National Library of Ireland for their efficiency and kindness in meeting my many requests. My task in completing the project was greatly assisted by the comments and suggestions of Professor Kathleen Boner, O.P. (University of Bophuthatswana), Fr Parig Digan (archivist, St Columban's Missionary Society), Sr Rita Dooney (archivist, Columban Sisters) and Hugh Brady (Viatores Christi), who read sections of the manuscript. I wish to acknowledge the kind permission of Fr Colm Cooke (St Patrick's Missionary Society) to use material from his M.A. thesis; also I am grateful to Fr Robert Trisco and Professor Andrew Walls, who allowed me to reproduce material first published in the *Catholic Historical Review* and the *Journal of Religion in Africa*.

Above all, I am indebted to the many people who responded so promptly to my letters of inquiry and questionnaires, whose names I am happy to record: Fr Con Clancy and Fr Frank McGovern (S.M.A. archivists, Cork); Fr N.-P. Douau (S.M.A. archivist, Rome); Fr Noel (C.S.Sp. archivist, Paris); Fr Leo Layden (C.S.Sp. archivist,

Dublin); Fr Michael Evans, S.M.A.; Br. Colman (Provincial, Marist Brothers); Fr Patrick Gantly, S.M.A.; Fr Gerard Marinan (Society of St Columban); Fr Séamus Galvin (Pontifical Mission Aid Societies, Dublin); Br. Matthew Feheney (Presentation Brothers); Fr Hugh Fenning, O.P.; Fr Tommy Greenan, S.P.S.; Fr Kevin Condon, C.M.; Br. Linus Walker (Patrician Brothers); Fr Henry Koren, C.S.Sp.; Br. Brendan O'Shea (Marist Brothers); Br. Austin Connolly (Irish Christian Brothers); Br. P. N. Dineen (Irish Christian Brothers); Fr Fergus O'Donoghue, S.J.; Fr Thomas Davitt, C.M.; Sr Pius O'Farrell, P.B.V.M.; Sr Philomena Jump, O.S.F.; Sr Angela Bolster (diocesan archivist, Cork); Sr Miriam Tracey (Holy Rosary Sisters); Sr Bertrand Flynn, O.P.; Bishop Joseph Whelan, C.S.Sp.; Bishop Richard Finn, S.M.A.; Bishop John Reddington, S.M.A.; Sr Patricia Langan (Assumption Sisters, Ballynahinch); Sr Catherine Dwyer, M.M.M.; Rev. Professor F. X. Martin, O.S.A.; Sr Koska McDonnell, O.L.A.; Fr Tom Riordan (Secretary, Medical Missionary Society, U.C.C.); Jarlath Dolan (Trócaire); Fr W. J. Mol, M.H.M.; Sr Miriam Cummins (St Louis Sisters); Mother M. Austin (Nazareth Sisters, London); J. W. Jackson (APSO); Sr Ann Marie Daly; Sr M. Magdalena (Mercy Convent, Baggot Street, Dublin); Fr Peadar O'Keane (P.P., Mallow); Fr Joe Egan, S.M.A.; Mgr F. Mocchiutti (Propaganda Fide Archives); Sr Monica McGinley (Medical Missions Sisters, Philadelphia); Rev. Dr James Good; Rev. Dr Alberto Olivoni; Dr Patrick Kiely, F.R.C.S.; Dr Eithne Conlan; Maurice Foley; Volunteer Missionary Movement Community, High Park, Dublin; Dr P. Urban Rapp (Augsburg); Fr Mario Marazzi (C.U.A. M.M.); Dr Robert F. O'Donoghue; Dr Joseph Barnes; Seán Kehoe; Paulo Danesi; Dr Julian Mac Airt; Fr Martin Walsh; Michael Ryan.

Lastly I want to thank Fr Bernard Cotter, S.M.A., for reading through the manuscript and helping in its final preparation, and Fr Bernard J. Raymond, S.M.A., who made his extensive photographic skills available in the preparation of the plates.

Introduction

I

IN 1967 Joseph McGlade's study *The Missions: Africa and the Orient* was published as part of *A History of Irish Catholicism* under the general editorship of Professor P. J. Corish. This slender volume marked the first attempt at a comprehensive and scholarly treatment of the Irish Catholic contribution to the evangelisation of non-Christian peoples in the modern period. Fr McGlade wrote at a time when little serious research had been conducted into the subject, and his achievement is all the more creditable on this account. In particular he succeeded in providing a remarkably thorough outline of the complex Irish contribution. At the same time the absence of a solid body of research inevitably produced weaknesses, such as the tentative treatment of the movement's origins. Moreover, the study suffered from a lack of contextualisation and the absence of an intellectual framework.

In the early 1970s the Department of Modern History at University College, Cork, then under the guidance of Professor Oliver MacDonagh, promoted a series of studies by postgraduate students on aspects of the modern missionary movement. These attempted to situate Irish enterprise within the wider context of Ireland's religious and secular history, and to consider also linkages with European expansionism. A more rigorous analysis of the movement's origins and structure was also a feature of these studies. The current volume is based on the fruit of this research and on a number of more recent studies conducted by Irish historians. It goes without saying that many avenues still remain to be explored relating to the course of the movement and its impact.[1] The following pages, therefore, provide little more than an introduction which, it is hoped, will stimulate further scholarship.

II

In this study the term 'modern Irish missionary movement' is used to describe Ireland's involvement during the nineteenth and twentieth centuries in the evangelisation of peoples and races to whom the Gospel was unknown and who are henceforth described as 'non-Christians'; it does not include the extensive outreach to Irish emigrant communities or to predominantly Christian countries.

Such a definition, together with the distinction it postulates, requires justification; for to reject that Irish priests and religious who went to Newfoundland, North America, Australasia, England and Scotland were also truly missionary would be extremely rash. What is suggested here is that there was a fundamental difference in the motivation and organisational structure of the two missionary thrusts which allows a separate treatment of each. Irish missionaries to non-Christian peoples drew their inspiration largely from the continental missionary movement under way since the early decades of the nineteenth century; its purpose was to bring the light of faith to 'the poor abandoned souls still plunged in the darkness of idolatry'[2] who would otherwise be lost according to the harsh neo-scholastic interpretation of the theological principle *extra ecclesia nulla salus* ('outside the Church there is no salvation'). The Irish model of organisation—that of the institute dedicated *exclusively* to the work of non-Christian missions[3] whose members, though assigned to mission jurisdictions,[4] continued to belong to the institute[5]—was also of continental provenance. In contrast, Irish missionaries to America, Australia, New Zealand and the other destinations of Irish emigrants were motivated, above all else, by a desire to sustain the faith of their compatriots, at risk through lack of pastoral care. Moreover, their method of organisation, for the most part, was based on a model already well established in Ireland before the Great Famine of 1845-49: that of the seminary training students for secular priesthood in designated jurisdictions to which they were formally attached[6] at ordination.

In terms of the Church's own understanding of evangelisation, too, this distinction may be further validated. The Church has traditionally maintained a separation between 'missionary evangelisation' and 'pastoral evangelisation', regarding the former as a special activity directed towards those who have never heard the Gospel, and the latter as the pastoral care of those fully incorporated into the Church. One of the most important of recent statements on evangelisation, *Evangelii nuntiandi* (1976), while asserting that both expressions are 'intimately connected and mutually enriching',[7] continues to maintain the distinction. It is possible to argue that Ireland's two overseas apostolic thrusts reflected these different models of evangelisation; that the movement to non-Christians mirrored accurately the Pauline prototype on which the Church's concept of 'missionary evangelisation' is largely based, while the Irish Church's outreach to its diaspora, although encompassing elements of the Pauline model, approximated more to the image of 'pastoral evangelisation'. Because of its importance for the framework of this book, it will be necessary to pursue this issue at some length.

The Pauline model of 'missionary evangelisation', emerging principally from the pages of the Acts of the Apostles, comprised five elements, namely 'commission', 'exile', 'primary proclamation', 'consolidation' and 'mobility'. Commissioned by his church of origin, Paul embraced exile 'for the sake of the kingdom';[8] he preached to those who had no knowledge of the Gospel; once Christian churches were established, he proceeded to new locations for the same purpose; finally he revisited the young churches to heal divisions and ensure doctrinal integrity. No one will dispute that missionaries who followed the emigrant Irish were exiles 'for the sake of the kingdom'. Nor can it be doubted that they were commissioned by their church of origin, albeit informally. On the other hand—and herein lies the heart of the distinction between these and others who went overseas—their mission was primarily a chaplaincy apostolate, directed at Catholics very many of whom were compatriots. It is true that there were some striking exceptions to this pattern and that in almost all instances their apostolate was never limited to the Catholic constituency; but the thrust of 'primary proclamation', an essential feature of missions to the unevangelised, was more typically a secondary consideration. Whether one can characterise this apostolate as a work of 'consolidation' in the Pauline sense is open to discussion. Paul sought to confirm the faith of lukewarm Christians and to recover those who had strayed from authentic profession and practice. For Irish missionaries in many theatres, especially South Africa and parts of North America, the re-evangelisation of lapsed Catholics was an important element of the pastorate. But, on balance, pastoral care of those already in possession of an authentic faith, through the provision of Mass, the sacraments and Christian education, formed the major portion of the work undertaken. Finally, with regard to 'mobility' it must be said that priests working in diaspora locations rarely transferred to new jurisdictions once the Church had been placed on a sure footing, although there was always a measure of internal movement. Some were on temporary assignment from

Ireland and returned to their dioceses of origin, but in most cases they were already incardinated[9] in the jurisdictions where they worked.

In contrast, those who left Ireland to evangelise non-Christian peoples provide a perfect paradigm of the Pauline model of 'missionary evangelisation'. Such missionaries were clearly exiles 'for the sake of the kingdom'. They were sent by their church of origin, being supported and encouraged by significant elements within their local communities. Their mission was to those to whom the Gospel had never been preached. Finally, once the local church had been founded and consolidated, the agencies to which they belonged tended to transfer them to other areas of need.

Contemporary theology presents *'missionary* evangelisation' (the apostolate of missionaries) as a particular aspect of a wider reality, namely the Church's *'Mission* of evangelisation' (the apostolate of all Christians). The significance of this will be explored later.[10] It has also greatly expanded the concept of *missionary* evangelisation. The profile of the missionary apostolate, presented in the Vatican II Decree on Missions (*Ad gentes*, 1965), in *Evangelii nuntiandi* and more recently in the encyclical *Redemptoris Missio* (1990) and vigorously elaborated in theological writings, stresses the continuing importance of primary proclamation and the foundation of local churches. But it goes much further, portraying the missionary as an agent of human development, liberation, dialogue with other religions, justice and social change. What distinguishes the missionary above all else, according to contemporary theological description, is a commitment to the various 'frontiers' of the Church's universal Mission, frontiers which are fundamentally spiritual but present themselves in many forms. In practical terms, frontier evangelisation implies a ministry beyond well-established Christian communities, to people who have never heard the Gospel, to those whose faith is seriously at risk, to those who have become alienated from the Church, to those who are radically opposed to the spirit of Christianity, and finally to those who are victims of ignorance, prejudice, oppression, deprivation and the other extreme manifestations of humanity's rejection of God. *Redemptoris Missio* regards the re-evangelisation of those who have abandoned the practice of their faith as 'new evangelisation', and not as 'missions to non-Christians'. Nonetheless, it emphasises that the boundaries between both forms of evangelisation cannot be easily drawn. (See Appendix C for a discussion of this.)

The grounds for applying the title 'missionary' to Irish priests and religious who served the diaspora in the nineteenth century extend beyond the invocation of those elements of the Pauline model which attached to their apostolate. It is true that those who served the diaspora can be called 'missionary' because they went into exile 'for the sake of the kingdom' and because their ministry was never confined to the Catholic community. But there were other factors bearing directly on their pastoral care of compatriots (and other emigrant Catholics) which distinguished them from counterparts in the continental European churches and which merit a different description of their ministry. A precedent already existed for the application of the term 'missionary' to pastoral evangelisation conducted in circumstances of extreme hardship and where there was a real danger to the faith of baptised Christians.

Irish and English priests trained on the continent and returning to their homelands during penal times were commonly described as 'missionaries'. It was the perilous nature of their apostolate and the parlous state of the home churches which placed these priests in a different category from those enjoying easy access to communities unhindered in the practice of their faith. Irish priests and religious who devoted themselves to the service of diaspora communities in the nineteenth century often had to contend with conditions which were scarcely less arduous. Those working in British colonies in the opening decades were subject to legal restrictions which greatly inhibited their apostolate. Throughout most of the century in all theatres there was a critical shortage of financial and human resources. The vast extent of jurisdictions in North America, Australasia, Canada, South Africa and the Caribbean necessitated extensive travel, a burden which was often compounded by poor communications and sometimes by a difficult climate. Inevitably, too, many of these priests had to endure long periods of isolation, a function of the immensity of the territories to which they were attached, the frequently fragmented nature of settlement and the scarcity of personnel. The emigrant communities, apart altogether from the distress of dislocation, lacked cohesion and were easy prey for proselytising agencies. Ignorance of their religion, superstition and apostasy—the fruit of pastoral neglect—were endemic in many communities, especially in the early years. Irish priests and religious who followed the emigrants overseas were effectively working on a frontier whose boundaries were as much spiritual, psychological

and social as they were geographic. It was hardly surprising, therefore, that the home church should confer the title of 'missionary' on
those who engaged in such work. Nor is it difficult to see how the
designation is justified in terms of contemporary mission theology.

The foregoing discussion represents an attempt to establish for this
book an intellectual framework which reflects the reality of history
and at the same time facilitates the task of documentation. The
postulation of separate models (based on distinctions relating to
motivation, organisational structure and theological notions of
evangelisation) permits a description, with some degree of accuracy,
of *some* aspects of the general missionary contribution. To attempt a
description of *all* aspects, however desirable, would be a task of
unmanageable proportions, given the current state of scholarship.

In defining the status of the various nineteenth- and twentieth-
century Irish missionary ventures, distinctions based on motivation
and structure may generally be applied without undue difficulty.
The determination of status by the application of theological models
also poses no great problem in the generality of cases. There were,
however, a number of enterprises which are difficult to categorise
with accuracy. The missions to South Africa and the West Indies are
a case in point. The Maynooth Mission to India, too, poses some
difficulties. The purpose of the missionary seminary of All Hallows
during its earlier years requires clarification. Later in this study it
will be necessary to examine these enterprises in order to ascertain
their precise status as works of missionary evangelisation.

Finally, it must be said that the distinction between Ireland's two
missionary thrusts in the modern period was one of kind rather
than degree. In terms of the Church's apostolic mission, both were
of vital importance.

III

From the conclusion of its early medieval mission to continental
Europe[11] at the close of the ninth century until the third decade of
the nineteenth century Ireland played virtually no part in Roman
Catholic missionary enterprise. In the period before the Reformation political and social disruption and internal ecclesiastical
problems were among factors which inhibited the development of a
missionary dimension. After the Reformation the Catholic Church

became increasingly preoccupied with problems of survival. Indeed (as has been mentioned earlier) from the seventeenth century, when candidates for priesthood were compelled to train on the continent, Ireland itself was regarded as mission territory both by the Holy See and by Irish clergy. It was only in the early nineteenth century, when the veil of penal legislation had finally been lifted, that participation in overseas missionary activity again became feasible.

In modern times Ireland's first missionaries came from the Protestant churches. The 'Irish Auxiliary' to the Society for the Propagation of the Gospel was founded as early as 1714. Members of the 'Auxiliary' were to work in the American colonies, in South Africa, India, Japan and West Africa. No less active was the Hibernian Church Missionary Society, founded in 1814. Many Irish men and women also were involved in English or international missionary agencies, such as the South American Missionary Society, the Church of England Zenana Missionary Society, the Bible Churchmen's Missionary Society, the Moravian Missions, the Baptist Missions and the Methodist Missionary Society. Among the home-grown agencies were the Irish Presbyterian Missions and the Mission to Lepers. The story of these Irish Protestant missionaries has yet to be adequately told. Although this study is focused on the Catholic missionary movement, a glance at the work of Protestant missionaries suggests that the scale of their involvement may have been proportionately as great as that of their Catholic counterparts.

IV

In Ireland the closing years of the nineteenth century saw the virtual resolution of the land and education questions, while the opening years of the twentieth century were dominated by the struggles for self-determination and ultimately national independence. The growth of the modern Irish missionary movement was another significant development during this period. While in recent years an increasing number of studies have set out to document the social and political upheavals, the missionary movement has received scant attention from historians. The reasons for this neglect are not difficult to uncover. Any historian approaching the topic quickly discovers that there exist a number of factors which hinder the work of documentation. In the first place, the Irish missionary's singularly poor standard of record-keeping (in contrast to his French counterpart) ensures that source material, when available, is often incomplete and disorganised. Secondly, almost all primary material is deposited in the archives or libraries of the mission dioceses, which are not always well organised, or in the holdings of the missionary societies and agencies where the rules for access are usually more rigid than in public archives and libraries. For example, up to very recently access to the archives of the Congregation for the Evangelisation of Peoples (formerly the Congregation for the Propagation of the Faith), undoubtedly the most important Catholic holding, closed after 1903. Thirdly, the most readily available accounts of the modern Irish missionary movement are to be found in the magazines and journals published by the missionary societies, compiled with a view to securing financial assistance and recruits and therefore selective in their use of material.

Again, there has been a marked reluctance among historians to regard the missionary movement as an important historical phenomenon. In this connection it may be said that while exaggerated claims have been made for Irish missionaries by advocates of the movement, the fact remains that large numbers of highly motivated men and women possessing a considerable expertise have gone (and continue to go) abroad to influence the developing countries in Africa, Asia and South and Central America. By 1965 Ireland had 7,085 priests, sisters, brothers and laity working in these regions, as well as hundreds more at home engaged in providing support services.[12] In 1982, reflecting a decline in recruitment, the number stood at a total of 5,613 priests, brothers, sisters and laity working in some 86 of the developing countries, including 142 missionaries from the Protestant denominations, working in ten countries.[13] The impact of these missionaries has been all the more notable because their activities were never confined to catechesis or administration of the sacraments. Almost everywhere and from the early days Irish missionaries provided schooling and health care, as well as responding to a variety of other social and human needs. Whether in other respects this influence was less benign is beside the point. Accusations of cultural arrogance, religious imperialism and collusion in colonial exploitation have always been placed at the door of missionaries, and the Irish movement has not escaped. The validity of such criticism remains to be tested. However, considerable doubt may be cast on attempts to implicate Irish missionaries in colonial exploitation.[14] Moreover, a recent study of 'conversion' in the

African context suggests that, whatever the intentions of missionaries, what took place was more in the nature of an interaction or dialectic between religious traditions.[15] Yet leaving aside the quality of their influence, which is not at issue here, there can be no doubt that Irish missionaries have made a considerable impact in the countries where they worked. By the same token, the experience of a wide variety of cultures and societies, mediated through returning missionaries, has had its effect on Ireland. Because of the traditional esteem accorded to missionaries, their opinions have helped to shape Irish attitudes towards the wider community and in particular to the poorer nations. It may be claimed that Ireland's exceptional concern[16] with the problem of world poverty in recent times owes much to the missionary factor.

V

The high point in the origins of the modern Irish missionary movement occurred between the years 1916 and 1937 when there was a dramatic increase in the number of indigenous institutes established specifically for missionary activity. There is, however, a common tendency among those who have written on the topic to assume that the movement began with the formation of the first of these institutes, the Maynooth Mission to China, in 1916, and that the movement's origins were wholly indigenous.[17] Such claims are unhistorical. Rather the 'explosion of interest' which commenced in 1916 was the result of forces which had been building up for years and which were by no means all local or indigenous. More accurately the missionary renaissance must be seen as the logical outcome of a slow, laborious but ultimately successful struggle since the fourth decade of nineteenth century. The fact of the matter was that during most of that century the Church's missionary movement to non-Christian peoples was regarded by many in Ireland with a certain suspicion because of its peculiar provenance. For missionary enterprise was essentially a continental preoccupation and especially the preserve of the French Church—a church which to many Maynooth-trained clergy had done itself no credit during the storm of the Revolution, showing little of the tenacity which had characterised Ireland's response to a more devastating and prolonged religious persecution. The subsequent difficulty of the French Church in combating anticlericalism and secularism, and its persistent problems with doctrinal orthodoxy and fidelity to Rome, added fuel to fire. Indeed, the French Church was accused not only of weakness but also, on occasions, of collusion in the promotion of French colonial ambitions. Such accusations had their roots in the understandable efforts of the French Church to reach an accommodation with anticlerical governments from the 1850s onwards.[18]

But even if it had been so disposed, the Irish Church was in no condition to participate, to any significant degree, in the work of 'non-Christian missions' (commonly but inaccurately termed 'pagan missions') during most, if not all, of the nineteenth century. Since the early part of that century its energies were almost totally absorbed in coping with the task of internal reform, with the need to provide for its growing diaspora and with its new role of leadership in the national life.

By the early decades of the twentieth century, however, the situation had been transformed. In the first place, the suspicion towards missions had been gradually eroded by agencies from the continent which had penetrated Ireland from the late 1830s. It was these also which were largely responsible for introducing the modern missionary impulse to Ireland. Secondly, by the end of the first decade of the twentieth century the Irish Church had fully overcome the problems caused by centuries of oppression and was at last unified, disciplined, organised, self-confident and capable of looking outwards beyond its diaspora. Thirdly, new cultural and political forces were stirring which favoured a national missionary movement. It was against such a background that the missionary renaissance of the twentieth century emerged.

PART ONE

The
Irish Background

ONE

The Irish Church
after Catholic Emancipation

I

THE middle years of the nineteenth century heralded a period of unprecedented growth in the Irish Church. The penal laws had been relaxed at the end of the eighteenth century, and the achievement of Emancipation, involving as it did a concerted mass movement among the Catholic population, created a new confidence. There were still some grievances outstanding, such as the position of the Established Church and the government's reticence on the question of Catholic education; but in the sphere of internal church organisation and functioning a new freedom had been granted. The foundation of six major seminaries between 1782 and 1837 (including Maynooth College in 1795) ensured that there would be a clergy capable of using this new-found freedom. In contrast to the clergy of penal times, who had been educated on the continent and were generally imbued with the conservative and reactionary ideas of the *ancien régime*, priests trained at home were, in the main, anxious for reform in social and political matters as well as in religious.[1]

From the second decade of the century onwards the Irish Church witnessed a sustained and substantial increase in its cadres of secular clergy, a spiralling in the numbers of regular clergy, women religious and brothers,[2] and a steady growth in church construction. In the post-Famine period this expansion was all the more striking since it took place at a time when the Catholic population was enduring considerable hardship and was rapidly declining because of high mortality and emigration.[3]

Undoubtedly the most pressing requirement for this emerging church was to weld its highly localised, quasi-independent diocesan organisations into a unified national structure, subject to a common discipline, adopting a common administrative code and subscribing to a single leadership. Even without any additional complicating factors, it was obvious that attempts to reorganise would not be easy, because of the strong tradition of local autonomy in the dioceses and the fact that the clergy were drawn from a wide variety of backgrounds. But another factor impinged: the new status and strength of the Irish Church since the repeal of the penal laws had placed it in a position of leadership in the social and political life of the nation. The controversy relating to the exercise of this role made its already onerous task of internal reorganisation and harmonisation even more difficult to accomplish.[4]

Nor were the Church's preoccupations limited to questions of internal reform or the problems of leadership. There was also the vexed question of Catholic education. In 1831 the National Schools system was introduced, and although there was dissatisfaction in some ecclesiastical quarters, Archbishop Daniel Murray of Dublin and the clergy of the *ancien régime* secured its acceptance. The arrival of Paul Cullen as Archbishop of Armagh in 1850 marked the beginning of a bitter campaign against the non-denominational system which was to endure into the last decade of the century.[5] In secondary education the situation was even more grave. Before 1878 no state provision for the promotion or support of Catholic secondary schools existed. Much agitation was required before the Intermediate Education Bill was eventually introduced in 1878. The 'university question' was scarcely less intractable. The non-denominational Queen's Colleges were generally unacceptable to the hierarchy, which in 1854 set up its own university. A long period of bargaining followed before an acceptable solution emerged in the first decade of the twentieth century.[6]

II

A further responsibility facing the Irish Church was her emigrants. In the half-century before the Famine (1845-49) almost a million had gone to North America, while at least half that number had emigrated to England and Scotland. Ever since the Famine, emigration to America, Canada, Australia and New Zealand had been gathering momentum. In the years 1850-60, it is estimated, the number of Irish in the U.S.A. increased from 962,000 to 1,611,000. By 1871 the figure had risen to 1,850,000, and in addition there were 200,000 Irish in Australia and 220,000 in Canada. Emigration to England and Scotland also continued on a significant scale. The number of people leaving Ireland annually in the second half of the nineteenth century fluctuated between 50,000 and 70,000.[7]

From the 1830s the mission to this diaspora became a major concern for the Irish Church. Increasing numbers of secular and regular clergy followed the emigrants, forming, in due course, the significant element in the emerging American and Oceanic Churches. The formation of an institute which was to cater largely for the needs of this diaspora took place in 1842. In that year Fr John Hand, from Phibsborough parish in Dublin, petitioned the Congregation for the Propagation of the Faith (henceforth cited as Propaganda Fide) for permission to open a 'foreign missionary seminary'.[8] The project was supported by Archbishop Murray, Daniel O'Connell and many of the leading Dublin clergy; Dr Paul Cullen, then Rector of the Irish College in Rome, also gave his support. On 28 February 1842 a rescript of approbation was received from the Holy See, and the seminary, named All Hallows College, opened in November. Hand's assertion that there were in Ireland 'some hundreds of young men . . . who would gladly offer themselves for the foreign missions' was fully justified. By late 1843 there were 46 seminarians in the college, and at the time of his death in 1846 there were 120 candidates for the priesthood under instruction.[9]

Before the foundation of All Hallows the diaspora was served from continental seminaries, such as the Collège du Saint-Esprit and the Sulpician colleges, by the religious orders and, increasingly, by Irish diocesan seminaries. St Kieran's College, Kilkenny, founded in 1782, was sending priests to Newfoundland and the maritime provinces of Canada from 1813; and in the decade immediately before the Famine the English Benedictine Dr W. B. Ullathorne, on his appointment to the Australian mission, recruited a group of students from St Kieran's. St Patrick's College, Carlow, which opened in 1793, provided some of the first Irish priests to serve overseas, including John Therry, who ministered in Australia, and John England, who later became Bishop of Charleston, North Carolina. Priests educated at Maynooth College, Ireland's national seminary, went overseas from the 1830s onwards, some recruited for Australia by Ullathorne and others to vicariates in India. St John's College, Waterford, founded in 1807, became a major source of supply for Newfoundland in the 1830s and 1840s, while St Peter's College, Wexford, established in 1819, formed a connection with the Cape Province in South Africa during the same period.[10]

Among the factors which drew many Irish clerics and religious overseas in the pre-Famine period were the steady stream of emigrants to British colonies since the closing decades of the eighteenth century, the repeal of laws against religious freedom culminating in the 1829 Emancipation Act,[11] and Propaganda's requests for administrators and priests to staff new vicariates. Indeed, as Fr Kevin Condon points out in his excellent survey of this subject, the decade before the Famine was 'one of the most active missionary periods of the century'.[12]

After the Famine priests continued to go overseas from the Irish diocesan colleges in increasing numbers, some for temporary service, many more offering permanent commitment, Nonetheless, the great majority of Irish priests serving overseas was supplied by Fr Hand's foundation. Between 1840 and 1900 All Hallows sent over 1,500 priests abroad, the vast majority to the new homes of the emigrant Irish.

III

From an early stage, too, Irish convents were active in supplying personnel for overseas apostolates. A group of five Sisters of Charity, from Stanhope Street Convent, Dublin, were among volunteers who accompanied Ullathorne to Australia in 1839. In the same year the Ursuline convent in Cork responded to requests for assistance from William Clancy, Vicar Apostolic of Georgetown, British Guiana. Dr Richard P. Smith,[13] first appointed a bishop in the West Indies in 1836 (and from 1851 Archbishop of Port of Spain), attracted a number of sisters (as well as priests) from his native diocese of Ardagh and from neighbouring Kilmore. Similarly, William Collier, an Irish national of the English Benedictine community, entrusted with the vicariate of Mauritius Island in 1840, was able to supplement volunteers from All Hallows with a group of Irish Loreto Sisters. In 1841 a contingent of Loreto Sisters and groups from the Presentation convents in Rahan and Maynooth accompanied Dr Patrick Carew to India. Presentation Sisters first went to Newfoundland in 1833, making nine foundations in the archdiocese of St John's and three in the diocese of Harbour Grace by the close of the century. By the same time there were seventeen Presentation foundations in eight U.S. dioceses and fourteen in seven Oceanic jurisdictions. The first Irish Sisters of Mercy to serve abroad went from Dublin to Newfoundland in 1842. In the following year a foundation was made in Pittsburgh by sisters from the Carlow convent. In 1846 sisters from Dublin opened a convent in Perth, Western Australia. The year 1849 saw two further Oceanic foundations: the Limerick convent provided sisters for Glasgow, while Carlow made its second extension to Auckland. Other Mercy foundations were made in Buenos Aires (1856), Brisbane (1860), Adelaide (1880), Belize (1883), Jamaica (1890) and South Africa (1897). Irish Dominican Sisters from Cabra made foundations in New Orleans (1860), Cape Town (1863) and Adelaide (1868); the Sion Hill convent established missions in Port Elizabeth (1867), Dongarra, New Zealand (1867) and Perth, Western Australia (1899); the Kingstown (now Dún Laoghaire) house sent sisters to New South Wales (1867). Irish sisters who went overseas during the nineteenth century were mainly occupied in education and child care (orphanages), although they also made their mark in nursing and other forms of health care.[14]

While Irish Christian Brothers were active in England from 1825, the first Irish institute of brothers to establish permanent works on another continent were the Patrician Brothers (Brothers of St Patrick), who went to Los Angeles in 1848. A foundation made by Irish Presentation Brothers in Pittsburgh three years earlier had been soon abandoned. Similarly, ventures by Patrician Brothers in Baltimore (1846) and Irish Christian Brothers in Gibraltar (1835-37) and Sydney (1843-47) had failed to endure. Irish Christian Brothers returned to Australia in 1869, establishing nineteen houses there before the end of the century. In 1876 they extended to New Zealand and Newfoundland, and in the same year they returned to Gibraltar. In the years 1890-94 they established five houses in India, and in 1897 made their first foundation in South Africa at Kimberley. Patrician Brothers commenced their Indian mission with a foundation at Calcutta in 1875. Five years later they came to Australia in the wake of the New South Wales Education Act of 1879 which made education 'free, secular and compulsory'. Responding to invitations from the local church, they founded schools in Maitland, Goulburn and Bathurst; in the early 1890s, on the invitation of Cardinal Moran, they came to Sydney. Presentation Brothers made foundations in England at Dartford (1878) and Orpington (1893); early in the following century they were to establish themselves in Canada. Irish brothers who went overseas during the nineteenth century were principally engaged in the provision of schooling and orphanages.[15]

IV

It is clear from the foregoing that from the early decades of the nineteenth century onwards the Irish Church was greatly pre-occupied with renewal and reform, Catholic education, political and social questions and the problems of the diaspora. One would hardly expect, therefore, to discover a notable interest in 'non-Christian missions', still less an organised apostolate. Such an interest and commitment could only be expected from a church which was sufficiently self-assured to look outwards beyond the diaspora, or which possessed a strong living tradition of mission to the unevan-gelised. The Irish Church, unlike its French counterpart, had no such tradition—the early medieval impulse had petered out before the tenth century—nor, as has been indicated, did it come to terms with its structural and pastoral problems until the close of the nineteenth century.

Yet it would be wrong to conclude that Ireland was altogether unmoved by the plight of the 'poor abandoned pagan souls' which was causing such a stir among continental Catholics. Fr John Hand was one of a number of clergy and laity who were deeply affected and who vigorously promoted the cause of 'non-Christian missions' in Ireland through the activities of the Association for the Propa-gation of the Faith (A.P.F). It would be equally untrue to maintain that Irish priests and religious who were stationed abroad ministered only to their compatriots or to Catholics. Irish missionaries in South Africa, the Caribbean and Mauritius, in particular, were involved in a apostolate to non-Christians as well as to Catholics. In other locations Irish personnel attached to French congregations often found themselves in the front line of non-Christian missionary enterprise.

Nevertheless, Ireland's commitment to 'non-Christian missions' in the nineteenth century never achieved the coherence of a move-ment. Those attached to continental agencies, as we shall see later, were in most cases unable to influence opinion at home; while the alumni of All Hallows and other colleges who went overseas were commonly regarded as pastors to the emigrants, although their apostolate inevitably encompassed a much wider constituency. The A.P.F., through its journal and its fund-raising activities, did help to promote an awareness of the continental movement, particularly among the laity. For many clerical supporters, however, the A.P.F.

was valued chiefly for its capacity to fund diaspora missions. In any case, there could be no question of an Irish movement, because 'non-Christian missions' failed to capture the imagination of those in leadership roles within the Irish Church, overburdened by other preoccupations and often distrustful of continental Catholicism.

TWO

The Role of
All Hallows College

THE relationship between Fr Hand's project and Irish missionary endeavour among non-Christians is a subject of some complexity. There can be no dispute that Hand's inspiration came from his contacts with the Association for the Propagation of the Faith, for which he was an organiser, and from his readings in the *Annals* of that association.[1] The *Annals* highlighted the work of primary evangelisation conducted mainly by continental missionaries in the Far East, Africa, Oceania, the Americas and the Caribbean. And yet, although Hand was probably better informed on this subject than most other Irishmen of his time, his college was to become a power-house for Ireland's great outreach to the diaspora. Statistics clearly bear this out. Of the 1,407 priests trained in All Hallows in the period 1840-96, 596 ministered in the U.S.A., 406 in Australia and New Zealand, 66 in Canada and Newfoundland, 176 in England and Scotland, 53 in India and South Africa, 42 in the West Indies, 6 in Mauritius, 5 in Argentina, and 1 in Scandinavia.[2] Irish diaspora communities were to be found in all of these missions with the exception of Scandinavia and Mauritius.

I

Whether Hand intended his foundation to develop in this way is to be doubted. Kevin Condon in his history of All Hallows maintains that there was a certain confusion surrounding the purpose of the seminary at the time of its establishment.[3] This is readily shown by an examination of various written proposals and submissions penned by Hand between 1840 and 1842. In his first attempt to canvass support, made in the autumn of 1840, Hand outlined at considerable length how the seminary should be financed, organised and governed. The question of what missions would benefit was not formally addressed, but his views may be inferred from a number of remarks made in the course of the paper. Students, he wrote, should learn to speak French, since the language 'may be necessary or very useful for them in some of the missions to which they may be sent'.[4] The *Annals*, he hoped, would assist in inspiring recruits

> to extend the Empire of Jesus Christ and to rescue from the slavery of the devil some of the millions of our fellow-creatures who are at present either buried in the darkness of idolatry, or labouring under the greatest spiritual distress from a want of priests.[5]

England, Scotland, the colonies, America and India, he wrote, were to be 'classed under the name of "Foreign Missions"'.[6] From these excerpts we may surmise that Hand envisaged a seminary which would provide priests mainly for the British and French colonies whose apostolate would embrace both primary evangelisation of indigenes and pastoral care of emigrants. Hand's *Circular to the Irish Bishops*, distributed in December of the same year, although less informative, disclosed a similar design. The object of the college, he wrote, would be:

> To promote the glory of God, to extend the kingdom of Christ, and to procure the salvation of numberless souls, who would otherwise be lost forever, seated as they are in the shadow of death, and having no one to break for them the Bread of Life.[7]

In the event, after permitting Hand an interview at their Dublin meeting on 5 February 1841, the bishops of Ireland rejected his scheme, although individuals such as Archbishop Daniel Murray encouraged him to persevere.

Hand's petition to Cardinal Fransoni, Prefect of Propaganda, for authorisation to open the college, made a year later while in Rome, contained the declaration that the college would provide 'for the spiritual distress now existing among the millions of *our Catholic brethren* in all the British colonies, in America, and in other countries abroad' [my italics].[8] This declaration marked an important departure from Hand's original scheme in that it omitted a specific reference to the French colonies and made no mention of primary evangelisation. Yet a *Prospectus* published by Hand in February 1842, after Propaganda had given its approval, indicated that the college would give equal priority to diaspora *and* non-Christian missions and commented on the latter in terms which reflected the influence of the continental movement:

> It is a lamentable truth, that 500 millions of our fellow-creatures throughout the world are, at this moment, buried in the darkness of idolatry, and given up to all the abominations of heathen superstition. It is equally true that, in the vast extent of the English colonies and America, there are millions of Christians of various denominations, and even of Catholics, perishing for want of spiritual food; and that there are but few, and in very many places, no missionaries to break for them the Bread of Life.[9]

II

This confusion concerning missionary objectives was part of a wider uncertainty which attended the project's planning phase. Such uncertainty was unavoidable, not least because the establishment of a missionary seminary had no precedent in the history of the Irish Church. Lacking guidelines from the past, Hand was faced with the daunting task of devising a method of financing the seminary as well as an appropriate system for its supervision and government. Hand had hoped that the bishops would assume responsibility, especially for the upkeep of the college. Their rejection of the scheme in its entirety appears to have been motivated by a lack of confidence in the youthful and inexperienced priest who appeared before them at their Dublin meeting. [10] But the hard-pressed financial circumstances of many dioceses certainly helped to influence the bishops' decision, making them reluctant to invest resources in a scheme which was bound to be costly and which at the end of the day might not succeed. Indeed, during Hand's lengthy absence on the continent (from February 1841 until June 1842), during which he studied models for his college and presented his case at Rome, there was a movement in Dublin to place the scheme in the hands of a committee of diocesan priests several of whom were associated with the Association for the Propagation of the Faith. The purpose, it seems, was to inspire greater confidence locally and to secure funding from the A.P.F.'s Dublin branch and from its Central Committee in Paris. [11]

It seems probable that Hand's preoccupation with the immediate problems of finance and organisation, even more pressing
after the bishops' rejection, left him little time to apply his mind
rigorously to the question of missionary destinations. When eventually he did address the issue in his petition to Cardinal Fransoni
his choice of the Irish Catholic emigrant communities over non-
Christian missions was hardly surprising. An enterprise catering for
both constituencies might have appeared unwieldy and over-
ambitious and therefore ran the risk of provoking a negative
response. Besides, Hand's supporters within the Irish Church were
clamouring for a college which would supply the diaspora, and their
views were almost certainly known at Propaganda. Archbishop
Murray was finding it increasingly difficult to meet the numerous
requests for personnel which came from the British colonies.[12] Dr
Cullen, for his part, although in Rome, was keenly aware that Irish
dioceses and the existing seminaries lacked the capacity to shoulder
the burden. Already in February 1840 he had received a letter from
Fr Myles Gaffney, Dean at Maynooth College, stating that the
supply of volunteers for India and Australia had greatly diminished.[13] Other bishops whose assistance had been solicited were
equally convinced of the need for an independent missionary
seminary to serve the diaspora.

While Hand's decision to highlight the needs of the diaspora
made good sense in the context of a petition to the Holy See, there
can be no doubt that he himself passionately believed in the
importance of both apostolates. On the one hand he shared with
leaders of the continental movement, like François Libermann, a
burning desire to bring the faith to those 'in the shadow of
darkness' through ignorance of the Gospel. On the other hand, as
Fr Condon points out, 'he was convinced that Ireland, as the chief
Catholic country in the empire, was the natural centre from which
Catholicism should reach out to the British colonies',[14] territories
which in many cases contained communities of Irish emigrants.
Hand had been greatly impressed by John England, Bishop of
Charleston, who in an article in the *Annals* made a strong case for
an Irish apostolate to emigrants in the southern states of the Union;
and he was influenced too by the appeals of Dr Ullathorne on
behalf of Australia. But he was equally moved by reports in the
Annals of the plight of the unevangelised in Africa and the Orient.
Thus, once the question of Roman approval was settled, he

proceeded to widen the seminary's scope to include non-Christian missions. His *Prospectus* of February 1842, aimed at attracting subventions from prominent Catholics in Rome and England, and which probably revealed his true state of mind, envisaged a seminary whose alumni would serve overseas wherever priests were required.

But while Hand intended his college to develop in this way, his Irish supporters remained adamant that it should concentrate on the needs of Irish emigrants in Australia and America and in those missionary jurisdictions already entrusted by Propaganda Fide to Irish ecclesiastics, such as Calcutta, Madras, the Cape of Good Hope, the West Indies and Mauritius where Catholic communities (containing in most cases an Irish component) already existed. The fact that after the Famine the main thrust of the college was directed towards Australia and America was perhaps inevitable. Indeed, already during Hand's short presidency of All Hallows the tendency to give first preference to emigrant missions had emerged. The seminary's interest in the Maynooth Mission to India was not sustained. And the expectation of Mgr Edward Barron, founder of the first nineteenth-century Catholic mission to West Africa, that the college would supply his vast vicariate with priests, was never fulfilled. By 1853, when Dr David Moriarty, President of All Hallows, published a *Prospectus* to raise funds, the priority of the diaspora was firmly established, although missions to the unevangelised still feature.[15] That the project should have developed in this fashion was not surprising, given the overwhelming preference of Hand's supporters for the diaspora, his own premature death and the haemorrhage of emigration which occurred in the post-Famine period.

THREE

The Irish Church and Non-Christian Missions, 1830–1880

THE principal Irish contribution to the evangelisation of non-Christians in the half-century which followed the disappearance of penal legislation in the colonies was made by priests and religious working in South Africa, the Caribbean and Mauritius and by Irish personnel attached to continental missionary agencies. The scale of this enterprise and its influence on the Irish missionary movement which emerged in the early twentieth century will form the subject-matter of this chapter. It will be appropriate, too, to consider at this juncture the Maynooth Mission to India. Although during the period under survey this mission was directed almost exclusively towards Catholics or those of Catholic parentage, and cannot therefore be considered as missionary enterprise to 'non-Christians', neither does it fit easily into the same category as the missions to Australia, Newfoundland, North America, England and Scotland. In the first place, there was no Irish settlement in India. The Irish in the region were almost all soldiers in the service of the East India Company and, later, of the British army in India. In the second place, these soldiers and their offspring from marriages or liaisons mainly with Eurasians or Indians, formed only a small grouping within the general Catholic community, while Christianity in all its forms represented a mere fraction of a population which was overwhelmingly Hindu and Moslem. It was the expectation of Propaganda Fide that the Maynooth mission should not only cater for the Irish and the wider Catholic community but also that it should reach out to non-Christians. In the event, the missionaries found it extremely difficult to discharge their responsibilities even to Catholics, and attempts to evangelise non-Christians were not to be made until long after the mission's direction had passed from Irish hands. Nonetheless, however we choose to classify the episode, it is a fact that the experience of failure by Irish secular priests who went to India was to have profound repercussions for future Irish enterprise in non-Christian cultures. It is primarily for this reason that a treatment of the subject is included in this section.

I

The Maynooth Mission to India

The Maynooth Mission to India began before the Famine, when the diaspora was still small. Calcutta and Madras, the principal cities of the province of Bengal (on the east coast), were the two centres of interest. It is estimated that by the early 1830s Bengal possessed some 25,000 Catholics, mainly Eurasians descended from the Portuguese soldiers and settlers of the sixteenth century. The Catholic community also included the so-called 'St Thomas Christians', originally from the Malabar (on the west coast), who, according to tradition, had first been evangelised by St Thomas the Apostle. Other Catholics in Bengal traced their religious ancestry to Francis Xavier in the sixteenth century. Some thousands more were employees of the East India Company, the instrument of British policy until direct British rule in 1858; of these the majority were Irish soldiers and their dependants.[1] Finally, there were groups of schismatics, largely of Portuguese origin. These had grown up in resistance to Propaganda Fide's long-standing efforts to suppress the *Padroado* (*Patronato*) arrangement whereby the organisation of missionary work and the nomination of bishops had been originally entrusted to the Portuguese authorities.

The Eurasian Catholics were an impoverished group and tended to congregate in the ghettos of Madras and Calcutta. The families of Irish soldiers, for whom little provision was made by the authorities, also suffered great hardship. In spiritual matters the East India Company, since its arrival, had rigidly excluded missionaries of all the Christian churches. Eventually after some thirty-four years of parliamentary agitation freedom to evangelise was accorded to the Protestant churches. And from the late 1820s well-funded Baptist, C.M.S. and Scottish Presbyterian missionaries were actively engaged in attempts to proselytise not only Hindus and Moslems but also the poorer Catholics. Orphanages and schools maintained by these missionaries were regarded by Catholic leaders as a serious threat to children of Eurasian origin and, most of all, to the orphans of deceased Irish soldiers.

In pursuance of Propaganda's efforts to eliminate the remaining vestiges of the *Padroado* legacy, and also in order to take advantage of the opportunities afforded by British expansionism in the region and the relaxation of penal legislation, Jesuits of the English province were introduced to Bengal in 1834 to staff the newly erected vicariate of Calcutta. However, within the space of four years sharp differences of opinion with Propaganda relating to policy led to the withdrawal of the vicar apostolic, Robert St Leger. Seeking a replacement who would be more amenable to its views (especially on the need for Catholic schools), Propaganda decided to transfer Dr Patrick Carew, formerly a Maynooth professor and at this time Vicar Apostolic of Madras, to the Calcutta jurisdiction. The appointment was made in the closing months of 1840.

Initially there were prospects for a worthwhile Irish involvement in Calcutta. In 1841 Bishop Carew brought out a group of twelve Loreto Sisters from Rathfarnham to take charge of an orphanage. A little later Dr Thomas Olliffe, Carew's deputy, returned from a recruiting drive in Ireland with three priests, eleven seminarians and a further group of Loreto Sisters. But soon the tide began to turn. In 1846 the English Jesuits were recalled to Europe after incessant squabbling with the bishop. Efforts to establish a teaching order patterned on the Irish Christian Brothers failed to prosper, while a preparatory seminary had to be closed because of the tragic deaths of three of its rectors in swift succession.[2] Most serious of all, the growth of the Irish diaspora in the aftermath of the Famine not only attracted away many likely candidates, but led several already committed to India to change allegiance. When Carew died in 1855 his successor, Dr Olliffe, soon came to the conclusion that only a religious institute could guarantee the regular supply of missionaries required to staff the vicariate. Accordingly in 1859 he relinquished responsibility to the Belgian Jesuits.

Irish involvement in Madras began in 1832 when Rome appointed Dr Daniel O'Connor, an Irish Augustinian, as vicar apostolic of the new vicariate of Madras. When Dr Patrick Carew—then a staff member at Maynooth—was designated to succeed him in 1838 a wave of enthusiasm swept Maynooth and many of the ablest men offered their services, including Fr John Fennelly, the college bursar.[3] Scarcely two years later, when Carew had been transferred to Calcutta, John Fennelly was appointed to succeed him. Fennelly's consecration at Maynooth in 1841 marked the high point of enthusiasm in Ireland. One of its more important manifestations was the decision by the Presentation convents at Maynooth and Rahan to accede to a request made earlier by Carew to send out contingents to Madras.[4] Shortly after their arrival the sisters took charge of an orphanage for the children of soldiers massacred in the recent Afghan War, previously in the hands of a group of pious ladies.

Bishop Fennelly soon realised that his vicariate could only flourish if a regular supply of priests was forthcoming from Ireland. Unconvinced that Maynooth was capable of meeting his requirements, he encouraged Fr John Hand, who at the time was proposing his scheme, to assume responsibility for India. But, owing to the factors outlined in the previous chapter, his hopes were not fulfilled, and by 1846 Hand was already writing to Fennelly apologising for the small number and poor quality of the 'Indian students'.[5]

In Maynooth itself interest died swiftly. Bishop Fennelly's younger brother, Stephen, had planned to come to Madras in 1844, hoping to bring with him a sizeable band of missionaries. However, by the time of sailing he could only muster one priest, three students, three brothers and five sisters.[6] When Stephen succeeded as vicar apostolic on the death of his brother in 1868 his first act was to return to Ireland in search of priests. Again the response was disappointing, and, like Dr Olliffe a decade earlier, he too was forced to the conclusion that any further attempt to maintain the mission as an Irish venture would be pointless. He stayed at his post for a further decade until such time as arrangements were made to replace the tired and ageing Irish contingent by members of Bishop Herbert Vaughan's St Joseph's Missionary Society, Mill Hill.[7]

The reasons for the failure of the Maynooth Mission to India are not difficult to uncover. The nature of the movement's motivation made it unlikely to succeed. The manner of its organisation and conduct, as well as changing circumstances in Ireland, made its demise inevitable. Much of the initial enthusiasm for India had been generated by the personal magnetism of Patrick Carew and the Fennelly brothers. Carew was regarded as a 'universal favourite' in Maynooth, where he had embarked on a promising career as Professor of Dogmatic Theology. And John Fennelly, as college bursar, also enjoyed a high degree of popularity.[8] But admiration for such men was altogether too insecure a foundation on which to build a successful enterprise. Had the movement been motivated by the spirit of missionary romanticism which helped to inspire the

French successes of the time—the sense of 'holy and sublime adventure for Christ's Kingdom'—it might have been better able to endure. However, there was no great concern within the Irish Church to bring the 'light of faith' to non-Christians in India. Instead the focus was placed firmly on pastoral care for Irish soldiers and their families and the protection of Catholic orphans from proselytisation by Protestant missionaries. The establishment of orphanages and schools by the sisters appeared to remove this latter threat. Already by September 1843 there was evidence that the enthusiasm of 1841 was on the wane. Stephen Fennelly, writing from Maynooth to his brother, commented on the increasing apathy among the students towards the mission. 'It would be well', he wrote,

> if something were done to render them a little more warm and enthusiastic on the subject. Some time ago it was only necessary to propose a Foreign Mission to the students and numbers of them generously offered themselves. This spirit . . . has gradually died away.[9]

Whatever prospects the mission had of surviving, the practical planning by the Irish prelates in India doomed it to certain failure. The volunteers went directly from Maynooth or their dioceses to the mission-field; and no one was assigned to supervise the flow of personnel from the homeland. Furthermore, conditions on the mission were difficult. The Portuguese schismatics in the region offered unrelenting opposition, while the mission's problems were compounded by a difficult climate and lack of funds. Finally, the catastrophe of the Irish Famine, which drew away many potential recruits to America and Australia, set a seal on the failure. Before the Famine the capacity of the existing Irish seminaries to supply overseas jurisdictions was already under strain. In its aftermath, when even the missionary seminary of All Hallows found itself unable to sustain an adequate supply of personnel to India,[10] only a special organisation capable of training its own priests could have hoped to succeed.

The only lasting Irish contribution to the Indian mission in the nineteenth century was accomplished by the sisters, and by brothers who set down roots from the mid-1870s. The Presentation Sisters survived the failure of the Maynooth movement and towards the end of the century were able to expand their educational activities beyond the Catholic community. Whenever continuity was threatened, small bands were dispatched from Ireland; Maynooth and Rahan sent reinforcements in the 1840s; in 1850 and on two subsequent occasions the Presentation convent at Mullingar provided personnel; in 1880 the Presentation convent at Castleconnell, Co. Limerick, came to the rescue, while in 1889 Presentation Sisters came out from Kilcock. The supply of Loreto Sisters to Calcutta was halted abruptly in 1844 when Propaganda ruled that according to their constitutions the sisters could no longer supervise a hospital entrusted to their care. Bishop Carew responded by re-forming the community into an independent diocesan institute. However, despite the rift, the Irish mother house continued to provide moral and financial support, and after reunion in 1881 the supply of personnel from Ireland was renewed. Thereafter the sisters expanded their apostolate in Southern India, providing (as they had always sought to do from the earliest days) educational services for children of all races. Brothers of St Patrick came to India in 1875 to take charge of the Catholic Male Orphan Asylum of Calcutta founded in 1840 by Bishop Carew. Benefiting from a regular supply of staff from Ireland, by the close of the century they had opened two additional establishments (schools) which catered for Indians as well as Eurasians and Europeans. Irish Christian Brothers began their apostolate in 1889 and within a decade had established six schools. In the following century they were to increase steadily their network of schools, catering for students of all races.

There is, however, an important reservation which prompts reluctance in stressing the significance of this enterprise by Irish religious for the missionary movement of the twentieth century—a reservation deriving from the Church's evaluation of the role of sisterhoods and brotherhoods in missionary activity. In theory, if not in practice, nuns and brothers were cast in the role of *assistants* or *auxiliaries* to the priest missionaries in the work of evangelisation. Had the Maynooth priests been successful, India would quickly have come to be regarded as an Irish mission. But with their departure, India was considered lost to the Irish Church, although the sisters and brothers continued to labour fruitfully into the twentieth century.

The experience of failure in India was etched deeply in the consciousness of Irish secular clergy. It was significant that the great missionary impulse of the twentieth century, spearheaded by Irish diocesan priests, found its outlet in Africa and China, and not in

India where the needs were equally urgent. The failure of the Maynooth venture may also have contributed to the suspicion with which some diocesan clergy tended to regard missionary projects in the years before the foundation of the Maynooth Mission to China. Perhaps such ventures were regarded as wasteful and not really the business of Irish secular clergy. This is a hypothesis which needs testing but seems probable. If it is accepted, then it must be regarded as an important factor in delaying the birth of the modern missionary movement. Finally, the experience of mission in India had at least one positive consequence, for when Irish diocesan clergy turned their attention to foreign missions early in the twentieth century they remembered the mistakes that had been made half a century earlier and established exclusively missionary institutes to ensure continuity and permanence.

II
The Mission to South Africa

If, in the early stages, many within the Irish Church had seen the mission to India as an attempt to provide for the diaspora, the same also could be said for initial perceptions of the South African mission. Yet in the case of South Africa too such perceptions were not always accurate, since, as will become apparent, more was involved than a chaplaincy apostolate to Irish expatriates and their descendants. The work, from its commencement, involved the wider European Catholic settler community and, with the passage of time, increasingly embraced those of mixed race and the African[11] population. Yet while the true nature of the Indian mission soon became evident, a similar clarification for the South African enterprise, and especially an appreciation of its dimensions as a mission to 'non-Christians', took longer to emerge. Part of the reason was undoubtedly the fact that the most signal advances in 'primary evangelisation' during the nineteenth century, namely the accomplishments of Oblate missionaries in Natal, appeared to have had no Irish connection; while the modest achievements within jurisdictions staffed by Irish missionaries occurred largely in the last quarter of the century and were insignificant in comparison with the triumphs of continental missionaries in the Far East, Africa and Oceania, as reported in the *Annals*.

There were also important differences between the Indian and South African enterprises which contributed to misunderstanding about the latter and account for its lack of impact on the Irish Church. The mission to India, through its association with May-nooth College, constituted a concerted effort by Irish diocesan clergy to manage and supply an overseas jurisdiction. To Irish secular clergy it possessed the coherence of a 'movement' in which they were intimately involved and whose fortunes they keenly scruti-nised. Inevitably its failure was bound to have repercussions for the future involvement of diocesan clergy in non-Christian lands. The mission to South Africa, in contrast, while drawing a handful of its personnel from the Irish diocesan clergy and from one diocesan seminary, was associated mainly with a variety of religious orders (several recruited from the continent and some from England) and especially with All Hallows College. Not least because of the pro-venance of its personnel, the mission tended to operate at a remove from the mainstream of Irish diocesan life. It is not surprising, therefore, that it was never to attract the same attention among the secular clergy as did India, and that until well into the following century an accurate understanding of its apostolate tended to be confined to those directly connected with the work.

In the event, alongside the pastoral care of European Catholics, the Southern African region provided a workable model of primary evangelisation although on a small scale. The Irish bishops who dominated the South African Church in the nineteenth century demonstrated that much could be done by securing the services of orders from Europe whose brief would be the evangelisation of Africans. At the same time they encouraged those whose principal charge was the care of Europeans to reach out also to those of mixed race and to Africans. It is true that there were disappointments, such as the decision of the Society of African Missions of Lyons, introduced by an Irish bishop, to withdraw from its mission. Moreover, the circumstances under which the apostolate was conducted were hardly conducive to the work of primary evange-lisation. Apart from a serious and persistent shortage of resources, the missionaries had to contend with the prior claims of a neglected Catholic community scattered over a wide area, disruptive conflicts between settlers and tribal groupings, deeply rooted prejudices against Catholicism among other Christian denominations, and an antagonism among many settlers towards the evangelisation of non-Europeans (and especially against the provision of schools, which were believed to promote insubordination).[12] Nevertheless, in spite of the problems and setbacks, by the turn of the century a solid foundation had been laid for the future of Roman Catholicism among Africans and people of mixed race. How the Church built upon this foundation in the twentieth century is not relevant here. A proper appreciation of the achievements of Irish missionaries in South Africa might well have helped to temper the disillusionment caused by the failure of the Maynooth Mission to India, promoting a greater willingness among diocesan clergy to support involvement in non-Christian missions at an earlier juncture.

Southern Africa in the 1860s contained four areas of European settlement: the coastal colonies of the Cape of Good Hope and Natal, and inland the Boer republics of the Orange Free State and the Transvaal.[13] The population of the Cape Colony was in the region of half a million, of whom 180,000 were whites and the remainder largely of mixed race (so-called 'coloureds')[14] and Xhosa-speaking Africans. Natal, with perhaps half the population of the Cape, had only some 18,000 settlers, the vast majority of the inhabitants being Africans (mainly Zulus). The Transvaal and the Orange Free State had white populations of 27,000 and 25,000 respectively, living among large numbers of Africans (mainly Tswana, Southern Sotho and Basutos).

The Church of the Reformation, or Dutch Reformed Church, which came with the Dutch East India Company, formed the largest Christian denomination in South Africa. Its Calvinist doctrines of predestination and election which were applied to relationships between settlers and other races, first in the Cape and later with particular fervour in the Boer republics, meant that there would be no great preoccupation with non-Christian evangelisation.[15] The Anglican Church came with the first English settlers at the turn of the nineteenth century. The sense of racial superiority which animated Anglican settlers was very different to that found among the Dutch, being based not on Old Testament fundamentalism but on modern theories of social evolution and imperialism. Such theories contained nothing which militated against the work of non-Christian missions. On the contrary, Christianising the African was acknowledged as an important part in the process of social and cultural regeneration which, according to theory, the European was bound to undertake on behalf of other less fortunate and backward races.[16] Yet until the time of Bishop Robert Gray in the Cape (1858) and Bishop J. W. Colenso in Natal (1847), the Anglican Church found little opportunity to engage in missions to non-Europeans other than those already living within or in the vicinity of settlements.[17] Scarcity of men and funds, as well as the continuing conflict on the Xhosa–Cape frontier, were at the root of the delay. The first systematic attempt at non-Christian evangelisation was conducted by determined missionaries of the German Moravian Brethren, who after an abortive start in 1737 established a mission some fifty miles from Cape Town in 1792.[18] The non-denominational London Missionary Society, which began its work in 1799, was the first of several evangelical groups to enter South Africa for the purpose of non-Christian missions. The Glasgow and the Wesleyan Methodist missionary societies, taking advantage of a more benign government policy towards British Nonconformist denominations, came to South Africa in the early 1820s. They were soon followed by the American Board Mission and the Paris Evangelical Society. These societies and others of a similar nature spread gradually throughout the territories which later were to form the Union of South Africa.

In the first half of the nineteenth century Christian missions made modest progress among those who had been already brought within the ambit of European settlement. Efforts to evangelise African peoples living beyond the frontier, however, met with strong opposition. Persistent wars between settlers and tribesmen made it hazardous for missionaries to engage in such work. Between 1779 and 1879 there were nine outbreaks of hostilities between Xhosa-speaking Africans and white settlers (although the former were effectively a spent force after the cattle-killing tragedy[19] of 1857). To the north there were major clashes between settlers and Zulus in 1838 and 1879, while in the interior the Voortrekkers were strongly opposed by the Sotho, Tswana and Venda. As *The Oxford History of South Africa* points out, up to the mid-1860s 'except in the Western Cape, Whites still lived in fear of attack from the Black enemy'.[20] In these circumstances the prospects for mission were poor, all the more so because with good reason Christianity was perceived as a weapon of colonial conquest. With considerable bravery some missions were indeed founded on the frontier and beyond, but only a few survived for any length of time. Even where missionaries were welcomed (as in the case of the Paris Evangelical Society and the Oblate Mission by King Moshesh in Basutoland) the motives were unrelated to religion, and traditional religion remained robust.[21] It was only with the subjugation of the tribes (self-inflicted in the case of the Xhosa) and the disruption of their political and economic life (a process assisted by the dislocation which followed the discovery of mineral wealth) that such missions began to prosper.[22]

Irish emigration to South Africa was never on a large scale. The first Irish to come to the region were soldiers attached to the British army which occupied the Cape in 1806. The earliest contingent of Irish settlers arrived in the same year, forming some 350 out of a total of 5,000 emigrants from the British Isles. In the 1840s these were joined by a few hundred more fleeing from the potato famine, part of a group of about 4,500 from the British Isles which helped to colonise Natal.[23] Further small bands arrived out from Ireland during the 1860s, settling in Cape Town.

The first Irish priest to minister in South Africa was Patrick Scully, who took up residence in Cape Town in 1820 when the right to worship and other civil rights were effectively extended to Catholics and Nonconformists. However, his stay was of short duration. More properly, the beginning of Irish missionary involvement in South Africa may be dated from the appointment in August 1837 of Patrick Raymond Griffith, an Irish Dominican, as Vicar Apostolic of the Cape of Good Hope. Griffith's appointment, made after consultation with Archbishop Murray of Dublin, followed a petition to the Pope by a group of Catholic laymen, including some Irish soldiers of the 98th Regiment. The burden of their plea was that, in the absence of a chaplain, many Catholics were resorting to the Protestant faith, while those who remained loyal found themselves cut off from the Church's sacramental life.[24] Representations too for the appointment of a pastor for Catholic settlers and soldiers had been made by Lord Glenelg, Secretary of State for War and the Colonies, acting on the advice of officials in the Cape. At that time the Cape region formed part of an unwieldy ecclesiastical jurisdiction, created in an era less favourable to Catholicism, which included Mauritius and Madagascar. The jurisdiction to which Griffith was appointed was formed by detaching these two islands.

Travelling to the Cape in 1838, accompanied by a small group of volunteers which included his sister, Margaret, and younger brother, Joseph (later ordained a priest), a fellow-Dominican (Fr George Corcoran) and a Franciscan (Fr Daniel Burke), Griffith found the faith of the scattered Catholic population seriously undermined through years of pastoral neglect. Giving priority to those already Catholic, he deployed his scant resources among his flock of French, Dutch, English, German and Irish. But his ministry was not confined to this group. In his diary Griffith records that he also directed his attentions to 'those who ought to be papists'. These included Catholics who had defected to the religion of their spouses and those whose parents were known to be Catholics but who had been raised as Protestants.[25] Griffith studiously refrained from proselytising among the various Protestant *communities* in his jurisdiction. W. E. Brown, in his history of the Catholic Church in South Africa, explains that such an initiative would have been unacceptable to the colony's ruling authorities.[26] Any such endeavour would have been likely to antagonise adherents of the Dutch Reformed Church, whose anti-Catholic sentiments were intense and who were already at odds with the colony's British administrators.[27] In the government view, the function of the bishop was to be chaplain to the Catholic community, for which purpose he was paid a state stipend. Nevertheless, harmony with the authorities did not preclude the reception of *individual* Protestants into the Church, and Griffith recorded a number of such admissions. Nor did the informal concordat with the government prohibit the evangelisation of Africans and those of mixed race. Initially Griffith's opinion of these groups echoed the harsh sentiments of locals.[28] But soon he was to make his own evaluation and began eagerly to promote their evangelisation. In a report to Propaganda Fide in July 1841 he urged the foundation of a mission among the 'Kaffirs' (Xhosa).[29] He explained that he had been unable to act because of the need to concentrate his resources for the benefit of Catholics and because he was unsure as to whether his jurisdiction extended beyond the Great Fish River where the Xhosa lived. What was needed, he told the Cardinal Prefect, was the assistance of a missionary order, and he suggested that an approach should be made to the Company of Mary (Marists). In his letter he also gave details of the type of apostolate which would have to be conducted if the mission was to succeed.[30] In the event, Propaganda Fide offered the mission to the Marists, but they declined, pleading extensive commitments in Oceania and the difficulties created by the continuing Kaffir Wars. As for the 'Hottentots and Bushmen' living in the vicinity of white settlement, evidence from Griffith's letters show that a small number—mainly concubines and their children—were received into the Church.[31] Griffith's correspondence also reveals that he would certainly have established schools for blacks and even a seminary to train black priests, had he the means.[32]

In 1847 the Cape vicariate was divided, and Dr Aidan Devereux, an alumnus of St Peter's College, Wexford, was appointed to the new jurisdiction, named the Eastern district. In contrast to the Western Cape, where non-Europeans formed an amorphous group of mixed-race coloured peoples, the Eastern vicariate, with its vast confines stretching far north to the Zambesi and including Natal to the east, contained large bodies of African tribesmen. At the outset of his tenure Devereux expressed hopes that a vigorous European Catholic Church would exercise a positive influence on this African constituency.[33] But he also planned a more direct form of influence. After carrying out an exhaustive tour of his vicariate he travelled to Rome in July 1848 to discuss the problems of his mission in person with Propaganda Fide.[34] His most important request was a development of the proposal made seven years earlier by Griffith. In order to tackle the problem of African evangelisation, he asked for the division of his vicariate and the introduction to the new territory of a religious order experienced in non-Christian evangelisation. Rome responded by detaching from the Eastern jurisdiction a third vicariate centred on Natal and entrusting it to the Oblate Fathers, whose missionary work in Oceania from 1836 had already won them acclaim in missionary circles.[35] The first concerted effort to evangelise Africans came in 1855 when Mgr Marie Jean François Allard, the new vicar apostolic, assigned two of his priests specifically for such work some ninety miles west of Pietermaritzburg. However, unsettled conditions in the region and the strong resistance of the tribesmen to Christianity put paid to this first initiative. A second attempt in the same region during 1860 also proved fruitless. Two years later, having visited Irish Catholics of the Orange Free State 'in order to learn about the dispositions of the natives'[36] and then going in among the Basutos, Mgr Allard saw hope for a successful enterprise. Later that year saw the commencement of an apostolate in Basutoland (today Lesotho) by the renowned Oblate missionary, Fr Gerard, whose labours produced the first large-scale conversion of Southern Africans to Catholicism. Mgr Allard, his successor in 1874, Mgr Charles C. Jolivet, and Mgr Anthony Gaughren (entrusted with most of Basutoland in 1886), all three of them Oblates, were to preside over the rooting of the Church among the Basutos and Zulus.[37]

Devereux, through his advocacy with Propaganda, must be credited with at least an indirect responsibility for these achievements. Within his own jurisdiction, preoccupied with consolidating the position of his Church and breaking down anti-Catholic prejudice, he relied on education as the principal means. His decision to invite a community of Assumption Sisters from France to open a school at Grahamstown in 1849 was motivated by a desire to improve the standard of education available to Catholics. A willingness to admit Protestant children to the school—availed of by many parents— won for his Church much goodwill.[38] That Devereux was unable to contemplate apostolic works for the benefit of non-Europeans is hardly surprising. A complement of three priests formed the total staff available to him when he became bishop. Although the number was to increase over the years, it was never adequate for the Catholics of Port Elizabeth, Grahamstown and the rural areas of European settlement. And even if he had had sufficient resources, the unstable political situation would have presented an insurmountable obstacle. The regular outbreaks of hostility between settlers and Xhosa-speaking tribesmen created a barrier to missionary activity which was as much psychological as physical, since at times of crisis the Church was inevitably drawn to take sides. For example, such was the case on the occasion of the Eighth Kaffir War. At its outbreak in December 1850 over a hundred settlers were massacred. According to a contemporary account, 'Along a line of fifty miles nothing was to be seen but a moving mass of farmers with their waggons, horses, sheep and cattle—all fleeing from one common enemy, all animated by one common impulse, fear.'[39] Bishop Devereux had St Patrick's Church in Grahamstown fortified as a shelter for the women and children. During the course of the three-year war the sisters taught in overcrowded classrooms, tended the sick throughout the town, and prepared the dead for burial. It should be stressed, however, that the Church's sympathy for the beleagured white community during this period was essentially humanitarian and bore no ideological or racial signification. Later, after the collective suicide of the Xhosa through the cattle-killing tragedy of 1857, Catholics both in the Western Cape and the Eastern Cape vicariates joined other Christians in the distribution of food and care of the sick. And eventually, after the Kaffir Wars had finally run their course,[40] the Church in the Eastern Cape was at last able to develop schools for Africans.

Fr James Ricards, also from St Peter's College, Wexford, was appointed bishop of the Eastern vicariate in 1871 and received from Rome (most likely during an audience with the Pope) explicit instructions as to how he should conduct his apostolate. In his book *The Catholic Church and the Kaffir* he records that he had been told:

> Attend first to the wants of the children of the household of the faith. When the wants of this portion of your flock have been provided for, turn your attention to the native population.[41]

Whether his predecessors also had received instructions is unclear. But it is likely that Bishop Griffith's statement of policy and particularly his solicitude for 'those who ought to be papists' reflected Roman guidance. Nor should the absence of a Roman injunction respecting the 'native population' appear surprising, given the critical state of the Catholic community at the time of Griffith's appointment in 1837. By 1871, however, the context was beginning to change; the Catholic constituency was better served (though inadequately), and with the gradual subjugation of the tribal groupings the evangelisation of Africans could now be contemplated. Whatever the truth about the Holy See's 'instructions' to the various bishops—there is no evidence of any formal brief—it is clear that all regarded the evangelisation of Africans as an important but *secondary* task, to be undertaken as soon as peaceful conditions obtained and as the ministry to Catholics of European descent was placed on a sure footing.[42]

But the task would not easily be accomplished. When Ricards took office he found himself scarcely able to cope with the requirements of the 5,000 European Catholics within his jurisdiction. Moreover, the struggle between settlers and tribesmen had not yet been finally resolved. It was almost a decade before he was able to consider plans for the 200,000 Africans within his vicariate. During those years he laboured to build up his staff until by 1879 he had increased numbers from five to twenty-one priests. His predecessor in the Eastern district, Dr Patrick Moran, had seen the merit of education as a means of developing the Church and in 1867 had invited Irish Dominican Sisters (from Sion Hill, Dublin) to open a school in Port Elizabeth for the children of white settlers.

Impressed by the results, Ricards brought out English Jesuits to Grahamstown, Marist Brothers (from Cape Town) to Port Elizabeth (1879) and Dominican Sisters from Augsburg (invited in 1876) to King William's Town. Finally satisfied that the infrastructure for the pastoral care of Catholics had been secured and that the political climate at last was right, Ricards now turned his attention to developing non-Christian missions. In the towns he established a small number of schools for blacks and coloureds. But his most signal contribution came in 1880 when he introduced a large group of Trappist monks from Bohemia whose brief was to work exclusively among the indigenous population.[43] These were subsequently to renounce their membership of the Trappist order and to become the Congregation of the Missionaries of Marianhill, thereafter conducting a fruitful apostolate among the Zulus of Natal. Bishop Ricards's concern also led him to request Propaganda to introduce missionaries to territories north of the Limpopo. As a result, in 1879 a group of Jesuits came to the area which today is called Zimbabwe to work among the indigenous population.

Thomas Grimley, appointed coadjutor to Griffith in 1861, and who in the following year succeeded the bishop as Vicar Apostolic of the Western district, was anxious at the outset of his tenure to develop non-Christian missions, especially among the Bantu in the central part of his jurisdiction.[44] Circumstances in the vicariate favoured such an apostolate, as the tribal population had long been pacified. After touring his diocese in 1862 he wrote to James O'Haire, an All Hallows student destined for South Africa, expressing his heartfelt concern for a wider apostolate:

> I have just returned from visiting a large portion of this vicariate. . . . In one village in one day I baptized four adults, two blacks, one Africander, and one young Scotchman. Oh! When shall I get means to erect a small church in every village? If I had the means to establish missions, thousands would become members of our holy faith. Oh! labour then, with the zeal of an Apostle, for this *really foreign* mission.[45]

In the event, Grimley was never to have sufficient resources for the systematic apostolate to Africans which he envisaged, but he made the best use of the means available. He assigned O'Haire to Malmesbury, urging him to pay special attention to the 'Hottentot

[Khoikhoi] community'. Nor was the evangelisation of non-Christians to be the special task of one priest. As we have seen, the bishop, on his first tour of the vicariate, baptised two blacks, and on a similar tour towards the close of his life he 'received five adults, two of whom were Zulu Kaffirs'. He also boasted to having a procession of blacks ('at least eleven') attending church ceremonies in Cape Town Cathedral, where in 1864 he also opened a school for African children, 'though it had to start with only three pupils'.[46]

O'Haire reported early successes among the Khoikhoi at Malmesbury, but he was soon called away to serve a settled white community, leaving the mission to be abandoned for six years. Yet the commitment to non-Christian evangelisation remained strong among the vicariate staff. O'Haire's description of his own experience provides eloquent testimony to this commitment and demonstrates how it was fulfilled:

> I have resided at the Cape for 12 years. . . . I moved through all classes in society from the governor to the most degraded beggar. I visited continually the prisons and hospitals, and houses of the people high and low, walked through streets, lanes, and polluted alleys, and met men of every colour, of every nationality, of every creed, of every position.[47]

Grimley, for his part, had been struck by Devereux's educational apostolate in the Eastern jurisdiction, and in 1863 and 1867 respectively he introduced Irish Dominican Sisters (from Cabra, Dublin) and Marist Brothers (a group from the French headquarters, but which included English and Irish) for school work among children of Catholic settlers. But also recognising the potential of the Catholic school for the evangelisation of non-Christians, he developed a small network of schools for coloured and Khoisan peoples, and these establishments were soon to benefit from government subsidies. His most cherished scheme for the evangelisation of Africans came towards the end of his life. Travelling to the Vatican Council in 1869, he suggested to Fr Augustin Planque, Superior General of the Lyons Society of African Missions (S.M.A), that his society should take responsibility for a part of the vicariate and should reorganise it along lines resembling the Paraguay Reductions.[48] At the time Fr Planque was searching for an alternative to the society's treacherous West African jurisdiction, which had already claimed many lives and had left many of his priests incapable of returning to the tropics. Efforts to secure a more salubrious mission where invalided missionaries or younger, inexperienced priests might be assigned had been in progress for some time without any real success. Grimley's offer, which included the proposal that the S.M.A. mission might be erected into a separate jurisdiction, therefore seemed an ideal solution. However, the bishop's untimely death early in the following year delayed the implementation of the plan.

John Leonard, formerly parish priest of Chapelizod, Dublin, succeeded Grimley in 1872. While his principal concern remained the settlers and their descendants, he did not confine himself to this apostolate. Leonard provided educational facilities for blacks and coloureds as well as whites. He sponsored important social services, too, for all races, such as the Institute for the Deaf and Dumb under the direction of Irish Dominican Sisters. He was also favourable to his predecessor's scheme for introducing the Society of African Missions and, against the advice of his vicar general, agreed to yield up the more developed and populous parts in the south of his juris-diction, including three promising stations, Georgetown, Mossel Bay and Oudtshoorn. The new prefecture, the Central Cape, was finally erected in July 1874, and a team of eight missionaries was entrusted with its care.[49]

The project was not a success. The priests were largely young and inexperienced, and most spoke no language other than French. The few experienced members who had worked in West Africa, and principally the superior, Fr Devernoille, found the Central Cape prefecture backward, the stations decadent, and the population sparse and scattered. Moreover, Devernoille was one of a group which was dissatisfied with Planque's leadership of the society and expended much of his energy in seeking reform of its government. In the initial stages some useful work was accomplished. A new station, Pella, modelled on the Reductions, was opened in the north-west of the prefecture, and prospects there were described as promising. But the morale of the priests remained low, and Dever-noille's defection from the mission and the society (reputedly to become a Protestant) signalled the beginning of the end. Planque had hoped that the boundaries of the prefecture might be extended north of the Orange River, where he saw better prospects for his men, but the Holy Ghost Fathers who had jurisdiction there were unwilling to yield up the territory. When in 1878 Propaganda entrusted the S.M.A. with a prefecture in the Gold Coast, where the climate was reputed (wrongly) to be temperate, Planque decided that the time had come to disengage. In 1881 the Oblates of St Francis de Sales replaced the S.M.A. in Central Cape, but refused to take responsibility for the direction of the prefecture. As a result, the jurisdiction reverted to the care of Bishop Leonard. The withdrawal of the S.M.A. proved a bitter disappointment to the bishop. Owing to a combination of circumstances outside his control, his hopes of repeating for his African population what the Oblates had accomplished for theirs in Basutoland and Zululand were to be sadly frustrated.

In 1886 the division of the Natal jurisdiction and the erection of the vicariate of the Orange Free State, entrusted to an Irish Oblate, Anthony Gaughren, marked an intensification of the apostolate to the Africans in the Transvaal, Basutoland and the Diamond Fields. Loreto Sisters from Navan, who first became involved in education in 1879, and the Irish Mercy Sisters (from Strabane), who came to Mafeking in 1897, were to provide an important resource for work among blacks.

No less important for the apostolate to Africans were the hospitals and orphanages opened in the third quarter of the century. Reference has already been made to the Institute for the Deaf and Dumb founded by Irish Dominican Sisters in the Western Cape. The Dominican Sisters in King William's Town established an orphanage in 1885 in the wake of the great depression which afflicted South Africa in the previous year, and also opened a school for the deaf. Visitation of the sick in their homes came to form an important part of their extensive apostolic repertoire. In 1882 the Nazareth Sisters, many of whom were Irish, came from their mother house in London to Cape Town to care for orphans and the aged; in 1884 and 1888 this institute made two further foundations, in Kimberley, where they took charge of the local orphanage, and in Port Elizabeth, where they cared for children and the elderly.[50] While in the early years many of these works were for the benefit of whites, by the close of the century the sisters had expanded their apostolate to include other races.

In conclusion, it will be seen that the mission to South Africa was conducted according to the following pattern. In the early stages priority was given to the needs of Catholic settlers and 'those who ought to be papists', although some efforts were made also to evangelise blacks and those of mixed race. As the Church gradually grew stronger it expanded its apostolate to Africans in areas outside European influence, while intensifying its ministry to those living within settlement communities. Throughout this process Irish priests, sisters and brothers were to make a major contribution. Those in positions of leadership played the crucial role. In the early years, when shortage of resources ruled out a direct apostolate, they stimulated action by Propaganda Fide on behalf of Africans; and as soon as resources became available they engaged in energetic and successful educational and social apostolates. It is true that the most striking work was accomplished by continental missionaries, by the Oblates and the Missionaries of Marianhill, and also by the Dominican Sisters in King William's Town. But each of these institutes owed its presence in South Africa to the solicitude of the Irish bishops for the black population. Some of the other orders and congregations introduced by Irish bishops came from England and Germany; and Bishop Devereux, as early as 1849, had introduced Dutch priests to the Eastern Cape vicariate. Yet during the nineteenth century the predominant tone of the South African Church remained Irish, not merely because most of the leaders were Irish-born, but because the greater part of the secular clergy came from Ireland and because many of those belonging to English and French institutes were in fact Irish men and women.

For the reasons outlined at the beginning of this section, the modern Irish missionary movement to non-Christian peoples drew little inspiration from the South African experience. There was, however, one link which merits attention. Fr James O'Haire, who severed his connection with the mission in 1875, was later to play a significant role in introducing to Ireland one of the continental institutes which exercised a formative influence on the modern movement.[51]

III

Missions to Mauritius and the Caribbean

During the nineteenth century Irish missionaries were also engaged in the evangelisation of non-Christians in Mauritius and the Caribbean. Mauritius had been annexed from the French by the British at the end of the Napoleonic Wars. From the second decade of the nineteenth century onwards, with the abolition of slavery in the sugar plantations, Indians were introduced as indentured labourers. Formerly part of a wider ecclesiastical jurisdiction which included the Cape of Good Hope, Madagascar, Australia and New Zealand, Mauritius became a vicariate in its own right in 1840. Irish priests who went there to work alongside English missionaries were all alumni of All Hallows College. As well as ministering to the wealthy European landowners in the island, they developed an apostolate to blacks and also to the Indians. But the scale of activity was small; in the period 1840-96 there were no more than a dozen Irish priests on the mission. Late in the century the priests were joined by a handful of De La Salle Brothers of the Irish province who took charge of schools previously managed by French Lasallians.

The commitment to the Caribbean was more substantial. Records from the *Irish Catholic Directory* show that up to 1849 sixty-one Irish priests served in the region. These included volunteers from a number of Irish diocesan seminaries, and also some priests from Ardagh and the neighbouring diocese of Kilmore recruited by Bishop Richard Smith, a native of Ardagh. Later these were to be joined by a handful of Irish Redemptorists and Irish Dominicans. But All Hallows was soon to become the chief source of Irish personnel, supplying forty-two priests by 1896.

Commercial links between Ireland and the Caribbean had first developed in the eighteenth century, leading to residence in the region by small numbers of Irish to supervise the trade. Catholic communities, composed mainly of English, French, Spanish, Portuguese and Irish settlers, as well as indigenous elements, already existed in Trinidad, Guiana, Grenada, Dominica, St Lucia, Tobago, St Vincent, St Thomas, St Christopher's and Ste Croix when Propaganda established vicariates in the Caribbean during the fourth decade of the nineteenth century. The indigenous Catholics had been evangelised by Europeans staffing the warehouses and offices of the trading companies. Nano Nagle, foundress of the Sisters of the Presentation, wrote in 1770 of her efforts to train Irish youths destined for the West Indies 'to be catechists to the natives'.[52] There were also Catholics of mixed race, born of unions between Europeans and the local population. The French Dominicans and continental missionary agencies, such as the Congregation of the Holy Spirit and the Sisters of St Joseph of Cluny, ministered mainly to the Catholic community but were also active in the apostolate to local inhabitants. However, efforts to evangelise Indians and Chinese introduced to cultivate the land in the place of the emancipated slaves were generally unrewarded. Dr Moriarty, President of All Hallows, in a fund-raising *Prospectus* of 1853 referred to 'the thousands of Irish and English Catholics in the East and West Indies' whom priests from the college were already serving.[53] The numbers of Irish had been swelled by political prisoners and felons deported to the British islands, a form of migration which was to continue into the 1880s.

Irish missions to the Caribbean in the nineteenth century were predominantly concerned with providing pastoral care for a Catholic community by no means exclusively Irish in its composition. Shortage of resources and the size of the Catholic community ensured that primary evangelisation of indigenes and other groupings could not be conducted in a systematic fashion, although this work was never excluded. Because of the strong historical links between Ireland and the Caribbean, and a tendency of reports from the region to feature this connection, the mission was commonly regarded as a diaspora commitment. In these circumstances it could hardly be expected to exercise a significant influence on the modern Irish missionary movement to non-Christian peoples which emerged in the twentieth century.

IV

Irish Vincentians in China

Irish Vincentians of the modern era developed from the small group of Maynooth priests (which included Fr John Hand) who were anxious to break new ground in the apostolate at home and formed themselves into a community based in Castleknock (near Dublin) in 1833. Six years later they entered into negotiations with the Congregation of the Mission in Paris and were subsequently incorporated as members.[54] In the early years they managed a small seminary, took charge of a church in the Dublin archdiocese (Phibsborough) and delivered parish missions in many dioceses. In time they were also to be caught up in the continental missionary movement.

The Congregation of the Mission (known as the Lazarists on the continent), founded by St Vincent de Paul in the seventeenth century, had combined a variety of apostolic works in France with missionary enterprise, mainly in the Far East. In the early years Irish

Vincentians making their novitiate in Paris were to be influenced by reports of the missionary activities of their French confrères, but scarcity of numbers and an accumulation of commitments at home prevented them from participating. However, from the early 1840s letters from the generalate describing the recent martyrdom of Vincentians in China and calling for volunteers greatly moved members of the Irish communities and could not be ignored indefinitely.[55] The first to offer his services was Michael Dowling, who went to China in 1851 and died there seven years later aged thirty-eight. In 1862 Thomas Fitzpatrick departed for Shanghai, where he ministered until his death in 1865. Fr Patrick Moloney was the last Vincentian of the Irish province to serve in China until the congregation reactivated its mission in 1919. He was to spend ten years at his post until his death in 1882.[56] Three Irish members of the Dutch province also worked in China. All three were students of philosophy at Mungret College (near Limerick), from where they joined the Vincentians in Pannigen, Holland, with the intention of going to China. Denis Nugent, who went to Pannigen in 1907, was ordained in 1913 and later became superior of St Paul's Seminary in Ning-po. Michael McKiernan joined the Vincentians in 1908 and after his ordination in 1914 worked in the Ning-po district. James Feely, who went to Holland in 1906, was ordained in 1916 and served in Kiang-si. These Irishmen chose to dedicate themselves to the service of China as a result of a visit to Mungret by a priest promoting the mission. The identity of the priest is unknown, but Fr John Fraser, a tireless traveller on behalf of the mission who visited Ireland canvassing support on a number of occasions, cannot be excluded as the animator. In the event, the Jesuits at Mungret advised the students to join the Dutch Vincentians, whose reputation in China was long-established. This recommendation merely highlights the fact that the Irish province of the congregation was no longer perceived as having a missionary dimension at this time.

Nonetheless, Vincentians of the Irish province were to exercise an influence on the evolution of the twentieth-century movement out of proportion to the scale of their actual involvement in the work of non-Christian missions. Vincentian spiritual directors attached to Maynooth College from 1886 were among the first to stimulate interest in the Far East among staff and students and played a part in nurturing the movement which produced the Maynooth Mission to China.

V

The Mission to Argentina

Although in recent decades South and Central America have become highly publicised theatres, Irish missionary endeavour was already well established in parts of the sub-continent during the nineteenth century. The influence of this earlier mission on the twentieth-century movement, however, must be considered negligible, for its focus was firmly directed towards Irish diaspora communities.[57] The principal destination for Irish emigrants was Argentina, where substantial settlement took place throughout the century. By 1850 some 5,000 Irish emigrants had set down roots; by the third quarter of the century the total number of Irish and Irish-Argentines was estimated to be in the region of 34,000, a figure which had more than doubled by 1900. During the second decade of the twentieth century there were in excess of 110,000 Argentinians of Irish extraction in place.[58]

In the main, the Irish gravitated to rural areas, where they formed tightly knit, almost self-sufficient farming communities. Little effort was made to integrate into the wider community until the twentieth century. Knowledge of Spanish was restricted to the minimum necessary for business transactions, while strenuous efforts were made to preserve inherited cultural and religious identity. In order to meet the expressed desire of Irish Catholics to have their own pastors, local bishops permitted the establishment of a system of chaplaincies to the Irish rural communities; and during the nineteenth century more than a hundred priests were assigned to service these chaplaincies.[59] That the contemporary movement drew little inspiration from such activity is, therefore, hardly surprising.

VI

The Role of Irish Religious Sisters and Brothers

Finally, we must consider the contribution of Irish sisters and brothers belonging to Irish or continental foundations who engaged in missions to non-Christian peoples during the nineteenth century and especially in the latter half of the century.[60]

Reference has been made already to the work of Irish Loreto and Dominican Sisters in South Africa and to Loreto and Presentation Sisters in India.[61] The Sisters of Mercy in Australia worked among

Aborigines as well as settlers from 1846. In New Zealand (1849) they laboured among the Maoris, while in North America they pioneered missions among Indians in Maine (1878), Indian Island (1878) and Dana Point (1879). Primary evangelisation formed an important part of their work also in Mafeking (1897), Belize (1883) and Jamaica (1890). The work of Presentation, Loreto, Dominican and Mercy Sisters in the second half of the nineteenth century, especially its later decades, constitutes the most impressive example of successful involvement by Irish religious among non-Christians. There is no evidence that the sisters were influenced to any great extent by the continental missionary movement to non-Christian peoples. Rather the four institutes, three of them founded by Irishwomen,[62] the fourth by Irish priests, went overseas in response to appeals, mainly from Irish missionary bishops. In this sense their work must be considered as part of Ireland's apostolic outreach rather than a manifestation of that zeal for non-Christian missions which inspired the continental movement.

From 1850 large numbers of Irish sisters and a handful of Irish brothers became involved in a missionary apostolate of a different character. Some of the sisters were from convents established by French congregations which had come to Ireland specifically to recruit for their own missions. The convent of the Sisters of the Good Shepherd at Limerick was such a foundation. In 1854 two Irish sisters of the institute, accompanied by three French sisters, left the mother house at Angers for Bangalore to work for Mgr Charbonnaux, the Vicar Apostolic of Mysore. Small groups of Irish sisters followed the same path at regular intervals.[63] In similar fashion Irish members of the Sisters of the Holy Family, based at Newbridge since 1875, worked on missions organised from their French mother house, mainly in Ceylon.[64] Other French orders were content to use Ireland as a recruiting ground without establishing convents. The Sisters of Our Lady of Apostles of Lyons recruited for eleven years before making an Irish foundation in 1887. Those recruited were sent to Lyons for their novitiate and thereafter to missions in Benin, Lagos, Elmina and Cape Coast. For over half a century before opening their house at Drishane (Millstreet, Co. Cork) the Sisters of the Holy Infant Jesus brought candidates over to France to train for French missions in India and Malaya.[65] The Sisters of St Joseph of Cluny, the largest of the French missionary congregations, opened a transit centre for recruits at Blanchardstown in 1861. During the space of thirty-eight years (1861-99) they sent 565 candidates to France, many of whom subsequently served in the colonies.[66] The introduction of a brief preparatory course after some years did little to change the complexion of the operation, since its purpose was to help the recruits adapt more easily to the French style of life. The Franciscan Missionaries of Mary recruited Irish women for forty-five years before making an Irish foundation in 1933.[67]

Reference has been made earlier to the contribution of the Irish Christian Brothers and the Brothers of St Patrick (1808) in India and South Africa. The De La Salle Brothers, founded in France at the close of the seventeenth century, recruited Irish-born personnel in North America, where they had been active since 1845. Records show that in 1863 fifty aspirants left Ireland to join the order's North American province. In 1865 a 'house of reception' was opened in Queenstown (now Cóbh) to supervise recruitment and transport of candidates for America, and some fifty passages from Liverpool were arranged in the same year. Young Irishmen continued to be recruited for the American province into the first decade of the twentieth century.[68] There was also substantial recruitment in Ireland by the De La Salle generalate. In the years before the establishment of an Irish novitiate in Castletown, Queen's County (Laois), in 1882, Irish aspirants went regularly to Paris for their initial training. And for a further decade many postulants continued to make their novitiate in Paris. Only from the mid-1890s did the majority who entered remain in Castletown for their formation.

The number of Irish or Irish-born Lasallians to serve in the order's missions to non-Christian territories was relatively small.[69] Many of those who went to Paris were retained in France to take the places of French brothers undergoing military service. However, a number of those recruited for America were reassigned to the Far East. In the British crown colony of Hong Kong over a dozen Irish were assigned between 1875 and the end of the century. Two Irish-born brothers, both belonging to the North American province, were sent to Singapore in 1852. A third died before reaching the same mission in 1853 and was replaced by a fourth, who later transferred to Penang. Irish-born brothers also served in Ceylon from 1887. Earlier in the century Irish members worked in a number of foundations made in India, none of which survived for long. Less than a dozen Irish brothers who entered at Castletown worked in Mauritius between 1882 and the close of the century.

It is difficult to estimate accurately the number of women and men who became professed members of continental foundations in the second half of the nineteenth century, but the figure was probably in the region of 600 to 800. It appears that there was little opposition within the Irish Church to such recruitment. At the time there was a dramatic increase in the numbers of those offering themselves for the religious life as nuns and brothers, so the leakage to France was easily absorbed. It may also be suggested that the absence of protest was related to the relatively low valuation placed on nuns and brothers by the Catholic community. During penal times it was the depletion of clerical ranks which had threatened the very existence of the Church, since it had struck at the core elements of Mass and sacraments. The reaction to this crisis in the restored order of the nineteenth century seems to have taken the form of an inflated reverence for priesthood, so strong as to overshadow the other categories of church membership. Thus while agencies seeking prospective nuns and brothers went largely unchallenged, missionary societies seeking candidates for priesthood were to have an altogether different experience, often meeting resolute opposition.

Perhaps a quarter of those who joined continental societies as nuns served in 'non-Christian' mission-fields; the proportion of brothers was significantly lower. However, neither group was to exercise an influence on the modern Irish missionary movement. This was scarcely surprising. In the first place, there was always a measure of ignorance about their activities. In the case of the sisters, the recruiting agents frequently gave it to be understood that the young ladies were destined for educational work on the continent. Secondly, in those instances where it was known that the sisters would work in non-Christian mission territories, the Irish Church appears to have been unmoved, a consequence perhaps of the low valuation placed on sisters at this time and the prevailing lack of enthusiasm for non-Christian missions. Thirdly, for all practical purposes, those who joined continental societies were lost to the Irish Church. Detached from their roots at the point of entry, they were subsequently discouraged from cultivating an Irish identity within their institutes and from maintaining links with Ireland. Finally, few of the sisters and brothers who worked in the French foreign missions ever had the opportunity of returning home to spread the missionary message.

PART TWO

The
Continental Background

FOUR

The Continental Missionary Impulse

URING the nineteenth century Ireland's contribution to Roman Catholic enterprise among non-Christians was unremarkable in comparison with that of France, Italy, Belgium and Holland; it also failed to match that of England, which had produced its own movement spearheaded by Bishop Herbert Vaughan's St Joseph's Foreign Missionary Society.[1] With few exceptions, the priests and religious of Ireland, if not the people, exhibited little of that burning zeal to evangelise non-Christians which was at the heart of the continental movement. And yet the opening decades of the twentieth century were to witness the development of a commitment within the Irish Church which was to place Ireland in the forefront of Catholic missionary enterprise alongside the leading European mission-sending countries.

The forces which wrought this transformation had been at work since the late 1830s. Their impact became apparent only at the beginning of the twentieth century, when the Irish Church finally emerged as a cohesive, self-confident institution capable of directing its considerable energies beyond the diaspora. Central to the missionary renaissance were the activities of a handful of French agencies which set down roots in Ireland during the second half of the nineteenth century. Building upon the work of the Association for the Propagation of the Faith, which had been active since the late 1830s, these provided the principal channel through which the continental missionary impulse entered Ireland.

I

In the final analysis, the continental movement can be considered less a new beginning than the revival of a great impulse, originating in the Counter-Reformation period but which had become dormant by the end of the eighteenth century. Yet there were important differences between the old and the new. The *Padroado* (*Patronato*) arrangement, whereby effective control over missions had been entrusted by the papacy to secular powers (Portugal and Spain), was now abandoned in favour of direct supervision by Propaganda Fide. The Popes of the modern era, unlike their predecessors, appealed directly to the peoples of Europe over the heads of their rulers, thus creating the context for the emergence of a great populist movement. By the same token, mission jurisdictions were increasingly entrusted to religious orders or missionary societies who nominated their own members as bishops; this ensured greater cohesion in the conduct of missions than had formerly existed. Above all, there was the recognition, for the first time since the Apostolic period, that women had a vital role to play in the work of missions.

The decline of the Counter-Reformation movement had been a gradual process. In the seventeenth century France replaced Spain and Portugal as the leading missionary nation; thousands of her missionaries were active from America in the Far West to China and Japan in the Far East.[2] In the eighteenth century, however, the quarrel with Rome over the Chinese and Malabar rites, the suppression of the Jesuits, and the hostile writings of the Encyclopaedists and especially Voltaire, led to a serious weakening of the missionary impulse. At the same time there was a growing laxity within religious orders and congregations in France.[3] It was no surprise, therefore, that when the Revolution broke out most of the agencies engaged in missions offered little resistance. By 1789 there were only some 300 missionaries still at work.[4] By 1800 the celebrated Paris Foreign Missionary Society, considered by many to rival the Jesuits as the pride of the seventeenth-century enterprise, had been reduced to a mere twenty-nine members; and other orders engaged in missionary activity showed a similar decline.[5] Nevertheless, the movement did not die, and a slender continuity was maintained throughout the revolutionary period by a handful of missionaries who remained at their posts.

The revival of missionary endeavour began in the second decade of the nineteenth century and grew in strength as the years progressed. The Society of Jesus, restored in 1814, reactivated its missions in Asia and established new foundations in Africa; within a century it had become again the largest of the Church's missionary agencies. The Association for the Propagation of the Faith, founded in Lyons in 1822, took on the responsibility of publicising the movement and of funding its missions, a task which had been carried out (rather inefficiently) by the Portuguese and Spanish governments during the era of the royal *Padroado*. Numerous additional lay agencies whose purpose was to assist clerical and religious missionaries were established during the century. The most notable were the Association of the Holy Childhood, founded at Nancy in 1843 to provide for children orphaned or enslaved in mission countries; the Apostolic Work Society, founded in France in 1838 to supply missionaries with *matériel* and especially liturgical equipment; the Society of the Orient, founded in Paris in 1853 to fund seminaries, education and health care in the Near East; and the Society of St Peter the Apostle, founded in Caen in 1884 to assist in the education of indigenous clergy. The Lazarists (Vincentians) set to work in the Middle East and China, while the Paris Foreign Missionary Society renewed its apostolate in China, south-east Asia and North America.

In addition, many new agencies, some exclusively missionary, others with a strong missionary orientation, came into existence and were assigned territories by the Holy See. The Oblates of Mary Immaculate (1816) worked chiefly in Canada, Oceania and Southern Africa; the Marists (1822) were entrusted with jurisdictions in New Zealand and Oceania; the Picpus Fathers (1805) had charge of Hawaii and the Polynesian islands; the Congregation of the Holy Ghost and the Immaculate Heart of Mary (1848) was allocated jurisdictions in the French colonies, mainly in Africa; the Missionaries of the Sacred Heart (1854) received responsibility for missions in South America; while the Society of African Missions of Lyons (1856) and the White Fathers (1868) were given territories in Africa. Also assigned to Africa were the Oblates of St Francis (1873) and the Fathers of the Sacred Heart (1877). Missionary institutes of priests and brothers founded elsewhere in Europe included the Foreign Missions of Milan (1850), the Verona Fathers (1866), the Society of St Joseph (Mill Hill, London, 1866) and the Missionaries of Scheut (Belgium 1862). Among new groups of women missionaries were the Sisters of St Joseph of Cluny (1806), the Religious of Our Lady of Lyons (1861), the Sisters of Our Lady of Africa (1869), the Sisters of Our Lady of Apostles (1876), the Franciscan Missionaries of Mary (1877) and the Daughters of the Sacred Heart (1882). A more complete list of the new foundations and the territories in which they ministered is provided in Appendix A.

II

This astonishing revival was caused by a variety of factors. First of all, in the opening decades of the nineteenth century there appeared a flood of romantic mission literature which effectively stifled the rationalist critique of Voltaire and led to a new enthusiasm among the young for the missionary life. Chateaubriand's *Génie du Christianisme*, first published in 1802, was a classic work in the new genre. Although often inaccurate and naive in its presentation of missionary life, the book's strong romantic flavour held an irresistible attraction for a generation which set a premium on the noble and sublime.[6] Equally popular were the *Lettres Édifiantes et Curieuses* and the *Nouvelles Lettres Édifiantes des Missions de la Chine et des Indes Orientales*, published between 1803 and 1824, which contained often idealised accounts of the Jesuits' continuing missionary activity. The *Annals* of the Association for the Propagation of the Faith, published monthly from 1823 and again written in the romantic style, soon became the movement's most influential literary source.[7]

A second factor which assisted the revitalisation of Catholic missions was the restoration of the French monarchy. The return to old political forms was accompanied by an upsurge of religious feeling and a return to traditional Catholic values; involvement in missionary activity again became fashionable in Catholic circles.[8] At the same time the freedom to organise mission cadres, which had been withdrawn since the Revolution, was now restored, thereby enabling the older institutes to re-form and new institutes to be founded. And this tolerance from the governing authorities persisted to a greater or lesser degree until 1870.[9] Moreover, the Revolution had ensured that those who were now prepared to engage in the task of reorganisation were men and women of the highest calibre, persevering in their faith and capable of exceptional endurance. The quality of their work was never more evident than in the period after 1870 when the institutes withstood the assaults of successive republican governments.

Again, the missionary movement benefited from the nineteenth-century interest in exploration, trading and the establishment of protectorates and colonies. During the century the French engaged in colonial ventures in Algeria, Tunisia, the Sahara, West Africa, Equatorial Africa, Madagascar, Djibouti, Cochin China and Oceania.

The missionaries sometimes preceded the administrators, often accompanied them, and always followed them. The association was mutually beneficial, for in the course of their work the missionaries tended to keep an eye open to French political interests, while, in return, during the anticlerical persecutions they were treated with a measure of leniency.

Another influential factor was the interest of the papacy. Gregory XVI (1831-46) had much practical experience to add to his deep concern for missions. As Prefect of Propaganda Fide from 1826 he had worked to restrict the influence of the *Padroado* (*Patronato*), establishing an approach which was to be vigorously pursued later in the century whenever the revival of secular control over missions threatened. During his pontificate he carried out a major restructuring of the Church's missions, forming more than seventy jurisdictions and appointing 195 missionary bishops.[10] Pius IX, glad to turn away from the intractable problems of his papacy in Europe, was particularly active (though his capable Prefect of Propaganda, Cardinal Alessandro Barnabo) in gathering together diffuse missionary jurisdictions into tightly-knit units and assigning them to new missionary societies which lacked the traditional political and territorial allegiances of the older orders. Leo XIII, with his surer touch for the concerns of the age, led the missionaries to the front line in the fight against slavery.[11]

The success of Protestant missions, at a time when ecumenism was unknown, served as a special incentive to the movement. Ever since 1790 Protestant missionary societies had been multiplying and were working in close liaison with English, Dutch, German and American trading and political interests. The fear that Africa and the Far East might be lost to Protestantism was a constant theme in Catholic literature urging the necessity of missions. Other relevant influences on the movement were the development of steam travel, railways and other modern systems of communication.

Finally, it is important to realise that the missionary movement was part of a much wider development occurring in many parts of continental Europe. For, during the whole of the century, and especially in the period 1815-71, there was a dramatic increase in the number of religious institutes devoted to teaching and to care of the poor, sick and aged, occurring first within French boundaries and then in the Italian peninsula, Belgium, Holland, the Rhineland and further afield. The causes of the wider movement need not detain us; in France the revival of religious feeling with the restoration of the monarchy was perhaps the most obvious catalyst; in Italy much must be attributed to a generation of outstanding priests and bishops.[12] It is well to note, however, that with the passage of time many of these institutes were caught up in the missionary movement to a greater or lesser degree; the tables in Appendix A give an indication of the date and extent of this involvement.

III

In summary, therefore, the roots of the modern continental missionary movement are to be found in a highly successful effort by French Catholicism to combine traditional virtues with modern values. The high regard for missions, which was an essential feature of the old order, had again manifested itself with the return to traditional political forms, but with a difference. Now it was fired by the spirit of romanticism; at the same time it formed a happy and productive alliance with the three great secular values of the age—geographical discovery, commercial expansion and colonisation. The confidence which enabled French Catholicism to harness modern values in a traditional cause was provided by the spirituality which attended the nineteenth-century religious revival. In contrast to the laxity which had characterised French Catholicism before the Revolution, the purged, post-revolutionary Church was notable for its return to the ascetical spirituality of the seventeenth century.[13] The premium now placed on obedience, devotion to rule and the spirit of self-sacrifice led to the growth of highly disciplined, self-confident organisations not only capable of embracing the most severe hardships but also able to make use of all the advantages afforded by the modern age without being compromised by its less attractive features.

The expansion of this movement beyond French boundaries occurred during the second half of the century, reaching across the Italian peninsula, Germany, Holland, and Belgium to England and finally taking root in Ireland. In general, its propagation tended to occur in two ways: in some instances the successes of French missionaries, communicated to the Catholic world through the growing network of missionary publications, inspired men and women in other countries to commence their own missionary activity; more frequently missionary agencies or institutes with missionary commitments opened branches in other countries to meet the increasing demands of their missions. In the case of Ireland the development was in the latter category. The Congregation of the Holy Ghost and the Immaculate Heart of Mary (C.S.Sp.), the Society of African Missions (S.M.A.) and other French institutes seeking English-speaking personnel entered Ireland in the second half of the century. The Association for the Propagation of the Faith had already been active there since 1838. In their efforts to raise funds or to secure and train recruits, these organisations were compelled to engage in extensive promotional activity, particularly in view of the apathy towards 'non-Christian missions' and their status as 'French' foundations. It was largely through such work that, in the last two decades of the century, a new enthusiasm for evangelising non-Christian peoples was generated among Irish Catholics.

FIVE

The Impact of the Association for the Propagation of the Faith

I

THE first of the continental agencies to come to Ireland, the Association for the Propagation of the Faith, established itself in Dublin in 1838 and soon had branches in all the dioceses. The A.P.F. was as much concerned with heightening missionary consciousness among Catholics as with the task of fund-raising. Its populist *modus operandi* was designed to serve both purposes. Employing a cell system based on tens and multiples of tens, the small weekly contributions of the poor were made to amount to substantial sums, and through this ingenious method large numbers of laity were made to feel intimately involved in the Church's missionary activity. It we are to judge from Irish remittances to the agency, it would appear that the laity was truly infected by an enthusiasm for the association and the missions which it sponsored. The annual accounts of income show that, within a short period of its introduction, Irish contributions to the A.P.F. had outstripped those from the rest of the British Isles, trebling the English and Scottish totals, while at the same time exceeding the subscriptions from Germany, North America, Portugal, the Low Countries and Spain. A slight decline during the second half of the century can be attributed to the effects of famine and emigration rather than to a slackening of zeal. In Ireland the A.P.F. organisers were mainly members of the diocesan clergy who acted with the consent of their bishops. In the event, some dioceses showed greater enthusiasm than others, but it is clear from the cumulative sum contributed annually that the A.P.F. also enjoyed a wide measure of support from within the Church's clerical ranks.[1]

Pope Gregory XVI's formal endorsement of the A.P.F. in 1840 doubtless influenced clerical attitudes, since, among other things, it freed the agency from any suspicion of Gallicanism or from suggestions that it favoured French colonial interests. The hierarchy's own public expression of approval, extended after the publication of Gregory's encyclical, was one among numerous similar declarations by bishops throughout the world. But the terms of the Irish declaration were particularly wholehearted and suggest something more than mere tolerance of an agency enjoying papal approval.[2] Indeed, strong support for the association already existed in senior church circles before the papal endorsement. Not only did Archbishop Daniel Murray of Dublin permit the A.P.F. to be established in his archdiocese, but he took an active part in the preparation of the inaugural meeting. He was to remain president of the Irish Standing Committee until his death in 1852, after which his successor, Paul Cullen, assumed the office. Charles McNally of Clogher and John Murphy of Cork were prominent among those bishops who actively promoted local committees in their dioceses. The diocese of Cork provided sums in excess of £800 annually to the A.P.F.'s coffers during Bishop Murphy's term of office.[3]

Evidence shows that there were those in the hierarchy who hoped that Irish dioceses might benefit from the agency's annual distribution of funds. But the principal reason for the bishops' enthusiasm was an awareness that the A.P.F. had already given subventions to overseas jurisdictions where Irish emigrants had settled or where Irish bishops, priests and religious were ministering. Among the 'resolutions' passed at the inaugural meeting, held on 18 April 1838 and attended by 'the Archbishop of Dublin and numerous dignitaries of the archdiocese', was one

> conveying to the Central Committees of Paris and Lyons the warmest thanks, not only of the meeting, but of Catholics generally, *for the promptitude and zeal with which they have on different occasions advanced a sum of more than 10,000 pounds sterling to the missions of the British colonies* [my italics].[4]

Irish ecclesiastics working overseas frequently chaired meetings of the Standing Committee when home on leave. Moreover, specific appeals to the Central Committees on behalf of Irish bishops were made from time to time, as on the occasion of the appointment of Dr William Walsh to a jurisdiction in Nova Scotia.[5]

The A.P.F. actively encouraged this perception of its role as underwriter for Irish concerns overseas. *The Address of the Central Committees to the Catholics of Ireland*, dated 18 September 1838, pointedly referred to the help already given to Bishop John England of Charleston, Bishop Patrick Griffith at the Cape of Good Hope, and Bishop William Clancy, recently appointed to Demerara. And in subsequent years the A.P.F.'s bulletin, in its appeal for funds, frequently alluded to its generosity towards Irish emigrants. A typical insertion to this effect was contained in an issue of the *Annals* for 1859:

> The Society has for many years past allocated annually the large sum of £40,000 to those countries in which most of the Catholics are either Irish or of Irish parentage. The Central Councils of Paris and Lyons have always been more generous in the distribution of the funds to those foreign missions in which Irishmen form a great portion of the Catholic population.[6]

It was, therefore, the expectation of securing funds for diaspora apostolates or for Irish ecclesiastics appointed to overseas jurisdictions (such as India or South Africa) at a time when local resources were already strained that formed the principal basis of episcopal support.

The expectation was to be fully realised. After the Famine, when the scale of emigration rapidly increased and circumstances became even more straitened, the A.P.F. provided considerable sums for the benefit of the Irish overseas, permitting the diminishing local resources to be concentrated on the task of reconstruction at home. The hundreds of churches, chapels, convents, monasteries and schools erected in the second half of the nineteenth century were a tribute not only to the generosity of the impoverished Catholic community and to the bounty of Irish emigrants but also to the effectiveness of the A.P.F. in fulfilling the promises made in its 1838 *Address* to the Irish Church. Those who hoped that the A.P.F. might also supply Irish dioceses with funds were to be disappointed. For a time sums were made available,[7] but the amounts were insignificant and the subventions were later discontinued. In November 1851 a memorial was presented by the Irish Standing Committee to the Central Committees 'praying that a grant be made to this Committee, to enable them to counteract the efforts being made to proselytize the destitute poor, particularly in the South and West'.[8] Although there is no record of the response, it is likely that the small grants made to Irish dioceses were intended for such purposes. However, departing from its policy of funding only vicariates and dioceses, the A.P.F. responded more generously to repeated appeals for help from All

Hallows College during the height of the Famine and in its immediate aftermath. Thereafter until 1875 All Hallows was to receive a
total of £14,960, which was of great importance to the survival of
the college.[9]

II

Before the summer of 1839 it is doubtful whether the A.P.F.'s
monthly bulletin, available only in French, had a wide circulation
in Ireland. According to the association's rules, each collector of ten
subscriptions was entitled to a copy of the *Annals*, 'to be by him
retained after the perusal of the other nine subscribers'. Few of
those with this entitlement had the capacity to read French, and it
appears that no serious effort was made to fulfil the requirement. In
the period before the A.P.F. came to Ireland, and in the months
between its establishment and the publication of an English translation, it is likely that the French version was read by a small number
of clerical and educated lay enthusiasts, although its publication of
accounts would also have been of interest to senior churchmen. In
October 1838, however, the first of what was known as the *Retrospective Series*—a selection of items from earlier editions translated
into English—was published in London, and in less than a year an
English-language edition of the *Annals* (an exact translation of the
French original) became available. Initially the English-language
version was translated and printed in Paris, but the problems of distribution made this an unsatisfactory arrangement. Proposals to
have the printing transferred to London and the distribution organised from Dublin and Edinburgh were reluctantly accepted by the
Irish Committee in April 1839. Two months later, however, the
Central Committees acceded to a request that the *Annals* be printed
in Dublin and distributed by the Irish Committee. The first issue
printed in Ireland (by William Powell of Thomas Street, Dublin)
became available in July 1839. Some years later the work of translation was also placed under the supervision of the Irish Committee.[10]

The contents of the *Annals* included letters from missionaries
written very much in the style of the *Lettres Édifiantes* (indeed, the
Retrospective Series presented itself as a 'continuation' of these *Lettres*),
details of departures to the mission-fields, obituaries of deceased
missionaries, and a comprehensive account of income and expenditure. The preponderance of material related to primary evangelisa-

tion in Asia and the Far East,[11] an apostolate conducted mainly by missionaries of the Paris Foreign Missionary Society, by Lazarists, Marists, Picpuciens and Jesuits. Reports, letters and articles on 'chaplaincy' missions, or apostolates to Catholic emigrant communities, in which Irish missionaries played an important part, were included but rarely highlighted. Indeed, much of the material from territories where significant European settlement had occurred dealt not with efforts to preserve or restore the faith among emigrants but with the evangelisation of indigenes. This was particularly noticeable in the accounts of missionary endeavour from the North American continent which dwelt on efforts to evangelise the 'savage Indian'. This pattern of preoccupation with an apostolate which, no matter how praiseworthy, became increasingly peripheral as the scale of European immigration increased was to persist down to the end of the century. Missions in Oceania received a similar treatment. The *Annals* provided graphic descriptions of missionary endeavour among the indigenes of the Sandwich Islands, Tonga and the other South Sea Islands; conversely, there is surprisingly little reference to missions among settlers in Australia. Accounts from New Zealand focused on the apostolate to the Maoris and rarely referred to emigrant missions.

Among the contributions from Irish missionary bishops were letters from John England, Richard Smith of Trinidad, Aidan Devereux of South Africa, and Patrick N. Lynch, who succeeded Bishop England in Charleston. All gave accounts of their work, thanked the association for moneys received, and pleaded for additional resources. It seems likely that their contributions did not always reflect what in practice was the primary concern of these missionary bishops, namely the pastoral care of European emigrants. Rather, in line with the emphasis of the *Annals*, they tended to give greater prominence to the work of primary evangelisation within their jurisdictions. Indeed, this self-consciousness was characteristic of almost all contributions from areas where Europeans had settled. For instance, Fr Baur, ministering to emigrants in Paulding, Mississippi, felt it necessary to emphasise that 'the priest here is as much a missionary as any place else in Africa', citing as evidence the lack of proper habitation, the wildness of the terrain and the poverty and ignorance of the sparsely distributed colonial population.[12]

Bishop England's letter to the Central Committees, published in 1838,[13] reflected a similar sensitivity. It is true that in the hope of attracting additional personnel to his hard-pressed jurisdiction, he reported on the large-scale defection of emigrants, calling it 'an emergency'. Fr John Hand, it seems, was particularly impressed by this portion of his letter. But, clearly anxious to impress the Central Committees of his zeal for non-Christian missions, England also wrote at considerable length on the question of evangelising blacks in his diocese. In this regard he blamed penal legislation in the period before the American Revolution for the lack of progress. Only with a large injection of fresh personnel, he argued, could a worthwhile apostolate to the black constituency be now undertaken.[14] England's successor, Bishop Lynch, writing in the *Annals*,[15] concentrated almost exclusively on the needs of the blacks and the measures he was presently undertaking on their behalf. Continental readers would have been pleased by his admission that 'For me, the happiest time in my ministry was the time I spent visiting the Negroes, going from Plantation to Plantation instructing and baptising them.' And they would have been impressed by his statement that he was 'looking forward to the day when Negroes will have a clergy, churches, schools, orphanages, religious communities'.[16] As it happened, largely as a result of circumstances outside his control, this was to remain little more than a pious hope. Devereux, writing from South Africa, took pains to highlight the 'non-Christian' missionary dimension of his apostolate, while Richard Smith, Vicar Apostolic of Trinidad, wrote about the zeal of the freed slaves and about the blacks.[17]

III

Although comprehensive records are not available, it is clear that the circulation of the *Annals* increased dramatically once the Irish Committee took control of publication. In the period before the transfer some 150–500 copies of each English-language issue were sent from France. The print-run for the monthly issues ordered by the Irish Committee from its Dublin printer in November and December 1839 was for 3,500 and 5,000 copies respectively, and by 1841 this had increased to an order of 12,000 copies for each issue. It is fair to assume that the Dublin-printed *Annals* were certainly read by the branch organisers, by educated lay subscribers and probably by most bishops. Moreover, some articles, letters and especially details of the 'annual distribution of the fund' were reprinted in Catholic newspapers and periodicals and also in the secular press; and this helped to further popularise the agency, as well as sharpening subscribers' perceptions as to the precise nature of its work. It appears that amongst the laity a real sense of commitment to 'non-Christian missions' developed alongside the natural concern for the apostolate to Irish emigrants. Later, when the continental missionary agencies entered Ireland, they were to draw their strongest support from those who had been contributing over the years to the A.P.F.[18]

Apart from the important reports of the disbursement of funds, which were always itemised in the greatest detail, and the infrequent accounts of work among Irish emigrants, the *Annals* would not have made congenial reading to the majority of Irish clergy and bishops. Its preoccupation with exotic places and romantic apostolates would hardly have appealed to men struggling to contend with the legacy of penal oppression and the calamitous effects of the Famine. Moreover, the stylised offerings, mainly by French missionaries, would have jarred on more pragmatic Irish sensibilities. By the same token, the journal's obsessive curiosity with the customs of remote tribes and other manifestations of a strong anthropological bias would not have been generally shared by the Irish clergy, who tended to be insular in their outlook.

SIX

The Congregation of the Holy Ghost
and the Immaculate Heart of Mary,
1858–1920[1]

I

THERE was no co-ordinated policy or plan to spread the continental missionary message to Ireland, still less to create an indigenous and autonomous missionary movement. The competitiveness which existed between the continental missionary societies of priests and religious, and which appears to have been actively promoted by Propaganda, precluded any common approach to the promotion of non-Christian missions in Europe; it also ensured that in the field the societies usually took the narrow view, putting their own interests above those of the wider movement.[2] The preoccupation with Ireland was typically self-serving. Since the early 1840s restrictions on French missionaries in the British colonies had made the introduction of British subjects essential if the missions were to be maintained. After efforts to recruit in England proved uniformly unsuccessful Ireland came to be regarded as a promising ground for candidates who would be trained on the continent and would work under the close supervision of continental superiors. And it was generally believed, such was the momentum of the Irish religious revival, that successful recruitment could be accomplished without the establishment of 'houses' and without necessarily harnessing the support of the local hierarchy and clergy.

From mid-century onwards these opinions were put to the test by several congregations of women religious and by some brotherhoods. As has been seen in Chapter 3, the results were most encouraging,[3] yet attempts to recruit candidates for the missionary priesthood undertaken by the Society of African Missions of Lyons from 1876 were strongly resisted by elements within the local clergy. Earlier in the 1840s and 1850s, when the Congregation of the Holy Heart of Mary and the Congregation of the Holy Ghost and the Immaculate Heart of Mary had made tentative efforts to secure candidates, the results were disappointing. Clearly much research is required before a satisfactory explanation can be offered for the different experiences. The circumstances in which recruitment to continental sisterhoods and brotherhoods took place have already been discussed.[4] It was suggested that the lack of opposition derived, among other factors, from the tendency to undervalue the vocation to sisterhood or brotherhood at a time when the priestly vocation enjoyed an excessive eminence. The prospect of losing priestly vocations to the continent at a time when there were still grave shortages at home and in the diaspora was bound to cause alarm in a church which had almost foundered for lack of priests in the previous century. The extent of the shortage at home was especially severe in the years before the Famine when the population was steadily increasing. Indeed, in 1840 the Church was less well supplied than it had been at the start of the century: in 1800 the ratio of priests to people had been 1:2,100, while in 1840 it had reached 1:3,000.[5] The fact that the insufficiency related more to a lack of places in seminaries than to a scarcity of candidates may not always have been appreciated. In the post-Famine period, although the ratio of priests to people steadily improved[6] as the population decreased and as additional space was made available in the seminaries, there were now the new demands of the diaspora to be met. There had always been a trickle of Irish students and priests to French dioceses and to orders like the Sulpicians. One may speculate that in the view of some Irish priests and bishops recruitment for the powerful continental missionary movement threatened to convert this innocuous outflow into a loss of damaging proportions. The status of the 'non-Christian' missionary movement as a French product may also have contributed to the opposition. For many Irish Catholics the French Church had proved unreliable during the revolutionary period, and its capacity to withstand the assaults of resurgent anticlericalism in the second half of the nineteenth century was considered suspect. By the same token, the strong Ultramontane sentiment which had the upper hand in Ireland up to 1878[7] would have encouraged distrust for a church whose loyalty to Rome had been traditionally weak. There can be little doubt, too, that the opposition was fuelled by a fear that, with a large outflow of priestly vocations, funds so badly needed in Ireland might also be diverted to France.

II

In the final analysis, it was precisely the institutes committed to recruiting candidates for the priesthood which were to play the leading role in introducing the continental missionary impulse to Ireland. Confronted with the resistance of significant elements within the local church and yet unable to turn elsewhere for English-speaking subjects, they were forced to adopt tactics altogether different from those originally preferred. Learning from initial attempts at recruitment that there could be little progress without a wide measure of local support, they were compelled to set down permanent roots and to engage in activities calculated to win the approval and trust of the Irish Church. The pioneers of this new approach were the missionaries of the Congregation of the Holy Ghost and the Immaculate Heart of Mary (C.S.Sp.).

The shape of the C.S.Sp.'s Irish undertaking was determined by the congregation's peculiar constitution and the needs of the Irish Church. Formed by a fusion of two ecclesiastical organisations, each with its particular charism and tradition, the congregation was eminently suited to respond to what was undoubtedly the most pressing requirement for Irish Catholicism during the second half of the nineteenth century—namely the construction of an efficient educational system.

The Congregation of the Holy Ghost had been founded in 1703 by Claude Poullart des Places to train students for the diocesan priesthood.[8] Renowned for the excellence of its tuition, its doctrinal orthodoxy and loyalty to the Holy See,[9] during the course of the eighteenth century the congregation was to train a body of priests which remained faithful during the Revolution. Suppressed in 1792, its seminary confiscated and its members dispersed, the congregation was unable to recover its earlier momentum in the first part of the nineteenth century. Efforts to regroup were frustrated by weak leadership and by the impossibility of accommodating, at one and the same time, successive political regimes *and* a Holy See deeply suspicious of any accommodation between church and state. Indeed, by the 1840s the outlook for the institute had become distinctly bleak.

Since the 1780s those ordained at the congregation's Paris seminary in the Rue des Postes (later in the Rue Lhomond) had been encouraged to go to the French colonies. It was the colonies too which attracted the attention of François Libermann, the convert from Judaism, who more than any other figure (with the possible exception of Cardinal Lavigerie) was to dominate the missionary renaissance in France. Possessing a passionate desire to serve the 'poor abandoned blacks' and in particular to save them from the threat of 'Protestant heresy', Libermann was dissatisfied with the existing colonial clergy. These, he maintained, were over-preoccupied with white communities, lacked zeal for the conversion of indigenous populations and paid little attention to the plight of slaves.[10] It was against this background that in 1841 he decided to found the Congregation of the Holy Heart of Mary specifically for the evangelisation of blacks. From the start his endeavour was beset with difficulties. Because the work proposed had already been entrusted by the Holy See to other agencies, not least Poullart des Places' institute, Libermann's missionaries were compelled to operate in areas which were generally considered unsafe for Europeans, or in regions where the political climate was unfavourable to French missionary enterprise.

The fusion[11] between the two institutes, arranged by Propaganda Fide in 1848, was designed to solve the problems of both congregations. Libermann brought to the foundation a vigorous and energetic leadership, a capacity to deal with government agencies, and an infusion of young and dedicated priests to staff its missions. The Congregation of the Holy Ghost brought its reputation for doctrinal orthodoxy and educational excellence, a tradition of long service to the colonies and, perhaps most important of all, the mission jurisdictions which Libermann's institute lacked.

III

It was the Congregation of the Holy Heart of Mary which first became interested in creating an Irish cadre of missionaries when in 1842 a prohibition on French nationals in the British colonies endangered her position in Mauritius. After some singularly unsuccessful attempts to recruit in England and Ireland, Libermann placed his hopes on Fr John Hand, who at that time was contemplating the establishment of his seminary. Libermann proposed that Hand could best serve the Church's apostolic mission by supplying students who would be trained in the congregation's seminary at Amiens. He also suggested the foundation of an Irish institute along the lines of his own in which Hand would be the superior general.[12] When after some vacillation the Irish priest decided to go his own way Libermann became despondent about the capacity of Ireland to produce missionaries and sought to solve his difficulties in the colonies by attempting to influence the British government (through Nicholas Wiseman, then Vicar of the London District)[13] to relax its restrictive regulations.[14] Again he was unsuccessful, and the problem was to remain unresolved for a further decade, despite fitful and always futile efforts at recruitment in Ireland and England.

It was under the leadership of Libermann's successor, Fr Ignace Schwindenhammer, that a concerted effort was made to institute a foundation in the British Isles. The problems of the fusion which had inhibited Libermann in his efforts to secure English-speaking subjects had now been resolved, and the congregation at last found itself in a position to deal forcefully with the continuing threat to its missions in the British colonies, especially Gambia and Sierra Leone. The danger of suppression after the upheavals of 1848 lent a new urgency to the question of expansion outside continental Europe.

Shortly before his death Libermann had already come to the conclusion that successful recruitment in the British Isles required the establishment of foundations, which would in turn require the goodwill of the local hierarchy and clergy. Schwindenhammer concurred with this view after efforts to secure recruits in Ireland (through Dr David Moriarty of All Hallows, Dr Thomas Bennett of the Carmelites and Bishop Dominick O'Brien of Waterford) and in England (through Dr Henry Edward Manning) had proved unproductive. The choice of Ireland in preference to England was easily made, for since the mid-1850s the congregation had been receiving indications from a number of Irish churchmen that it would be welcome in Ireland to assist in the work of Catholic education. This development was not altogether unexpected. Relations between the Holy Ghost Fathers and the Irish had always been cordial. Irish priests and bishops working in the United States of America and the colonies had cultivated friendships with priests educated at the Rue des Postes, and prelates en route to Rome often stopped off at the Holy Ghost headquarters to seek new recruits for their missions. Again, during his years at the Sulpician seminary at Issy (1827-37) Libermann had made a profound impression on Irish seminarians, some of whom now occupied influential posts in Ireland. Relationships were consolidated in Rome, where from 1853 the Congregation of the Holy Ghost had assumed charge over the French seminary, and in Paris, where the Irish College was situated in the same *quartier* as the Holy Ghost headquarters. Doubtless the Irish were also influenced by the fact that under Schwindenhammer the congregation was vigorously developing its educational dimension. Indeed, between 1852 and 1862 Schwindenhammer was to open several seminaries, colleges and industrial schools, in contrast to a single new mission station in Africa. In all, during his term of office (1852-81) he was to found more than thirty colleges and seminaries.[15]

The congregation's decision to take advantage of the favourable attitude among Irish churchmen was not arrived at without misgivings. It was clear from the outset that it was the congregation's reputation for educational excellence and not its missionary dimension which attracted the Irish.[16] Accordingly there could be no alternative to the provision of schools which would inevitably place a strain on resources. There were also certain misgivings as to the capacity of Irishmen who might join the congregation to function effectively as missionaries. Libermann's experiences had led him to the opinion that the Irish lacked the 'spirit of generosity' which he found in other races—a view which was to be repeated by leaders of the Society of African Missions of Lyons and which also gained currency in official circles in Rome.[17] Yet these objections were by no means insuperable and, weighed against the paramount necessity to procure English-speaking priests and the need to establish the congregation outside continental Europe, were eventually overruled. It was seen that despite its drawbacks the foundation of schools would provide at least a base from which recruitment might proceed, although it was realised that such activity would have to be conducted judiciously so as not to attract the censure of a Church unsympathetic to the 'pagan missionary cause'. On the other count, there was the argument that the long period of seminary training in France and careful supervision in the mission-field could help to wean away the Irish from their attachment to '*la vie confortable*'.

IV

In 1859, responding to repeated invitations and finally overcoming its scruples, the congregation dispatched Fr Marie-Louis Holley[18] to negotiate an Irish foundation. On his arrival Holley received a request from Bishop David Moriarty of Kerry[19] to undertake the management of his new seminary in Killarney. Bishop O'Brien of Waterford[20] signalled his willingness to allow him to open a school in his diocese.[21] Holley and his superiors, however, were anxious to settle the congregation in Dublin, which possessed the largest Catholic population and the greatest concentration of resources. Paul Cullen, Archbishop of Dublin, was initially reluctant to accommodate the institute, fearing that his already overtaxed diocese would be unable to support a new foundation. Fortunately for the congregation, Dr Bartholomew Woodlock of All Hallows and Dr Thomas Bennett, the influential provincial of the Carmelites—both firm supporters of the C.S.Sp.—intervened forcefully and persuaded Cullen to grant a conditional permission. An Irish house was duly opened in Blanchardstown, to the north of Dublin, in October, and in the following summer the community transferred to Williamstown House, later Blackrock College, in the city's southern suburbs.

Fr Jules Leman, superior of the Irish foundation, and his superiors in Paris hoped that the secondary school which opened in 1860 would provide candidates for the missionary priesthood and revenue for the congregation's Irish works. But the main prospect for the future lay with the junior scholasticate (or secondary school for aspirants) which opened at the same time in Blackrock and was designed to ensure that those prepared to commit themselves to the congregation would be brought firmly within its ambience from the earliest stage.[22] In the final analysis, the success of the congregation's Irish enterprise depended upon its ability to preserve the delicate balance between its commitment to education and its commitment to the formation of aspirants in the scholasticate. But it was apparent from the start that the balance could not easily be maintained.

Ironically, what undermined the congregation's strategy was the resounding success of the school as an educational establishment. By the end of the 1862 school year Archbishop Cullen was sufficiently impressed to preside at the distribution of prizes.[23] The 1863-64 school year was even more successful, with the college taking second place in the Catholic University examinations. In the following year, with seventeen distinctions in the examinations, Blackrock became the leading college in the university.[24] Similar performances were maintained year after year until the university's closure in 1880. But these achievements invariably brought an ever-increasing number of applications to enter the school, with a corresponding need for extensions to the existing buildings; there was also a natural determination to maintain the high academic standards. As a result, shortage of funds became an endemic problem, and the little which was available went to the upkeep of the schools rather than to the poorly equipped scholasticate. More damaging was the circumstance that, in the efforts to maintain academic standards, it became impossible to provide sufficient formation staff for the scholastics, and aspirants were henceforth integrated in the school.

The opening in 1864 of another secondary school and scholasticate at Rockwell, Co. Tipperary, to serve the south of the country, increased the congregation's prestige in educational circles but added to its financial burdens and demands on personnel. St Mary's College, Rathmines, which opened as a day school in 1890, placed a further strain on resources. Until 1924 and even later financial and staffing difficulties regularly reached critical proportions.[25]

Throughout this period there was no shortage of applications to join the congregation, a consequence of its growing prestige through educational work at a time when recruits to the religious life were at a premium. Yet the number of those persevering to ordination was disappointing. From the establishment of the Blackrock scholasticate in 1859 until 1917 a total of 924 aspirants were accepted. Of these, 158 were ordained, while 22 more made their final profession, yielding an average perseverance rate of 19.5 per cent. In the Rockwell scholasticate an average perseverance rate of 16.9 per cent was recorded between 1865 and 1924; or, from an intake of 449 candidates, 65 were ordained, while 11 made final profession without seeking ordination.[26] These figures were far from satisfying by any standards. A leakage rate of 60–70 per cent over the total term of training (scholasticate, novitiate, prefecting,[27] philosophy, and theology), lasting from ten to thirteen years, would have been acceptable. Losses of 80 per cent and 83 per cent were exceptionally high. Even more disturbing was the fact that almost all of those who abandoned the congregation did so during their scholasticate years in Ireland. Defection from the senior levels of training in France was rare.[28]

Undoubtedly there were some who had joined the scholasticates to secure a good and economical education; there must have been others who used the congregation's facilities as a stepping-stone to priesthood in diaspora dioceses. There were also those who joined the congregation attracted by its conspicuous educational dimension, but when gradually confronted with the prospect of a missionary career, became discouraged and severed the connection. But the major cause of the high defection rate was generally acknowledged to be the absence of proper facilities in Ireland for training aspirants.[29] And this, in turn, was due to the overriding necessity to maintain the schools. Many held that the scholasticates should be completely separate from the schools, for, it was argued, contact with the secular atmosphere took its toll. But efforts to solve the problem along these lines were frustrated by the continuing lack of funds and by the insufficiency of capable personnel.

The intention, therefore, that the Irish foundation would provide a substantial body of missionaries for C.S.Sp. jurisdictions in British Africa was not to be realised during the first half-century of the congregation's presence in Ireland. By 1893 there were 89 Irish ordinations, but because of the need to maintain the schools only 18 found their way to Africa. Of the remainder, 14 were assigned to Trinidad, where they worked mainly in colleges; 13 went to the United States of America, where some missions to blacks were established; while 4 were assigned to France to teach in seminaries and colleges. Forty priests were retained in Ireland for school work. The number of professed brothers during the same period slightly exceeded that of priests; and a similar proportion was kept at home to help with the running of the schools. In 1901 there were 46 brothers working in Ireland.[30]

There was, nonetheless, some notable field-work, particularly on the west coast of Africa, in the British colonies of Sierra Leone, and later in Nigeria, where talented missionaries like Fr James Browne (Pro-Vicar Apostolic of Sierra Leone) opened up new territories and set high standards, thus helping to confound those who held that Irishmen were incapable of performing as successful missionaries. But measured against the large-scale activity in Africa by French, Belgian, German and Italian missionaries, Irish Holy Ghost personnel made little impact until the third decade of the twentieth century.[31]

V

Even though by the turn of the century its original objective in coming to Ireland remained largely unfulfilled, the Irish C.S.Sp. foundation did much to change local attitudes to the 'pagan' (or more accurately 'non-Christian') missionary cause. The congregation had been active in promoting its African missions as soon as its reputation in education permitted it to do so. For example, Fr Leman had founded an 'Association for the Propagation of the Faith to Blacks', managed a lottery to raise funds for the missions, and organised and delivered lectures and talks on missionary subjects.

But it was only in the last years of the century, when a measure of control had been brought over school staffing and financing, that it became possible to mount a determined promotional campaign. In 1897 a special team, headed by a skilled publicist, Fr Jean-Martin Ebenrecht, a native of Alsace, was formed to spread mission awareness throughout the country. Ebenrecht preached numerous 'missions' or retreats in which he featured foreign missions.[32] He also edited an influential front-page column in the leading Catholic weekly, the *Irish Catholic*, in which he described the exploits of Holy Ghost missionaries on the west coast of Africa.[33] Special prominence was given to the achievements of Irish members of the congregation; Fr James Browne, his successor in Sierra Leone, Mgr John O'Gorman, and Fr Joseph Shanahan (later Vicar Apostolic of Southern Nigeria) were most frequently mentioned. Impassioned appeals for supporting the congregation's anti-slavery campaign and a novel scheme to raise revenue by collecting used stamps all helped to sustain interest. By such promotional work, and especially by the emphasis on the Irish contribution, the congregation helped to create the climate which made the later missionary movement possible.

If the promotional campaign was to benefit the Irish missionary movement as a whole, it was the schools which in the long run were to serve the congregation best. It was true that between 1859 and the late 1920s the commitment to Irish education seriously compromised the congregation's effectiveness in recruiting and training missionaries. Yet the financial difficulties were eventually brought under control, and the rate of perseverance among candidates increased correspondingly as additional funds were invested in training facilities and as greater numbers of students from the congregation's secondary schools—mostly of high calibre—made their way into the Holy Ghost seminary at Kimmage, Dublin. In retrospect, therefore, if the extensive educational base built by the pioneers fell short of expectations, in the long term it was to ensure that the Congregation of the Holy Ghost would become Ireland's largest mission-sending agency.[34]

SEVEN

The Society of
African Missions, 1878–1920[1]

I

A SECOND French missionary institute instrumental in awakening Irish interest in non-Christian missions was the Society of African Missions of Lyons (S.M.A.), which first came to Ireland in 1878, also in search of priests for its missions in the British colonies. The decision by the S.M.A. to make a foundation in Ireland was the result of a combination of chance and necessity; the latter was imposed by the circumstance that in 1876 the two most important missions serviced by the society were in Lagos and South Africa; chance operated when Fr Augustin Planque, the S.M.A. Superior General, came to look for a base from which to recruit English-speaking personnel for these missions.

It was in the South African mission that the idea of recruiting *Irish* missionaries originated. The first S.M.A. group arriving there in 1873 was received by the Irish priest James O'Haire (mentioned in Chapter 3),[2] acting for his bishop, Dr John Leonard. A good relationship was established, and in discussions during the next few years O'Haire suggested to the French that they would best meet the demands of their English-speaking missions by recruiting Irish students for the society. He went even further (influenced also by a falling out with his bishop) and volunteered his own services, which Lyons accepted. Had not O'Haire intervened, it is likely that Planque would have turned to England rather than Ireland. He had useful contacts there since 1870, when anticlerical riots in Lyons led him to transfer several of his seminarians to Bishop Vaughan's missionary establishment at Mill Hill, London. Nor, like Fr Libermann, was his estimation of the Irish missionary potential high. On the contrary, he had been influenced by reports from South Africa which denigrated the Irish and claimed that O'Haire was the only true missionary amongst them.[3]

From the outset, in its efforts to establish itself in Ireland, the S.M.A. had to contend with considerable clerical hostility. To an extent the problem was self-inflicted, a consequence of the unorthodox and often extravagant tactics of O'Haire, who was soon compelled to withdraw from the project, and the ineptitude of his successor, François Devoucoux, the first superior appointed by the society. However, at a deeper level there was the reluctance by clergy to accept in their midst an unknown French foundation promoting a scarcely popular cause and which was unlikely to make the slightest contribution to local needs.

O'Haire, who arrived in Ireland in the summer of 1876, spent two years touring the country before he could obtain permission to establish a house. Eventually Bishop William Delany of Cork gave his consent in 1878 on the understanding that the society would limit its activities to recruitment and fund-raising. During the next four years when, in contravention of the agreement with the bishop, S.M.A. priests built a church and opened a small 'apostolic school' or junior seminary, there was strong opposition from local clergy; and the bishop, with full justification, would almost certainly have expelled them from his diocese had he not fallen ill. In the event, the church was closed to the public, and permission to collect funds was withdrawn. Meanwhile the number and quality of those dispatched from the school to the S.M.A. seminary in Lyons failed to impress the society's leaders. This too was largely a consequence of the failure to win the trust and favour of the clergy. The accepted method of recruitment among religious institutes and seminaries at the time was to seek suitable candidates through local clergy. Because of clerical hostility, this channel was almost completely closed, and the society was forced instead to rely on advertisements placed in Catholic newspapers and reference works like the *Irish Catholic Directory*. The applicants obtained through these channels were usually of poor calibre and frequently included those who were unable to obtain recommendations from their local clergy for diocesan colleges. By the close of 1882 the Irish foundation was in some disarray, its staff demoralised, its student complement reduced to a meagre seven, and its church still closed to the public.

The appointment of Fr Joseph Zimmermann as superior in Cork in January 1883 marked a turning-point in the foundation's fortunes. Zimmermann, who hailed from Switzerland, was a man of rare quality, a graduate of the Dominican university at Fribourg but with a common touch and a sensitivity to local feelings which none of his French predecessors possessed. Aware that his superiors were disappointed with results and might well withdraw from Ireland, Zimmermann set about the task of reviving the foundation. Already within months of his arrival he had identified the reasons for his society's failure to make progress. He saw that the C.S.Sp. had won acceptance because of its reputation for orthodoxy and loyalty to Rome, as well as its impeccable credentials in the field of education. The S.M.A., in contrast, had come empty-handed and was perceived as a typical Gallican organisation bent on filching funds and priestly vocations.

Zimmermann had no great love for the French. As a young priest he had taught in the society's seminary at Lyons, experiencing there a measure of cultural arrogance among other staff members who felt that Frenchmen alone were capable of functioning effectively as missionaries. He concluded that if the Irish foundation was to have any prospect of success, it would have to shed its French characteristics; nor had he any reservations about flying in the face of society authority in order to secure this objective. In the years 1886-91, acting in concert with one of two Irish members of the society, Fr John Barrett, Zimmermann developed a strategy which was to change radically the direction of the foundation. From its inception the branch had endeavoured to raise funds mainly in England, and by 1890 substantial sums had been gathered. Zimmermann resolved that henceforth efforts should be made to retain these moneys and the proceeds of further collections under the control of the Irish branch; furthermore, he determined to seek authorisation from Rome for the training of candidates in Ireland rather than in Lyons and for their subsequent assignment to mission-fields entrusted to the Irish branch and administered from Cork.

Zimmermann never fully revealed his intentions to his superiors, but when the ruling council of the society eventually learned that funds were being withheld, it demanded an explanation. Replying that the benefactors, in most cases, had insisted on their subscriptions remaining in Ireland, Zimmermann declared his hands were tied. This disingenuous response concealed the fact that it was the Cork superior who had persuaded supporters to prohibit the alienation of funds to France.

The key to the success of Zimmermann's strategy was his capacity to win support from bishops and diocesan clergy. During the early years he sought to establish the good reputation of the society in the diocese of Cork, no easy task in view of the hostility of certain prominent local clerics and low morale among his confrères. Refusing to be intimidated by his opponents, while at the same time offering the services of his priests[4] to those better disposed, he hoped to gain acceptance for his community. Eventually his efforts bore fruit, assisted in no small measure by the arrival of the missionary-minded Dr Thomas O'Callaghan, O.P., who succeeded Delany as bishop in 1886. Thereafter Zimmermann set about cultivating leading figures in the Irish Church, suggesting that the time was ripe for the inauguration of an indigenous missionary enterprise to non-Christian peoples. Zimmermann's advocacy of an Irish enterprise was particularly appropriate, for by the closing decade of the century the Irish Church had solved most of its domestic problems, the task of internal reorganisation was almost complete, the education question was well in hand, and the diaspora communities were producing their own clergy in increasing numbers. In all his contacts Zimmermann emphasised his distrust of the French and his desire to bring to birth a distinctively Irish movement which would revive the glories of Ireland's illustrious missionary past. Eventually, in 1902, his efforts were rewarded when O'Callaghan and Robert Browne, a former President of Maynooth and at the time Bishop of Cloyne, with the blessing of Cardinal Michael Logue, agreed to become trustees for the foundation's funds. Later, in 1905, a second trust involving John Healy, Archbishop of Tuam (a historian who was greatly attracted by the prospect of an Irish missionary renaissance), was established. The formation of the trusts made the Irish funds secure. But their significance went deeper. By the agreement of the bishops to participate, a policy of direct episcopal involvement in the affairs of the Irish branch was initiated. On a wider level, it signalled that the 'pagan' missionary cause was now no longer a matter of peripheral interest to Irish bishops.

II

The support of Bishop Thomas O'Callaghan was of critical importance to the success of Zimmermann's plans. His predecessor, Bishop Delany, was already in his seventy-fifth year and in declining health when he admitted the society to his diocese. By 1880 the effective administration of the diocese had fallen into the hands of Dean

Henry Neville, the vicar general, who had taken a distinct dislike to the foundation. When Bishop Delany asked for a coadjutor in 1883 it seemed likely that Neville, a former Rector of the Catholic University and the bishop's own choice, would be appointed.[5] Had the appointment proceeded, there can be little doubt that Zimmermann's scheme would have foundered. Neville's failure to gain the nomination was due to the intervention of ecclesiastical opponents who vigorously promoted the candidacy of Thomas O'Callaghan, then Prior of San Clemente in Rome. From the outset of his episcopacy[6] O'Callaghan was impressed by the personal and priestly qualities of the S.M.A. superior. As an early token of approval he lifted the prohibition on fund-raising, permitted the opening of the S.M.A. church to the public, and restored to Zimmermann the right to hear confessions in the diocese which his predecessor had withdrawn. Well acquainted with the Church's efforts to evangelise non-Christian peoples through his contacts with Propaganda Fide, and anxious that Ireland should participate, O'Callaghan was immediately receptive to Zimmermann's proposal for an Irish movement. He was also soon convinced that the Swiss priest could provide the necessary leadership. Thereafter, until Zimmermann's removal by his superiors in 1913, he was to play a leading role in the promotion of the scheme.

Scarcely less important to the success of the project was the support of a wealthy Catholic layman, Lieutenant-Colonel Llewellyn Blake.[7] Unlike the Holy Ghost Fathers, whose fee-paying schools provided a reliable (albeit inadequate) source of income, the S.M.A. was wholly dependent on private subscriptions. During the first fifteen of the thirty years he spent in Cork Zimmermann was compelled to devote much time and energy to fund-raising in Ireland, England and America. The relatively substantial sums which he and his colleagues raised during this period were sufficient for existing needs; however, they fell far short of the amounts necessary for the comprehensive training programme for large numbers of students which Zimmermann's scheme required. It was the intervention of Colonel Blake which was to provide a solution to this difficulty. From 1899 until his death in 1916 Blake subscribed in excess of £20,000 towards the education of students and made over his estates in Mayo and Galway for use as houses of training. At his death he bequeathed eight-fifteenths of his assets, amounting to a sum of £60,000, to the society's benefit. Not only did Blake provide most of the society's financial means, but his intervention on its behalf was an important factor in winning the support of the Cardinal and bishops. His advocacy, both in Irish clerical circles and at Rome, of a distinctly Irish enterprise, free from continental control, won for that concept a measure of acceptance which Zimmermann, despite his exceptional powers of persuasion, could never have achieved alone.

Blake's interest in missions predated his association with the S.M.A. After the death of his wife without issue in 1891 he began to look for suitable Catholic charities to endow. He gave small sums of money to Fr Anthony Boyle, a Vincentian involved in sponsoring Chinese seminarians, and contributed more generously to Bishop Benziger in Southern India. Fr Nicholas Dillon of the Franciscans (brother of John Dillon, M.P.) and Fr Daniel Lynch, a C.S.Sp. missionary working in Sierra Leone, were also in receipt of his charity. The circumstances of Blake's first contacts with Zimmermann are difficult to determine. One source suggests that in 1899 the colonel sent 5s each in response to five charitable appeals in the *Irish Catholic* and was so impressed by the warmth of Zimmermann's acknowledgment that he immediately donated a burse of £500.[8] Although this account has the flavour of legend and is unsupported by documentary evidence, it may well have been true. Appeals in the *Irish Catholic* were commonplace; Blake was seeking suitable outlets for his benefactions; and Zimmermann was always careful to respond to donations, no matter how small, by lengthy letters expressing deep gratitude and describing the nature of his work as well as his own straitened circumstances.

Blake appears to have been endowed with an unsentimental, disciplined piety; and in business affairs he was decidedly shrewd. It is clear that not only was he deeply impressed by the sincerity of Zimmermann's expressions of gratitude, but also that the sound practical sense which the Cork superior displayed found resonances in his own temperament. Zimmermann helped to foster his interest by revealing detailed information about the society, its finances, prospects and internal politics and by seeking his advice in directing the Irish branch, an approach which had already proved successful with previous benefactors. More important, he gradually introduced Blake to his unique vision of Ireland's missionary future and in particular to the role which he had marked out for the Irish branch of the S.M.A.

The most obvious effect of Blake's largesse was that it enabled Zimmermann to develop his work with facility. Freed from the burden of undertaking arduous collecting tours, within three years he was able to raise the number of students attending the apostolic school to 50 and was also catering for 35 French priests (who taught in the school, learned English, or simply convalesced after tours of duty in Africa). In addition, he saw to the needs of a community of between 25 and 30 missionary sisters of the order of Our Lady of Apostles (founded by Fr Planque) which he had first introduced to Ireland in 1887. When it became necessary to purchase a second house and add a wing to the school the Blake funds covered the cost. More important, in the longer term, Blake's donation of property and burses for the training of students greatly strengthened Zimmermann's position when he came to argue his case for autonomy in Rome.

III

In 1905, as soon as the formation of the trusts was accomplished, Zimmermann travelled to Rome (ostensibly to obtain a papal honour for Blake) and submitted the first of a series of petitions to Propaganda Fide informing the Sacred Congregation that the time was ripe for the development of an Irish 'pagan missionary enterprise' and that the Irish branch of the S.M.A. was eminently suited to spearhead the movement. He requested that S.M.A. headquarters should be instructed to authorise the Irish branch to train its students in Ireland, and that specially designated mission territories should be confided to the society's Irish members. He argued that Egypt, which had been under British control since 1883, would be an appropriate location for such an enterprise because French missionaries were no longer acceptable there. Appended to the petition were letters from Cardinal Logue, Bishop O'Callaghan, Archbishop Healy, Bishop Browne and other leading Irish ecclesiastics declaring support for these projects and confidence in Zimmermann. Through the good offices of Fr Thomas Crotty, Prior of San Clemente, who had been enlisted by O'Callaghan, Zimmermann obtained interviews with Cardinal Merry del Val, Secretary of State, and Cardinal Gotti, Prefect of Propaganda Fide, and other influential officials in the Vatican. The society's leadership, which had first been alerted to the petition when Propaganda requested its views on the matter, informed the Sacred Congregation that since Zimmermann was attempting to disrupt the unity of the society, he must be withdrawn.

Officials at Propaganda, in an effort at compromise, rejected the Irish petition but informed S.M.A. headquarters that Zimmermann's recall would be inopportune in view of the wide measure of support he commanded from within the Irish hierarchy.

Between 1907 and 1910 Zimmermann was to make four further excursions to Rome, bearing impressive dossiers containing submissions of the type already described but, in addition, seeking the concession of provincial status for the Irish branch, and always armed with numerous letters of recommendation from his Irish supporters. Lyons continued to dispatch its own representatives, arguing against the Irish position and seeking Propaganda's consent to Zimmermann's recall. By 1910 the affair had become something of an embarrassment at Rome and the Holy See could no longer procrastinate. In July of that year the *plenarium* of cardinals authorised to adjudicate the case decided that the Irish branch should be raised to provincial status with a large measure of autonomy, and that it should be allowed to train priests, retain funds, and be assigned specific mission territories. At the same time sanction was given for Zimmermann's recall, while the new province was awarded the extremely hazardous mission of Liberia instead of Egypt.[9]

The reaction of the Irish hierarchy to Zimmermann's removal was even greater than Propaganda had anticipated. Many of the bishops made strong representations to have the decision reversed. Zimmermann, believing his work incomplete, made every effort to stay at his post, even orchestrating a series of petitions from his lay supporters, including Colonel Blake. But Rome remained firm. The society's leadership withdrew Fr Stephen Kyne, an Irish member trained at Lyons, from his mission in Liberia and appointed him to govern the new province in the French interest. Strongly opposed by the bishops and local clergy, he soon found the strain unsustainable and resigned his position. His successor, Fr Maurice Slattery, during the subsequent decade experienced serious difficulties in maintaining the province. But he was made of sterner stuff than his predecessor, and the growing support for non-Christian missions and the firm financial base laid by Zimmermann made it possible for him to bring the Irish province through the crisis. During the 1920s and 1930s the province consolidated its position and in subsequent decades became one of the larger institutes working in the African theatre.

Zimmermann's importance for the missionary movement of the twentieth century extends beyond his work on behalf of the S.M.A. During his thirty years in Ireland he played a major role in persuading leading churchmen that the time had come to inaugurate an indigenous non-Christian missionary enterprise. This achievement was quite distinct from his success in promoting the S.M.A. as the vehicle for such a movement. For with his departure and the withdrawal of support from his institute, the interest in non-Christian missions remained firm. Subsequently it contributed in no small degree to the readiness with which the Irish Church responded to a historic initiative by Irish diocesan priests to found a mission to China.

IV

It would be unhistorical to attribute the new missionary awareness spreading through Ireland in the first decade of the twentieth century exclusively to the activities of the C.S.Sp. and the S.M.A. By the turn of the nineteenth century other organisations were playing a part. During the last two decades of the century the institutes of women religious which hitherto had confined their activities to recruitment began to set down roots and to train candidates in Ireland. Some of the older-established orders also felt encouraged to engage in what was gradually becoming an acceptable form of the apostolate, while those already involved were moved to increase the scale of their commitment. Graphic accounts of the exploits of these Irish missionaries, emphasising the heroic quality of their work, now began to appear regularly in the Catholic press and occasionally in the secular press, alongside accounts of their better-known C.S.Sp. compatriots. The awareness which this created made it possible to mount extensive fund-raising campaigns in Ireland which in turn generated further interest.

Despite this flurry of activity, however, it would be wrong to claim that the modern Irish missionary movement was a reality at the close of the nineteenth century. It was true that the interest in Irish missions to non-Christians was beginning to gain momentum. But the hierarchy and the rank and file of the clergy still remained generally uncommitted or distrustful; while the support of the laity, although wholehearted, reflected more a commitment to the continental movement and a general enthusiasm for all things religious than a discriminating support for a new Irish initiative. It was principally the activities of the C.S.Sp. and the S.M.A. in the opening decade of the twentieth century which brought the idea of foreign missions to the centre of the stage and created the environment in which an Irish movement at last could be inaugurated and flourish.

PART THREE

Birth of an
Indigenous Movement

EIGHT

The Maynooth Mission
to China

THE formation of the Maynooth Mission to China (St Columban's Foreign Mission Society) in 1916 was the great watershed in the history of the modern Irish missionary movement. It marked the point where growing awareness and acceptance of the missionary ideal was transformed into actual commitment on a large scale. In the years immediately following the society's foundation enthusiasm for missions manifested itself in a dramatic increase in volunteers. The Columban seminary, opened in 1918, could hardly cater for the large number of applicants, while older missionary institutes, like the C.S.Sp. and the S.M.A., as well as those other congregations and orders which had taken on missionary commitments towards the close of the nineteenth century, now found a ready supply of highly motivated candidates. The Irish Vincentians re-established a presence in China, sending ten priests to that mission-field before the first Columban arrivals in 1922. Institutes hitherto lacking a missionary dimension changed course, while those already engaged in non-Christian missions intensified their activities. Above all, there was the extraordinary release of creative energy which issued in the formation of four additional Irish missionary bodies within the space of two decades: the Missionary Sisters of St Columban (1922), the Sisters of the Holy Rosary (1924), St Patrick's Missionary Society (1932) and the Medical Missionaries of Mary (1937).

I

Most commentators trace the origins of the Maynooth Mission to the Canadian priest John Fraser, who in June 1911 addressed the students and staff of Maynooth College on the subject of China, where he was a missionary.[1] Fr Anthony Boyle, one of the two Vincentian spiritual directors at the college, is rightly credited with having first promoted China at Maynooth; but it was Fraser who remained indelibly imprinted in the memory of John Blowick, co-founder of the Maynooth Mission, as the catalyst.[2] Yet Fraser's address took place against a background which was equally important to the origins of the Columban foundation. The fact that he could address the Maynooth community on such a topic shows the extent to which the Irish Church had changed. Maynooth was no longer the national seminary of a defensive, inward-looking Church, struggling to meet myriad commitments at home and on the diaspora. Had such been the case, Fraser would scarcely have been permitted to speak in the college. On the contrary, Maynooth was now the principal training-ground of a strong, self-confident Church, capable of new undertakings overseas. A signal proof of the Church's health was the fact that it now enjoyed an over-supply of priests. Ever since the construction of additional buildings in the 1840s and 1850s there had been larger numbers of admissions to Maynooth and larger ordination classes. Similar construction programmes had been undertaken in other seminaries supplying the Irish Church. Already by the mid-1860s there was an over-supply for the home mission and the dispatch of the surplus on loan to the diaspora had become commonplace. By the beginning of the twentieth century bishops in Ireland rarely objected when a priest on temporary mission sought an extension of his tour or requested excardination[3] so that he could remain abroad permanently.

II

The initial response to Fraser's appeal took the form of a substantial financial contribution towards the education of Chinese priests.[4] The available evidence suggests that it was Fr Boyle, already engaged in this work,[5] who took charge of the collection. The fact that no one offered to go to China was understandable. No Irish missionaries were active in that theatre; besides, the requirement of learning an alien language was bound to discourage potential volunteers who, in the normal course, would have only two to three years available for missionary work. Moreover, some in Fraser's audience, aware that the college's only previous missionary venture had failed,[6] may have felt that success in the work of non-Christian missions required experienced missionary agencies like the C.S.Sp., and the Mill Hill Fathers, or the more recently founded Catholic Foreign Missionary Society of Maryknoll.

While passing through North America on his return to China, Fraser met Edward Galvin, a young Cork diocesan priest whose temporary mission in Brooklyn, New York, was coming to a close. Galvin did not relish the prospect of returning to the routine of parish life in Ireland. Adventurous by nature, during his stay in America he had already evinced a strong interest in non-Christian missions, notably in China and Africa, and on one occasion had volunteered to work among Indians in Arizona. Immediately captivated by Fraser's description of China, he wrote to his bishop seeking permission to go there as a missionary. Bishop O'Callaghan, who as shown in Chapter 7 was a long-standing supporter of non-Christian missions,[7] readily gave his consent. Galvin settled quickly into his new surroundings and within two years had persuaded two diocesan colleagues, Joseph O'Leary from Cork and Patrick O'Reilly from Meath, to join him in China. Later the small group was supplemented by two volunteers from All Hallows College, Fr Andrew McArdle and Fr John P. Conway.[8]

For a while it seemed that the remote Chinese mission was destined to remain a peculiarly exotic form of mission for a handful of wilder spirits like Galvin and his companions. Then fate took a hand in the shape of the First World War, which precipitated the sudden withdrawal of large numbers of European missionaries from the territory. Aware of the resources available in Ireland and exhilarated by the prospects for mission in China, the Irish group decided to seize the opportunity. Already they had discussed the feasibility of securing from Rome the exclusive charge of a jurisdiction. Now, in view of Propaganda's anxiety to replace those who had gone to the war, there seemed every likelihood of success provided they could demonstrate Ireland's capacity to supply priests. It was O'Leary who first urged Galvin to found an Irish missionary society for China, persuading him to return to Ireland for this purpose.

The ground had been well prepared. Ever since his arrival in China four years earlier Galvin had written numerous letters to colleagues at home encouraging interest in the mission. The priests who joined him were no less active in pleading the cause of China's conversion and stirring Irish consciences by their accounts of the appalling human suffering caused by floods and other natural disasters which they had witnessed at first hand.

Galvin's return coincided with the final illness and death of his bishop in June 1916. Thus he was compelled to seek the approval of Dr Daniel Cohalan, administrator of the diocese, whose support was vital if the scheme was to proceed. Cohalan had been a supporter of Fr Zimmermann in his efforts to establish an Irish missionary movement spearheaded by the Society of African Missions. Sharing in the general disenchantment at Zimmermann's removal and the failure to reinstate him, Cohalan had turned against the society. Yet his interest in missions remained undiminished, and he readily approved Galvin's scheme. Taking an active part in the preparations, he suggested the inclusion of Maynooth in the title of the proposed foundation, arguing the great advantage of association with Ireland's national seminary. He also introduced Galvin to Dr James McCaffrey, a vice-president of the college who was known to be sympathetic to the cause of non-Christian missions. McCaffrey immediately offered his support and suggested the formation of a national committee to plead the cause of China before the hierarchy.

No less important for the success of the scheme was the interest of John Blowick, a twenty-seven-year-old Maynooth professor, who agreed to Galvin's suggestion that he should resign his chair in the faculty of Theology and join in the enterprise. There were other volunteers, including Fr Edward McCarthy and Fr James Conway of the Dunboyne Institute, but Blowick's participation was the most eagerly sought after by Galvin. Already a man of some stature in the Irish Church despite his youth, notable not only for his scholarship but for his administrative skills, he was clearly the man to put the scheme on its feet.

The committee formed to make the case for China before the hierarchy consisted of Dr Cohalan, Dr McCaffrey, Dr John F. Hogan, President of Maynooth, Fr Blowick and Fr Galvin. Within a matter of weeks they had formulated a set of proposals which were submitted in the form of a memorial to the hierarchy's October meeting in 1916. The memorial proposed that the hierarchy should petition the Holy See for a vicariate in China and suggested the establishment of a house in Ireland to supply priests and funds for the vicariate. It was also suggested that the hierarchy should authorise designated Irish priests to conduct the scheme.

The success of the submission required a willingness on the part of the bishops to release priests and students, and it was a hesitancy in this regard which prompted an initial reluctance to grant approval. But, swayed by the advocacy of Blowick and his supporters, the bishops finally withdrew their objections and the meeting gave its sanction.

At its commencement the Maynooth Mission to China, or St Columban's Foreign Mission Society, as it later came to be called, had a membership of eight priests. An appeal for funds to provide a seminary, conducted during the autumn of 1916 and through 1917, met with an overwhelming response. In less than a year an impressive sum had been raised and a large number of applicants had presented themselves for admission. By July 1917 Rome had signalled its approval to Cardinal Logue, and in January 1918 the institute's seminary at Dalgan Park, Shrule, Co. Galway,[9] opened its doors. By 1979, some sixty years later, the institute, now international, had 884 members (mostly Irish, but also including a number from Australia and the U.S.A.), working in Japan, Korea, Pakistan, the Philippines, Taiwan, Chile, Peru, Fiji, Burma, Hong Kong, Britain, the U.S.A., Australasia, Rome and Ireland.[10] It had also been instrumental, through the action of Fr Blowick, in founding a congregation of sisters, the Missionary Sisters of St Columban (1922), which by 1970 counted some 300 members.

III

The foundation of the Maynooth Mission to China coincided with a period of profound and revolutionary change in Ireland's political history. Over the years a number of writers have commented on the relationship between the missionary renaissance and the Easter Rising of 1916. Some maintain that the political upheaval exercised a powerful inspirational influence on the missionary movement. Others go so far as to suggest a direct causal relationship, describing the Maynooth Mission as a religious expression of the spirit of enthusiasm and self-sacrifice generated by the Easter Rising. What may be said of such interpretations?

It would be plainly unhistorical to characterise the missionary awakening, embodied in the Maynooth scheme, as a by-product of the Rising. The scheme had already been proposed and planned during the period 1912-16, before the outbreak of the rebellion in Dublin, when Galvin and his companions were resident in China. Galvin himself, on hearing of the fighting, feared that it might interfere with his plans. Had the Rising never occurred, the Maynooth Mission would have gone ahead successfully, because Ireland was already interested in non-Christian missions and capable of a profound commitment.

In the final analysis, the effect of the Rising was to make Catholics more receptive to the missionary movement. In its aftermath there was indeed a 'smouldering emotionalism' abroad in the land, and there was much talk of sacrifice, especially among the young. There is no doubt that the Maynooth Mission and the other missionary agencies drew advantage from such sentiment. Yet it is important to emphasise that widespread approval for the Rising took time to emerge. Not all young people were immediately swept away by admiration for Pearse and his fellow-revolutionaries. Tens of thousands were at that very time fighting in Flanders, France and other theatres of war, and they and their families were dismayed and confused by the events in Dublin. The leaders of the Maynooth Mission were acutely aware of these feelings. Fr Blowick records that during the initial fund-raising campaign for the new society he and his colleagues

> carefully avoided political discussion of any kind and when we were asked whether we were Sinn Féin or not in tendency, we always replied that we had given no thought to politics but that we concentrated all our attention on the work we had in hand.[11]

The enthusiasm for the national struggle and its fallen heroes took hold only after the Great War, with the growth of Sinn Féin and the disillusionment which followed the cessation of hostilities on the continent. It must be said that this enthusiasm was somewhat dampened by the Civil War and its legacy of bitterness. Nevertheless, at least among the young, a willingness to endure sacrifice and to undertake heroic action for the sake of the nation continued to manifest itself and made the notion of a national missionary effort attractive to those seeking an outlet for their idealism.

While the Easter Rising and the subsequent struggle for independence created an environment favourable to the missionary cause, there were other influences which merit attention. Patrick Callan, writing in *Archivium Hibernicum* (1986),[12] asserts that enthusiasm for the Great War, so marked in clerical circles in the early years of the conflict, gave way to war-weariness and was transferred to zeal for missions. Michael O'Neill, in an impressive (though yet unpublished) paper dealing with the early development of the Maynooth Mission, suggests instead that the relationship between 'war-weariness' and the missionary movement was more a 'coincidence in time'.[13] There is certainly no evidence that in the early years those who founded the Maynooth Mission saw 'war-weariness' as a factor which would aid their efforts. Nevertheless, after the armistice several supporters of the movement writing in missionary magazines drew object lessons from the Great War, dwelling on the themes of 'misplaced idealism' and 'wasted effort' and calling for a redirection of zeal to missionary enterprise.[14] Fr O'Neill also offers the intriguing thesis that the missionary movement provided Irish Catholics with an opportunity to turn away from the 'war within the Irish national conscience' over the legitimacy of physical force, which had convulsed the minds of Irishmen and especially clergy since the time of the Fenians.[15] It is likely that many of those who joined the missionary movement suffered no qualms of conscience about the means used to prosecute the national struggle. Yet O'Neill's thesis merits serious consideration. Although constitutional nationalism was overtaken by events, many from within that tradition, and most notably senior members of the Irish Church, were uncomfortable with the triumph of militarism. The missionary movement unquestionably provided a form of idealism to which Irish nationalists from all traditions could subscribe. It also provided those who were weary with the perennial problem of political violence with a vehicle of national regeneration which they could recommend without reservation.

Finally, there can be no doubt that the cultural revival exercised a profound influence on the missionary movement. The invocation of Ireland's history, literature and language created a fertile soil for the seed of revolution. But the missionary cause also benefited, since the new consciousness of 'Irishness' which the revival promoted also included Ireland's traditional devotion to missions and love of 'the Faith'. The Maynooth Mission to China represented itself to the Irish public both as an extraordinary expression of zeal for the Faith and as a re-enactment of Ireland's illustrious missionary past, and it was this which brought it within the realm of the new cultural idealism.

NINE

Bishop Joseph Shanahan
and the Foundation of
St Patrick's Missionary Society [1]

A KEY figure in harnessing the flood of enthusiasm unleashed by the Maynooth foundation was Joseph Shanahan, the C.S.Sp. missionary who in 1905 had been nominated Prefect Apostolic of the Lower Niger (south-eastern Nigeria). He was to play a central role in establishing two of the four new missionary institutes and was indirectly responsible for a third. It is regrettable that no critical biography of Shanahan has yet been published (although a life of the bishop by Desmond Forristal is shortly due to appear). Fr J. P. Jordan's book *Bishop Shanahan of Southern Nigeria*[2] is essentially an inspirational work, though singularly well written. Of the four institutes founded between 1922 and 1937, only one has been subjected to critical scrutiny, namely St Patrick's Missionary Society, although a study of the Maynooth Mission is currently in hand and a recent biography of Marie Martin[3] provides a useful introduction to the history of the Medical Missionaries of Mary.

I

St Patrick's Missionary Society, established in 1932, was the child of several influences and circumstances. First of all, underlying all missionary developments of the period, there was the interest in non-Christian missions which had been developing since the 1880s and which had quickened into active participation with the formation and success of the Maynooth Mission to China and the achievement of national independence. Secondly, there was the increasing number of secular diocesan priests available and willing to go on temporary mission not only to the diaspora but now also to non-Christian mission-fields. As has been mentioned earlier, temporary mission to diaspora locations had been a feature of Irish diocesan life since the 1860s. The opening decade of the twentieth century saw a change in the pattern. By that time, although North

America was making greater demands than before, the needs of most other missions and, above all, England, which traditionally had absorbed the greatest number, were being met by All Hallows, Carlow, and other colleges supplying the diaspora. The result was that Maynooth priests available for temporary mission had fewer outlets in traditional areas and began to look at other options, including non-Christian mission-fields.[4]

Thirdly, there was the circumstance that the Maynooth Mission to China was unwilling to accept temporary volunteers. Learning the lesson of the ill-fated Maynooth Mission to India, Fr John Blowick was determined to assure a regular supply of priests for his mission and felt that dependence on temporary volunteers would not achieve his purpose. He also feared that circumstances at home might change, causing the flow of volunteer priests to dry up, as it had done in the case of the Indian mission. A further reason for excluding those seeking temporary mission was the realisation that such priests would have insufficient time to study the local languages necessary for a successful apostolate in China.[5]

Fourthly, there was the predicament of Joseph Shanahan, who had been promoted Vicar Apostolic of Southern Nigeria in 1920 only to find himself facing a serious staffing problem. Early in his long missionary career (he first went to Africa in 1902) he had become convinced of the value of education as a means of establishing the Church.[6] Now as bishop of a large jurisdiction at a time when opportunities for educated Africans were multiplying, he was more anxious than ever to develop schools. However, most of the priests at his disposal belonged to the French province of the C.S.Sp. and were generally unsuited to teaching. Not only did these priests lack the necessary fluency in English, but they were disinclined to see the merits of education as a means of evangelisation. Moreover, for reasons of nationality they were becoming increasingly unacceptable to the British authorities in Nigeria. Requests to his superiors for additional Irish priests, made while he was prefect apostolic, had met with a poor response because of the congregation's heavy commitment to education in Ireland. In 1920 prospects of obtaining the men required were scarcely more encouraging. Faced with this growing crisis, therefore, Shanahan determined to recruit secular priests available for temporary mission. Such priests, he felt, would be eminently suitable, since schooling and day-to-day business in the colony was conducted in English and they could be put to work as soon as they arrived.

Shanahan, who received his new appointment while on leave in Ireland, was friendly with Mgr James McCaffrey, already mentioned in connection with the Maynooth Mission to China. McCaffrey was now President of Maynooth, and it was in this capacity that he offered to introduce Shanahan to Cardinal Logue, who had arrived at the college for a meeting of the hierarchy. Shanahan eagerly availed of the opportunity and requested permission to recruit diocesan priests who would serve for three-year tours of duty in Nigeria. The experience gained in Africa, he assured the Cardinal, would be of considerable benefit to the Irish Church after the priests returned to their dioceses. Logue, who already had a lively interest in non-Christian missions—stimulated in no small degree by his contacts with Zimmermann a decade earlier—did not need to be convinced. He suggested that a five-year term would be more appropriate and invited Shanahan to address the assembled bishops on the subject. Shanahan spoke, in the words of one observer, 'as never before or since'[7] and received authorisation to canvass volunteers among Maynooth students. In order further to publicise the opportunities in Nigeria, he chose to be consecrated bishop in the college chapel (on 6 June 1920). The first Maynooth volunteer to come forward was a student named Patrick J. Whitney, due to be ordained in the college that summer. In all, ten of the students who heard Shanahan's appeal in 1920 ultimately went to Nigeria.

II

Shanahan's staffing problems also extended to nuns when the Sisters of St Joseph of Cluny, who had worked in south-east Nigeria since 1888, decided to withdraw.[8] Various efforts to attract Irish and British replacements were unproductive. However, a number of individuals, aware of Shanahan's predicament, did offer their services. One was an Irish Sister of Charity (of English birth), Mary Magdalen Charles Walker, who obtained permission from her superiors to go to Nigeria.[9] Her major contribution was to be the foundation in 1923 of an institute of African sisters, the first of its kind in Nigeria. Of much greater significance for the Irish missionary movement, however, were two other volunteers, Agnes Ryan and Marie Martin, both laywomen, who came to the bishop's assistance in May 1921. Impressed by the work of these lay missionaries, Shanahan suggested that they should form the nucleus for a congregation of missionary sisters which he had determined to found for his vicariate. Agnes Ryan, who was invalided home after five months, readily agreed. Marie Martin, who was to remain on in Africa until March 1924, also joined in the scheme, although she was already beginning to develop ideas for a missionary congregation which were substantially different from Shanahan's. Subsequently she withdrew from the project in 1926 in order to pursue her own inspiration, eventually founding in 1937 the Medical Missionaries of Mary, an institute exclusively dedicated to health care and related apostolates.[10]

Shanahan had originally intended to found the sisterhood in Nigeria, but later, for reasons which are unclear,[11] he changed his mind. In 1923, back in Ireland for medical treatment, he laid the groundwork for the new congregation (named Sisters of the Holy Rosary), obtaining permission to establish a convent in the diocese of Kilmore, locating a suitable property near Killeshandra, Co. Cavan, and assembling a group of seven (led by Agnes Ryan) who were sent to the Dominican Sisters in Cabra for their novitiate. He also entrusted two of his volunteer priests, P. J. Whitney and Thomas Ronayne, with the task of gathering funds for the new convent to be built at Killeshandra. Already in Nigeria Whitney had displayed exceptional leadership qualities, and these were to become even more evident during the two years spent fund-raising for the convent. Granted access to Irish dioceses because of his Maynooth connections, he approached his task with energy and ingenuity. His most important additions to the existing repertoire of funding techniques were the placement of appeals and articles in the provincial press and a scheme for harnessing support in the National Schools of Ireland. During these years too he also found time to liaise between potential Irish recruits and the vicariate, arranging the dispatch of several volunteers, mainly from Maynooth.

The experience of fund-raising, conducted throughout Ireland between January 1924 and February 1925, was to have a profound effect on Whitney and Ronayne. During this period they realised that there would be no real difficulty in raising the £30,000 needed to build the convent. Everywhere they found that the people were enthusiastic about non-Christian missions, especially those staffed by Irish personnel. They also discovered, within the ranks of the diocesan clergy and the student body in Maynooth, many who expressed a desire to serve in Nigeria. These experiences left Whitney and Ronayne in no doubt that if they wanted to found a missionary society for Africa, the human and material resources were ready to hand.

Indeed, they were already thinking along these lines.[12] For during their years in Nigeria they had shared with their colleagues a number of difficulties arising from their status as unattached individuals which only membership of a group or a society could resolve. First of all, they had learned from their observation of Holy Ghost colleagues that membership of a society would provide better working conditions on the mission. In contrast to Holy Ghost priests, whose interests were protected by local society superiors, the Maynooth volunteers were completely at the disposal of the bishop and could find themselves appointed to assist French C.S.Sp. priests with whom they had little in common. Membership of a missionary society would give them the right to negotiate with the bishop the terms of their placement, enabling them to work together or with congenial Irish C.S.Sp. colleagues. Secondly, Whitney and Ronayne felt that a society would ensure proper care for priests forced to return home because of illness. As matters stood, invalided missionaries—and there were several—were cast back on their own resources. Thirdly, it was clear that a society would be better able to organise the recruitment of volunteers for temporary or indeed permanent mission in Nigeria.

III

Early in 1925 Whitney decided to take measures towards the establishment of a society of missionary priests. He wrote to Shanahan proposing the foundation of a 'Mission House' to cater for priests on leave or in ill-health. He also requested that the bishop should commission a priest to undertake the recruitment and organisation of diocesan volunteers. Bishop Patrick Finegan of Kilmore, who had welcomed the Holy Rosary Sisters into his diocese, encouraged Shanahan to accept. Shanahan, for his part, saw merit in any proposal that would ensure a greater supply of resources for his vicariate. With this in mind, he authorised Whitney to recruit and raise funds on his behalf. He also agreed to appoint Bishop Finegan as superior of all secular priests working on behalf of the vicariate in Ireland. Finally, he signalled his approval of the proposal to establish a mission house.

However, within a matter of months pressure from his C.S.Sp. superiors in Paris (who were anxious to retain the vicariate exclu-

sively for the congregation) forced Shanahan to withdraw his authorisation. This setback was the first of a series which placed the
project in serious doubt. Close on the heels of this first disappointment, Whitney received news that Shanahan's health was deterio-
rating and that he had been compelled to seek a coadjutor who, as it
then seemed, would replace him in the near future. The danger to
the scheme, in Whitney's view, was that Shanahan's successor, likely
to be chosen from the Irish province of the C.S.Sp., might take a
different view on staffing and abandon the practice of recruiting
priests for temporary mission. Thirdly, the withdrawal of Whitney's
commission to recruit led, in a relatively short time, to a serious
falling off in the number of those offering themselves for Nigeria.
Finally, Whitney's own standing in Ireland suffered a damaging blow
when he was forced to resign from the Holy Rosary project because
of a disagreement with Agnes Ryan and Bishop Finegan over methods of promotion. Whitney returned to Nigeria in 1926 depressed
at the turn events had taken. But on his arrival he was greatly
heartened to discover that the diocesan priests in the vicariate were
clamouring for the formation of an Irish missionary society for Africa
and wanted him to be their leader in accomplishing the scheme.

In 1927 Shanahan, whose health was still precarious, attended
the C.S.Sp. general chapter in Paris and returned to Nigeria armed
with proposals which, it was hoped, would defuse the objections of
the Irish volunteers. The main proposition was that the diocesan
priests should become associates of the C.S.Sp. Not surprisingly,
this suggestion was rejected out of hand. Moved by the firm insis-
tence of his Irish volunteers that they should be allowed to organise
themselves into a society, Shanahan finally decided to risk the wrath
of his superiors. Together with Whitney, Bishop Finegan and another
volunteer missionary, he signed a 'Declaration of Intent', proposing
that 'The best means to attain the evangelization of the eight million
souls in the vicariate and the temporal and spiritual safeguarding of
the Maynooth priests . . . is the formation of a new society.'[13] In June
1928 he won Rome's blessing for the scheme, only to be told
categorically by his French superiors that he himself should play no
part in founding the society. He had no option but to comply.

IV

It was at this juncture that Archbishop Arthur Hinsley, the Apostolic
Delegate, or Vatican representative for the region, took up the cause

of the diocesan volunteers. His intervention was timely, for there could be no question of progress without the support of a high-ranking cleric with missionary responsibility. Hinsley had visited Southern Nigeria in 1928 and had been impressed by the great opportunities for Catholic education which British colonial policy afforded missionaries. During his visit he had discovered that the French were reserved about the vicariate's education policy, were scarcely tolerated by the British because of their nationality, and were ill-equipped to teach school through the medium of English. It was obvious to him that the introduction of Irish priests was the answer. And since the Irish province of the C.S.Sp. did not seem to be able to supply sufficient priests, he decided that the organisation of the diocesan volunteers into a society was now a matter of urgency.

In November 1929 Hinsley arranged an interview for Whitney in Rome with Cardinal Van Rossum, Prefect of Propaganda, at which the Irish priest applied for permission to establish a new society to aid in the evangelisation of Africans. The Cardinal, who had been briefed by Hinsley, gave his verbal approval. Final approbation, it was indicated, would depend upon the attitude of the Irish hierarchy. Although the blessing of the hierarchy seemed probable and the eventual success of the scheme assured, the final phase was marked by a new series of setbacks. A benefactor had offered Whitney a property in Co. Wicklow, and the local bishop, Matthew Cullen of Kildare and Leighlin, gave permission for the establishment of a 'rest house' for convalescent missionaries. Soon after he changed his mind when he learned that a fully-fledged society was to be established, arguing the poverty of Ireland, the large number of religious societies already in his diocese, and the difficulty which was bound to arise with local clergy over access to public oratories which the institute would be entitled to establish. Perhaps a more fundamental reason for his change of heart was a series of warnings by people close to the scheme or with interests in Southern Nigeria. A prominent C.S.Sp. priest who was closely associated with the Nigerian mission, Dr Edward Leen, prophesied the society's failure for reasons which were tendentious. More accurately, a falling out with Whitney was at the root of his opposition. Also, it seems, Shanahan expressed misgivings, saying that the enterprise would have to be financed in Ireland and pointing out that Whitney was no longer attached to his jurisdiction. Clearly Shanahan too had fallen out with Whitney, whose abrasive temperament did not make for easy relationships.

Notwithstanding these setbacks, Whitney presented his case before the Standing Committee of the hierarchy in January 1930 and received a positive response. Bishop Cullen was sufficiently impressed to relent in his opposition, and so the property in Wicklow again became available. Rome's official approval followed soon on the hierarchy's sanction. The society, named after St Patrick, was formally constituted on St Patrick's Day, 1932. It was entrusted with two districts (Calabar and Ogoja) in Eastern Nigeria which in 1934 were erected into the prefecture of Calabar. Some ten years later, at the time of Whitney's death in 1942, St Patrick's Missionary Society counted a membership of 34 priests and had 51 seminarians in training. By 1988 the membership had expanded to a figure of 394 priests serving missions in Nigeria, Kenya, Zambia, Malawi, Brazil, Sudan, South Africa, Zimbabwe and the Cameroons.[14]

TEN

The Development
of Medical Missions

I

IN the modern period the work of Christian missions was spearheaded by the Protestant churches. In Africa Protestant missionaries were in the field almost half a century before their Catholic
counterparts, while in Asia they soon outnumbered the remnant of
Catholic missionaries who had survived the collapse of the early
modern movement. Already by the 1830s they had developed many
of the evangelising techniques which were adopted subsequently by
Catholics, including the use of catechists, the ordination of indigenous ministers, the provision of schools, and the establishment of
orphanages, leper settlements, dispensaries and hospitals. From the
outset Catholic missionaries were impressed by the achievements of
Protestants in the field of health care. Other techniques pioneered
by Protestants excited less enthusiasm, and some provoked criticism,
such as the early ordination of indigenous ministers. But in all
theatres the selfless and efficient work by Protestant medical personnel won unstinted admiration. Such work was plainly a powerful
instrument of evangelisation, since those who benefited were also
likely to be converted. But what most commanded respect was the
capacity of Protestant missionaries to alleviate human distress and
especially to combat the endemic diseases associated with mother-
hood and infancy.

Catholic missionaries contemplating a medical apostolate found
themselves inhibited by church law. *Norms for the Approbation of
New Institutes*, issued by the Holy See in 1901 (and repeated in
1921), prohibited religious from giving aid in childbirth and from
attending women in maternity homes; while the *Code of Canon Law*,
published in 1917, forbade the practice of medicine and surgery.
Up to the twelfth century religious had been free to engage in all
aspects of health care without restriction, and through their skill

and dedication, especially during the Crusades, they had won a reputation second to none in the western world for tending the sick. The twentieth-century prohibitions were the latest in a series dating from the twelfth century, which were based on a fear that the practice of certain medical and nursing skills could constitute a threat to chastity and consequently to vocation.[1] It is true that in theory the canonical prohibition, at least, was not absolute, since the *Code* made provision for the practice of medicine and surgery by way of indult (dispensation) from the Holy See. But in practice very few exceptions were made (for clerics), and none to benefit women religious. In these circumstances missionary bishops anxious to provide proficient maternity care were compelled to rely on lay personnel. But this could never be a satisfactory solution. In many mission territories, especially in Asia but also in Africa, local custom frequently required women doctors for attendance on female patients. Since the acceptance of women into medical colleges in Europe was a relatively recent development[2] and because at this epoch highly motivated Catholics tended to join religious congregations, it was difficult to find suitable staff. Moreover, in an era when government subventions for health care were rare, few bishops could afford the expense of remunerating lay professionals adequately for their services.

The lifting of the prohibition against the practice of maternity nursing occurred late in the history of modern Catholic missionary enterprise, in 1936, although pressure for change from missionary bishops and other interested parties had been building up since the opening decade of the twentieth century. The publication of the Instruction *Constans ac Sedula*,[3] authorising the practice of midwifery by religious, and indeed appealing for religious congregations to undertake maternity and child-care medicine, was to have the most far-reaching consequences. A comment by a proponent of the change in the American *Ecclesial Review* (1936) aptly summarised the significance of the Instruction:

> Opening the door of opportunity to Sisters to qualify themselves professionally for the medical care of women and children in foreign mission lands is as much an innovation today in the recognized activities of religious women as was the education of youth, nursing the sick, and care of the aged and poor, outside the cloister, in the 17th century when St

Vincent de Paul founded the first community of non-cloistered Sisters.[4]

The Instruction, which also heralded a significant liberalisation in the Holy See's attitude to the granting of indults (effectively permitting religious to practise medicine and surgery), paved the way for the foundation of Ireland's first congregation devoted exclusively to health care, the Medical Missionaries of Mary; and it also prompted many of the existing missionary congregations of women religious, such as the Sisters of the Holy Rosary, the Sisters of St Columban and the Sisters of Our Lady of Apostles, to expand the scope of their apostolate. In terms of the contribution to the countries where they laboured, the benefits were incalculable.

II

The publication of the Instruction of 1936 marked the culmination of a lengthy campaign by clergy, religious and laity who saw the church ban as outmoded and inappropriate in missionary situations. From the turn of the century onwards a small number of bishops and prefects apostolic in India, China and Africa had made representations to the Holy See and canvassed the support of high-ranking churchmen in Europe and America in favour of a change in church legislation. No less active in seeking support were a handful of religious and clergy, including two Irish women, Mother Kevin (Keaney), a missionary in Uganda, and Mother Xavier (Murphy), superior of the Presentation Sisters in Southern India. In the latter stages of the campaign the interventions of Arthur Hinsley, Archbishop of Westminster and a former Apostolic Delegate to Africa, and Archbishop Dougherty of Philadelphia were to prove of crucial importance. But the success of the movement owed most to the powerful advocacy of three lay missionary women doctors for whom the revocation of the ban and the formation of medical religious congregations became something of a crusade.

Agnes McLaren was a Scottish Presbyterian who converted to Catholicism late in life.[5] As a young woman she had been active in the suffragette movement and other causes which bore on the dignity of women. Keenly interested in matters affecting women's health, in 1876 while in her thirty-ninth year she conceived the idea of becoming a doctor, but was unable to gain entrance to medical schools in the British Isles, which were then closed to women. Refusing to be deterred, she sought the help of Cardinal Manning and through his good offices was able to commence her studies at the medical school of Montpellier. In 1878 she qualified and in the same year took the examination of the Royal College of Physicians, Dublin (the first institution in the British Isles to open its doors to women), with a view to practising in Scotland. Considerations of health led her instead to the south of France, where she combined a practice among the English colony with dedicated service to indigent women and children.

After her conversion to Catholicism in 1898 Agnes McLaren interested herself in the work of missions and invited recuperating missionaries to her home in Cannes. It was from Mgr Dominick Wagner, a Mill Hill missionary and Prefect Apostolic of Rawalpindi, that she first learned of the great need for women doctors in the Far East, where custom so often prevented sick women from attending male medical practitioners. And when, during a visit to Cannes in 1904, Mgr Wagner disclosed his plans for a hospital in Rawalpindi to cater exclusively for women in purdah, Dr McLaren offered to promote the project. Already well known in Rome through her activities in the movement to abolish the state regulation of vice, she obtained personally a blessing for the project from Pius X, sought and received the approval of the Irish, English and Scottish Primates, issued a prospectus, and gathered together a committee of interested Catholics in England (the London Medical Mission Committee) under the patronage of Cardinal Bourne for the purpose of funding the hospital and providing staff.

By 1907 the committee had raised the necessary finance and there remained only the question of staff. At the outset of her campaign Dr McLaren had hoped it might be possible to secure a change in church legislation or at least that a dispensation might be obtained which would make it possible to place the hospital in the hands of religious. During her visit to Rome in 1905 she had broached the issue but had received little encouragement. Now in 1908 she returned to Rome, where again she met the Pope and also officials at the Congregation for Religious and at Propaganda Fide, as well as the heads of several religious orders. On this occasion she made detailed submissions, citing urgent necessity and historical precedent,[6] but again received an unfavourable response.

In 1909, now in her seventy-third year, Agnes McLaren travelled to India to oversee the opening of St Catherine's Hospital in

Rawalpindi. Here she was to experience at first hand the difficulty in relying on lay staff to maintain medical missionary establishments. The London committee had found it extremely difficult to find a suitable medical director. Eventually a doctor had been engaged, but within a matter of months in Rawalpindi she abandoned her post and returned home. This occurrence convinced Dr McLaren and her supporters more than ever of the necessity for a change in church legislation. After a brief sojourn in India she returned to Europe in search of a new director for St Catherine's and also doctors requested by six bishops for hospitals they wished to open for treatment of women's illnesses. At the same time she intensified her efforts to change attitudes towards the practice of surgery and obstetrics by religious, visiting many European countries, including Ireland, and speaking on the subject to bishops, religious and laity. She also made several trips to Rome, bearing letters of support from bishops in India and presenting an impressive dossier drawing on her experience of conditions in the field. Among her submissions was the proposal that doctors who joined religious orders should be permitted to practise after final profession And in an effort to counter the principal opposing argument, namely the threat to vocation, she invoked the Soeurs Hospitaliers[7] and the Soeurs de la Charité Maternelle of Metz—orders devoted to the care of women whose members were authorised to take a modified course in midwifery although forbidden to practise—as examples of the fruitful combination of religious life with the medical apostolate.

Agnes McLaren died in 1913 while preparing for her sixth visit to Rome. Although a papal declaration encouraging nursing sisters to take state examinations, issued in 1911, gave some grounds for hope, her appeals proved unavailing during her lifetime. Yet her eloquent advocacy did much to promote an awareness of the difficulties caused by the canonical prohibition in mission countries, creating a solid body of opinion in favour of change and also helping to bring the matter under scrutiny in Rome.

A second influential campaigner in the cause of Catholic medical missions was Margaret Lamont,[8] who like Dr McLaren hailed from Scotland and was a convert. Having graduated from the London School of Medicine for Women in 1895, Dr Lamont had served as an Anglican missionary in India, New Zealand, Egypt and San Francisco for some sixteen years before becoming a Catholic. Later she was to work in China, finding herself the only Catholic woman doctor among some 200 Protestant medical missionaries. Dr

Lamont's experience of the prejudices concerning the treatment of women made her an impassioned exponent of participation by religious in all aspects of health care. An ability to write well and a readiness to put pen to paper caused her views to become widely known in church circles both in America and Europe, while her medical work in the Far East gave her ideas added credibility. In 1914 she won the prize for an essay sponsored by the Catholic Medical Missionary Society of America, an agency established in 1912 in connection with the Catholic Foreign Missionary Society, Maryknoll, to promote interest in medical missions. In this and many other essays and articles she pointed with excellent practical sense to the isolation suffered by individual Catholic women doctors working in alien cultures, and urged the creation of medical congregations which would provide support and continuity. The services supplied by such congregations, she maintained, should be dictated by local need and, if required, should include obstetrics and other branches of medicine forbidden to nuns. Aware that church law stood in the way of such institutes, she urged her readers to join those already campaigning for a change of attitude on the part of the Holy See.

The ardent hopes of Agnes McLaren and Margaret Lamont for a new approach were to receive a measure of fulfilment in the life and work of a third lay pioneer of Catholic medical missions, Anna Dengel.[9] It was in the latter years of her life, while seeking a replacement for St Catherine's Hospital, that Agnes McLaren had come into contact with Miss Dengel, a native of the Austrian Tyrol who was anxious to pursue a career as a medical missionary. Encouraged by Dr McLaren and accorded a scholarship by the London committee, Anna Dengel commenced studies at the medical school of University College, Cork, in 1914 on the understanding that after qualifying she would serve five years in India. The Cork college was particularly appropriate, for not only did it supply a degree acceptable to the authorities in India, but its President, Sir Bertram Windle, a convert to Catholicism and a medical doctor, was already well aware of India's need for women doctors since a visit to the college by Dr McLaren in 1912. Indeed, it was Dr McLaren who recommended the Cork medical school to the committee and in the months before her death made the necessary arrangements for Miss Dengel. Anna Dengel qualified in 1919 and after a brief period in England served for four years as medical director of St Catherine's

Hospital in Rawalpindi. Her experiences in India soon convinced her that the only adequate response to the medical needs of women lay in the establishment of communities of nuns capable of providing comprehensive health care.

In 1924 Dr Dengel travelled to the U.S.A.[10] to procure funds and additional staff for an extension to St Catherine's Hospital planned by Mgr Wagner's successor, Mgr Winkley, M.H.M. During her lecture tour she discussed the possibility of founding a medical congregation with two of her sponsors, Fr John Considine, a Maryknoll missionary, and Dr Paluel J. Flagg, a founder of the Medical Mission Board in New York. They introduced her to Fr Michael Mathis of the Congregation of the Holy Cross, who had already failed in an attempt to supply lay nursing staff for India and who shared Dr Dengel's convictions concerning the need for a missionary sisterhood. Fr Mathis encouraged Dr Dengel to establish a society and also proposed a means for circumventing the Church's legislative impediments which appeared an insurmountable obstacle to any such scheme. He suggested that members of the society should take private rather than public vows. According to church legislation they would therefore have the status of lay sisters belonging to a 'pious society' and would not be subject to the provisions of church law applicable to religious. In 1925, with the approval of Archbishop Curley of Baltimore, Anna Dengel established her community, named the Society of Catholic Medical Missionaries, whose members were bound by a missionary oath and private vows. From 1927 the community dispatched doctors and nurses to India. When in 1936 the Church's prohibition was lifted sisters from the community were at last free to take public vows, and the institute was formally constituted a religious congregation in 1941. By 1980 the society had grown to a strength of 700 members of eighteen nationalities working in five continents and thirty-three countries.

In the period following the establishment of her community Anna Dengel played a leading part in the campaign to have the church legislation revised, persuading bishops and priests to write to the Holy See and to make representations when they visited Rome. She herself travelled to Rome on six occasions in connection with the cause. In 1935, as part of a process of investigation into the issue of 'religious medical missionaries', the Prefect of Propaganda solicited a report from the Apostolic Delegate in Washington (Archbishop A. G. Cicognani) on Anna Dengel's institute and received a response which praised the work of the community and the spirit which animated its activities.[11] Archbishop Dougherty of Philadelphia, in whose diocese the community was located, was sufficiently impressed to submit memoranda on two occasions urging a change in church law. In 1929 he wrote to Pius XI detailing the appalling predicament of women in the Orient through lack of adequate professional care and the great good which could be accomplished by sisters qualified as doctors, midwives and obstetrical nurses. The response to this memorandum recorded that the issues raised were under consideration. A second memorandum submitted by the Archbishop in 1935 was answered by the publication of the Instruction of 1936,[12] although in the final analysis the Holy See's declaration must be seen as the result of pleadings since the opening decade of the century.

III

From the outset Irish sisters, both in the diaspora and non-Christian mission-fields, combined education, catechesis and care of orphans with a medical apostolate. Sisters of Mercy assisted Florence Nightingale in nursing the sick and wounded during the Crimean War. In India care of the sick in the neighbourhood of convents formed an important part of the sisters' work. In Africa, especially in the tropical regions, every convent had its dispensary giving daily treatment to the sick. Sisters also visited the sick in their homes, and many gave their lives in this service during epidemics.[13] There is evidence too that some sisters attended maternity cases before this was expressly forbidden in the Roman directive of 1901. However, for the most part, the nature of the medical and nursing care provided was rudimentary. And even after 1911, when Pius X encouraged religious to become nurses and authorised them to take state examinations, missionary congregations were slow to respond, not least because their members continued to be excluded from maternity nursing, which was manifestly the greatest area of need. It was only with the removal of the ban that sisters were sent in numbers for training.

From 1908 Agnes McLaren had approached various congregations in Ireland and England urging them to train sisters in those branches of medicine which were open to them for missionary service and to undertake the training of laywomen as doctors, and also seeking to interest them in the campaign to remove the legislative impediments. Although the congregations she canvassed agreed that these were praiseworthy objectives, they were reluctant to train personnel for the Far East or to become involved in the movement to open maternity medicine to religious. Many regarded her proposals as idealistic and unreal in a Church which was traditionally conservative; some told her that the expense of educating laywomen as doctors was prohibitive; and there was also a certain acceptance for the view that maternity nursing was an indelicate and unsuitable occupation for nuns. Such attitudes were also encountered by another campaigner for the removal of the Church's ban who visited Ireland in 1919 in search of medical staff for a mission hospital in Uganda. This was Mother Kevin (born Teresa Keaney in Co. Wicklow), one of a small group of Irish women and men who espoused the cause of medical missions and played a significant part in the crusade inaugurated by Agnes McLaren.

A member of the Franciscan community of St Mary's Abbey, London, Mother Kevin was to become one of the great figures of the Church's modern missionary movement, establishing her own missionary congregation (with its headquarters in Ireland) as well as an institute of African sisters. She had first gone to Africa in 1902 with a group of five from her convent at the request of the Vicar Apostolic of the Upper Nile (Equatorial Africa), Bishop Hanlon, M.H.M. Early in her missionary career in Uganda Mother Kevin was struck by the inadequacy of the Church's response to sickness and disease. With the active support of her bishop, she set up several dispensaries, clinics and a hospital; yet the lack of trained personnel among the vicariate staff and the difficulty in recruiting lay doctors greatly limited the effectiveness of her apostolate. During the East African campaign of the First World War, when injured African soldiers serving in the European armies were brought to her hospital at Nzambya, the deficiencies were cruelly exposed, although she was to be honoured with an M.B.E. for her efforts. Above all, however, it was the inadequacy of maternity and child-care services in Uganda which caused her anguish, for in spite of the best efforts of Protestant medical missionaries, little progress had been made in these branches of medicine over the years. After the war the government authorities made a concerted effort to tackle the problem, encouraging the churches to intensify their efforts and offering financial incentives. The Protestants responded by establishing a

Maternity Centre which yielded excellent results. The authorities also indicated their willingness to fund a Midwifery Training School for African nurses and to entrust it to any agency capable of providing tuition and management. Eager to make a contribution to the government's campaign and anxious that young Catholic girls who wished to participate should receive midwifery training in a Catholic environment, Bishop Biermans, M.H.M (Dr Hanlon's successor since 1912) requested Mother Kevin to take responsibility for the project.[14]

Both Bishop Biermans and Mother Kevin had long since concluded that the major obstacle to the development of a meaningful Catholic medical apostolate was the legislative prohibitions. The bishop had already raised the question in Rome and with leading ecclesiastics in England. Mother Kevin, who returned to Europe in 1919 to attend the general chapter of her institute, took the opportunity to further promote a revision of church law. Moreover, on hearing that some individual permissions had been granted,[15] she sought for herself authorisation to qualify and practise as a midwife. In Ireland she received sympathy from the churchmen she approached, but no official encouragement. During her visit too she was disappointed at the reaction of some religious with whom she had discussed the question and who showed little enthusiasm for her ideas.[16] In England Cardinal Bourne, Archbishop of Westminster, whose interest had first been aroused by Mgr Wagner and Agnes McLaren, arranged for her to take a modified obstetrics course with the Soeurs de la Charité Maternelle in Metz, but he was unable to provide her with a dispensation to qualify or practise. He and other churchmen whom she met intimated that the matter of the prohibitions was now under consideration in Rome, but that a change of such importance could not be expected to occur for some time. Mother Kevin returned to Uganda disappointed that her own application to qualify and practise had not been judged expedient, but content in the knowledge that Dr Evelyn Connolly, a laywoman from Dublin, recently qualified, had committed herself to take responsibility for the Midwifery Training School. The school opened in 1921, and Dr Connolly, who came initially for a three-year tour, stayed for a decade before joining the Franciscan missionaries.

Mother Kevin's failure to secure a dispensation was understandable, given the fact that the *Code of Canon Law* published in 1917 had effectively reinforced the prohibition issued in 1901, and indeed had extended its scope to include all branches of medicine and surgery. Yet dispensations had been granted in the past. Between the establishment of Propaganda Fide in 1622 and 1904 four had been accorded to missionaries (although none to nuns) for the practice of medicine and surgery under strict conditions.[17] Up to 1919 some appeals had been made to Rome by bishops in India for individual exemptions, though without success. In 1921, a year after Mother Kevin returned to Uganda, one bishop from India persuaded Rome to allow his own group of sisters give assistance in obstetrical work, although it is unclear whether the permission was confined to lay sisters.[18] The dispensations which had come to the notice of Mother Kevin probably related to earlier cases in India where local ecclesiastical authority had granted exemptions in specific circumstances without reference to Rome.[19] The Holy See, it appears, was either unaware of such permissions or turned a blind eye.

Eight years later another Irish missionary, Mother Xavier (Murphy), superior of the Presentation convents in Southern India, hoped to obtain an authorisation for her sisters to attend maternity cases when the Sacred Congregation for Religious permitted the order to take charge of a hospital at the Railway Colony, Golden Rock, Trichenopoly. In the event, some individual sisters who had not yet taken final vows were allowed to train as midwives. But this was an unsatisfactory solution, since it deprived these sisters of full membership of the community to which they belonged. Thereafter Mother Xavier was to make repeated efforts to secure for professed sisters permission to train as maternity nurses, travelling to Rome in 1933 in order to plead the case before Pius XI. When three years later the Instruction *Constans ac Sedula* was issued Presentation Sisters in Southern India, whose novitiate was situated in England, were among the first to qualify as midwives and maternity nurses.

IV

In her quest to find a doctor for the Midwifery Training School in Uganda Mother Kevin had visited the National Maternity Hospital, Holles Street, Dublin, in August 1919. There she met Frances Lady Moloney, widow of the former Governor of the Windward Islands, who had just completed a six-month course in midwifery to prepare herself for medical missionary work in the Far East.[20] Lady Moloney was the leader of a small group which, it was hoped, would form the nucleus of an organisation of women to serve in China. She had first come forward in response to an appeal by Fr John Blowick made at a public meeting in the Dublin Mansion House on 11 October 1917. At the meeting the superior of the Maynooth Mission to China had proposed the establishment of 'a new congregation of nuns vowed to the medical care of the sick in non-Christian countries and whose members would be properly qualified in medicine, surgery and midwifery'.[21] Two other members of the group, Agnes Ryan and Marie Martin, had been introduced to Lady Moloney by Fr Thomas Ronayne, a diocesan priest whose request for permission to join the Maynooth Mission had recently been denied (his subsequent involvement in Bishop Shanahan's missionary schemes is outlined in Chapter 9). Agnes Ryan, a teacher by profession, immediately resigned her post and commenced medical studies in U.C.D.; while Marie Martin, who had served as a V.A.D. during the Great War, went to England for further nursing experience and later to Holles Street to qualify in midwifery.

It was hardly surprising that Irishwomen, inspired by the Maynooth Mission to China, should have wished to make their own contribution to the movement. However, the fact that medical work should have featured so prominently in their plans requires some explanation, since there was no obvious precedent for such an apostolate. The inspiration came primarily from the small band of Irish priests led by Edward Galvin who had worked in China since 1912. They had left their supporters in no doubt of the great need for a medical apostolate in the Far East and had highlighted maternity care as a special area of concern.[22] Thus when the Maynooth Mission was formed the provision of doctors and nurses for China became an urgent priority. It is probable that some of those associated with the scheme were also influenced by the writings of Margaret Lamont available in the pages of the *Tablet* and other Catholic publications. What is certain is that a number of those close to the scheme drew strength from the life and work of Agnes McLaren. Lady Moloney had met her in Rome during a short residence in that city in 1912. Although she had no intention of engaging in medical missions at the time, Dr McLaren's emphatic views on the necessity for a medical sisterhood gave encouragement when later she decided to devote her life to China. John Blowick too was deeply impressed by Dr McLaren, and even while wrestling with the dual tasks of supervising the Maynooth Mission and organising

his women volunteers he found time to translate a French biography of her into English.[23]

In June 1919 Fr Blowick was to write to a correspondent that the
plans for the proposed foundation were 'not very well defined'; and
it is evident from other sources that among the issues unresolved
was the question as to whether the institute should be constituted as
a religious body or a lay association. Among the advantages of the
latter was that its members would require no special dispensation to
engage in midwifery and other branches of health care closed to
religious. Moreover, not all of the original group who responded to
Fr Blowick's Mansion House appeal were attracted by the religious
vocation. However, as the project matured it became clear that only
a religious sisterhood could guarantee the required level of continuity,
stability and commitment.[24] The question of the apostolate to be
pursued by the new institute or association had been resolved at an
earlier stage, certainly by the close of 1918. Priests of the Maynooth
Mission who had studied conditions in China were anxious that
provision should also be made for the education of women. When
efforts to secure Irish teaching sisters seemed unlikely to succeed it
was decided that members of the new institute would be trained in
social and educational fields as well as in medical work.

How the leaders of the scheme proposed to deal with the Church's
legislative prohibitions remains unclear. Blowick was well aware of
the situation, informing the Mansion House gathering that 'the
project of founding an order of nun-doctors' had 'not yet been
approved'. The matter, he said, had been 'referred to the Congregation of Bishops and Regulars', which had 'postponed approval
pending the fuller investigation of the whole matter'.[25] It is probable,
however, that he saw the removal of the impediment as imminent
or, at least, believed that those with the 'forbidden skills' would be
permitted to use them after religious profession.[26] Blowick wrote to
Lady Moloney in August 1918 saying he felt sure 'that when we are
ready to appeal to her, Rome will be quite willing to grant almost
anything we ask'.[27] Lady Moloney, for her part, attributed Agnes
McLaren's failure to make progress in Rome to 'her being at the
time a fairly recent convert'.[28] In any case, the acquisition of professional qualifications was considered a matter of urgency by all
concerned with the scheme, and in July 1919 Blowick was able to
inform Fr Charles Plater, S.J. (an English correspondent) that three

Nano Nagle. Nano Nagle, foundress of the
Sisters of the Presentation, had a deep concern
for the evangelisation of 'pagans' in the West
Indies. Presentation Sisters worked in India
from 1841.

Catherine McAuley. During the nineteenth
century her Irish Sisters of Mercy worked in
'pagan mission' apostolates among Aborigines,
Maoris and American Indians, as well as in
South Africa, Belize and Jamaica.

Frances Teresa Ball. She established the Irish
foundation of the Institute of the Blessed
Virgin Mary (Loreto Sisters). Members of
her institute worked in India from 1841
and in South Africa from 1879.

John Hand. Founder of All Hallows
Missionary College in 1842. Alumni
from All Hallows provided the mainstay
of the Irish diaspora. From 1840-1900 All
Hallows sent over 1,500 priests abroad,
the vast majority to the new homes of
the emigrant Irish.

John Fennelly. College Bursar at Maynooth, appointed Vicar Apostolic of Madras in 1841.

Patrick Raymond Griffith. Appointed bishop of the Cape Vicariate in 1837 and first of several Irish-born bishops entrusted with jurisdictions in South Africa during the nineteenth century.

Joseph Zimmermann. Superior of the Society of African Missions in Ireland. He did much to promote the idea of an Irish missionary movement to non-Christian peoples.

Joseph Shanahan. Bishop Joseph Shanahan C.S.Sp. played a key role in establishing the Sisters of the Holy Rosary and St Patrick's Missionary Society.

John Galvin and John Blowick, founders in 1916 of St Columban's Foreign Missionary Society (the Maynooth Mission to China), the first of Ireland's indigenous missionary institutes.

P.J. Whitney. First Superior General of St Patrick's Missionary Society.

Agnes Ryan. Lay missionary in Nigeria from 1921 and co-founder of the Missionary Sisters of the Holy Rosary in 1924.

Marie Martin. Mother Mary Martin founded the Medical Missionaries of Mary in 1937, an institute devoted exclusively to medical and related apostolates.

Lady Frances Moloney. With Fr John Blowick she founded in 1922 the Missionary Sisters of St Columban.

Teresa Keaney. Mother Kevin, veteran missionary in Uganda, foundress of an African Sisterhood and of the Sisters of Our Lady of Africa.

Fr Jules Leman. First C.S.Sp. Superior in Ireland.

O.L.A. SISTERS INTERRED OUTSIDE IRELAND

NAME		PLACE	YEAR	AGE	NAME		PLACE	YEAR	AGE
SR. DOMINIQUE	RIORDAN	NIGERIA	1878	23 YRS.	SR. URBAIN	McMAHON	NIGERIA	1910	22 YRS
SR. FELICITE	KIRWAN	NIGERIA	1878	22 YRS.	SR. HERACLIDE	TOBIN	EGYPT	1910	22 YRS
SR. VINCENT		NIGERIA	1879	23 YRS.	SR. THEOTIQUE	FORAN	NIGERIA	1913	31 YRS.
SR. CECILIUS	O'RIORDAN	NIGERIA	1887	31 YRS.	SR. CLAUDE	LOOBY	NIGERIA	1915	29 YRS
SR. SYLVIUS	MURPHY	NIGERIA	1888	30 YRS.	SR. DANIEL	MALONE	FRANCE	1916	59 YRS
SR. CASTULE	GRIFFIN	FRANCE	1889	20 YRS.	SR. SAMUEL	KELLY	NIGERIA	1918	60 YRS
SR. IGNACE	HOWARD	GHANA	1892	31 YRS.	SR. SALVE	LYONS	EGYPT	1918	44 YRS
SR. THECLE	MORAN	REP. OF BENIN	1893	27 YRS.	SR. M. OF EGYPT	TWOMEY	GHANA	1918	59 YRS.
SR. IPHIGENIE	MacENERY	NIGERIA	1894	23 YRS.	SR. CYRION	McMAHON	EGYPT	1921	33 YRS.
SR. JEAN	HOWARD	GHANA	1895	32 YRS.	SR. CECILIA	KEATING	GHANA	1922	26 YRS.
SR. ZENON	O'SULLIVAN	GHANA	1896	24 YRS.	SR. COLMAN	KEOHANE	GHANA	1927	27 YRS.
SR. NEMESE	ENNIS	NIGERIA	1897	32 YRS.	SR. ROGAT	McGORTY	FRANCE	1927	46 YRS.
SR. PERPETUA	DWYER	REP. OF BENIN	1900	28 YRS.	SR. SERAPION	McCORMACK	GHANA	1929	50 YRS.
SR. AGATHON	WALSH	NIGERIA	1900	26 YRS.	SR. FINBARR	BARRY	FRANCE	1929	24 YRS.
SR. DONAT	ROWAN	GHANA	1901	30 YRS.	SR. FIDELE	ABRAHAM	EGYPT	1930	84 YRS.
SR. IPHIGENIE	EVANS	GHANA	1902	35 YRS.	SR. CLAUDIEN	O'MAHONY	FRANCE	1930	57 YRS.
SR. MARK	McCARTAN	GHANA	1902	45 YRS.	SR. MAURA	HIGGINS	NIGERIA	1932	24 YRS.
SR. ANTOINE	FOUHY	REP. OF BENIN	1906	35 YRS.	SR. BERNARDINE	McCLEMANS	FRANCE	1935	38 YRS.
SR. ROSULE	HARTIGAN	NIGERIA	1907	31 YRS.	SR. ANTOINETTE	BARRY	ITALY	1934	35 YRS.
SR. ARCADE	NANGLE	FRANCE	1907	32 YRS.	SR. ETHNEA	HEANEY	GHANA	1938	34 YRS.
SR. GERANCE	McCARTHY	NIGERIA	1908	31 YRS.	SR. FIDELIS	TUOHY	NIGERIA	1938	26 YRS.
SR. JULIE	AHERN	FRANCE	1908	31 YRS.	SR. ANNUNCIATA	O'SULLIVAN	NIGERIA	1939	29 YRS.

O.L.A. Tombstone. Commemorative plaque to Irish members of the Sisters of Our Lady of Apostles buried in Africa. Note the early ages of death.

Edel Quinn. Envoy of the Legion of Mary in East Africa.

Edwina Gateley. Founder of the Volunteer Missionary Movement which established itself in Ireland from 1972.

Viatores. Group of Legion of Mary members containing several of the early leading figures in the Viatores movement formally established in 1965.

candidates for the projected sisterhood were already training as nurses, while a fourth was studying medicine.[29]

The decision of two of these candidates, Marie Martin and Agnes Ryan, to opt for Africa rather than China has never been satisfactorily explained. In the autumn of 1920 Agnes Ryan entered her fourth year of medical studies, while Marie Martin commenced a course in midwifery in the National Maternity Hospital which she completed in February 1921. Yet scarcely three months later, in May 1921, as recounted in Chapter 9,[30] both went to Nigeria as lay missionaries. It would be convenient to attribute this change of direction to the publication of *Norms for the Approbation of New Institutes*, issued by the Holy See in 1921, which reiterated the prohibition of 1901 and made it clear that maternity medicine would be forbidden to religious for some considerable time to come. However, the decision taken by Marie Martin and Agnes Ryan in February predated the publication of the *Norms* by some weeks. There is no doubt that both were moved by the appeals of Mgr Joseph Shanahan, the newly appointed Vicar Apostolic of Southern Nigeria, who had returned to Ireland for his consecration in June 1920 and was seeking replacements for the Sisters of St Joseph of Cluny, who had withdrawn from his jurisdiction. No less important was the influence of Fr Ronayne, a confidant of both women, who himself had recently volunteered for Africa and after an initial refusal had finally obtained his release from the Dublin archdiocese. Yet it is unclear whether Shanahan offered them the opportunity of putting their medical skills into practice or whether they sought such an opportunity. Since Agnes Ryan abandoned her medical studies within a year of completion in order to go to Africa, it is unlikely that her motivation was to engage in medical work. Marie Martin, in view of her subsequent history, may well have seen in Shanahan's appeal the only means by which her desire to engage in a medical apostolate could be fulfilled. Yet both women would have been aware when they responded to Shanahan's urgent telegram for assistance in February 1921 that they were destined to take the place of Cluny Sisters, whose work had been in education; and on arrival both were entrusted with charge of a boarding school vacated by the sisters. Later when Marie Martin requested permission to engage in medical work the bishop 'reminded her that she had been allowed into Calabar solely as a teacher', although he permitted her to give first aid whenever assistance was needed.[31] Whatever her motivation in 1921, Marie Martin was later to withdraw from Bishop Shanahan's scheme to establish a missionary congregation from among the vicariate's lay missionaries, in order to pursue the foundation of a medical sisterhood.

V

In the interval between the foundation of the Sisters of St Columban (1922) and the Sisters of the Holy Rosary (1924) and the publication of the Instruction *Constans ac Sedula* (1936) members of both institutes concentrated largely on an education apostolate. Medical work was undertaken, but was necessarily curtailed by the existing ban on medicine, surgery and maternity nursing. Marie Martin, as has been mentioned, spent some fifteen years before her vision of forming a congregation devoted exclusively to medical missions became a reality. During this period she refused to be deflected from her purpose despite many disappointments and recurring ill-health. Finally in 1933, on the advice of her spiritual director, who believed (rightly) that the long-awaited withdrawal of the Church's prohibition was imminent, she began to draw up detailed plans for a medical missionary congregation.[32] One of those she consulted was Anna Dengel, who had engaged in a similar exercise in 1925.

Marie Martin's institute, the Medical Missionaries of Mary, was effectively founded in 1936, when a Roman permission was accorded. Members of the congregation trained as nurses and (from the mid-1940s) as doctors, dispensations to practise medicine and surgery being readily obtained from the Holy See. Within fifty years of its foundation the institute, now international in its composition, had some 450 members working in Ireland, England, Angola, Ethiopia, Kenya, Malawi, Nigeria, Tanzania, Uganda, Brazil and the U.S.A.[33] The older institutes of women religious engaged in missions reacted to the publication of the 1936 Instruction by qualifying members as nurses and doctors. By 1955 the Sisters of the Holy Rosary had 45 of its 108 members trained for medical work and ministering mainly in West Africa.[34] Within thirty years of the Instruction the Sisters of St Columban listed 9 doctors and 42 nurses among its membership of 297.[35] The Sisters of Our Lady of Apostles, which in 1936 had only two trained nurses from its membership of 112, entered the 1970s with 83 of its 289 members qualified as nurses or doctors.[36] In 1973 the Franciscan Missionary Sisters for Africa, the institute founded by Mother Kevin in 1952, but which had been functioning as a province of the Franciscan Sisters of the Five Wounds (St Mary's Abbey) since 1937, had 74 of its 251 members trained for medical work.[37]

VI

Despite the new freedom granted by the 1936 Instruction and the wholehearted response of the Irish sisterhoods, demand for medical staff continued to outrun supply, especially in Africa. In British territories government subventions and mission strategy from the early 1930s had combined to produce a rapidly expanding educational sector which placed heavy demands on personnel. In the post-war period significant increases in subventions both for education and medical work led missionary bishops to open up new channels of supply. Congregations lacking a missionary dimension, such as the Sisters of St Louis, involved in education in Ireland, and the Irish Sisters of Charity, working primarily in health care, were invited to assume responsibility for schools, hospitals and clinics in Africa. Recruitment of lay graduates for secondary schools was also undertaken and proved most successful. However, efforts to recruit Irish lay personnel for medical work met with mixed fortunes. Newly registered doctors were generally reluctant to go to Africa because the Irish Medical Association, which supervised conditions of employment at home, refused to recognise experience acquired in mission hospitals for those resuming the practice of their profession at home. The grounds for the objection was the absence of appropriate consultant staff to supervise mission hospitals. Doctors with a measure of experience were equally discouraged because the rigid and highly competitive career structure of their profession meant that those who took time off to work for missions ran the risk of falling behind colleagues who remained at home.[38]

The Medical Missionary Society (M.M.S.),[39] established in University College, Cork, in May 1942, was one agency which sought to address these obstacles. This society had been inspired by a visit to the college in 1941 by Mgr Thomas McGettrick (of St Patrick's Missionary Society), Prefect Apostolic of Ogoja in Southern Nigeria. He came in search of replacements for doctors supplied by a German lay missionary institute who had been interned following the outbreak of the Second World War. His failure to secure the services of a single graduate prompted a number of staff members to take action.[40] The principal architect of the Medical Missionary Society was the college chaplain and lecturer in medical ethics, Dr James Bastible (who had known Anna Dengel while a student at Cork in 1918),[41] although Alfred O'Rahilly, registrar of the college and a champion of many Catholic causes, almost certainly had a hand in its foundation. Included in the society's executive council were several members of the Guild of St Luke and SS Cosmas and Damian, a medical-ethical association based in the university which had been first introduced to Ireland in 1931.[42]

Under the chairmanship of Dr Patrick Kiely, Professor of Surgery in the medical school, and the patronage of the Bishop of Cork, the society sought to promote an interest among medical students in the missions, provided scholarships for candidates who pledged six years' service overseas[43] and also supplied *matériel* for its volunteers and for mission hospitals. In addition, the M.M.S. processed requests from bishops and missionary societies for medical staff, advertising in the professional journals in Ireland and Great Britain and referring applicants to prospective employers. From 1953, in response to representations from missionaries, the society was to extend its activities to the recruitment of graduates for teaching in secondary schools.

The society's activities were funded by the subscriptions of members (mostly doctors in the Munster region), by grants from the Medical Guild, by bursaries from the missionary societies and by benefactions.[44] The most notable benefactor was a Mr John F. Crowley, a Cork landowner and industrialist, whose interest in medical missions had been cultivated by Professor Kiely and by Dr Jeremiah Foley, a Master General of the Medical Guild, who was to play a leading role in the activities of the M.M.S. until his untimely death in 1950. Dedicated to the memory of Dr Foley, the 'Crowley–Foley Trust', as the endowment was designated, became available from 1952 and amounted to a sum of £4,000. Interest from this sum was to provide a major source of funding in subsequent years.

All in all, the Medical Missionary Society became an important resource for the Irish missionary movement. Nevertheless, its effectiveness in supplying personnel for medical work was inhibited by the problems of reintegration which were never satisfactorily resolved.[45] From its inception the society engaged in extensive promotion in the university and further afield, circulating literature and sponsoring public lectures by missionaries and by members of the society who had served overseas. Doctors taking up mission posts were offered a three-month preparatory course embracing surgery, gynaecology and pathology. A short course in tropical medicine was also made available. The initial response to the campaign was encouraging. In the first ten years of its existence a total of fourteen Irish doctors went to the missions under the aegis of the society. However, the impetus was not sustained, and with the passage of time it became increasingly difficult to attract volunteers. Records show that between 1942 and 1975 thirty Irish doctors were placed in mission hospitals through the agency of the society. In addition, some forty-five doctors responded to advertisements placed in journals and were referred to missionary employers. Perhaps a quarter of these inquiries came from Irish doctors. Many of the other applicants were from overseas countries (mainly India, but also the Philippines, Canada and South Africa), and of these a sizeable proportion were not accepted because of inadequate qualifications.[46]

The scholarship scheme proved especially disappointing. Between 1942 and 1955, out of an estimated total of twenty Irish scholarship-holders, only five later served in mission hospitals. In many cases those who opted out reimbursed the society. These figures prompted a decision in 1958 to restrict scholarships to fourth-year and final-year medical students. From this time the number of scholarship-holders steadily declined, and the balance of the society's expenditure went on subventions to mission hospitals, grants to individual doctors for equipment, and on the advertising of posts for medical and teaching graduates. By 1964 only a single Irish student held a scholarship for medical studies, while in the same year £600 of the total expenditure of £944 went in grants to mission hospitals. In 1965 a bonus scheme was introduced which offered £500 to any doctor completing two years in a mission hospital who had not previously benefited from a M.M.S. scholarship. The allocation of nine scholarships to sisters representing five missionary societies in 1967 marked a radical new departure, and five of these sisters eventually qualified and served overseas. From an early stage the society had contemplated the education of Africans in the Cork medical school. At least one African, from the Republic of Liberia, arrived at the college in the late 1940s but did not persevere. Other Africans, mainly priests, were sponsored by missionary societies and took arts and science degrees from the mid-1950s. From 1962, however, a small number of Nigerians, one a religious sister, were given scholarships by the M.M.S. Of these, three qualified as doctors, while a fourth took a degree in agricultural science at University College, Dublin.

The introduction of the bonus scheme and the decision to sponsor religious and overseas students merely highlighted the difficulty in attracting Irish lay medical students and doctors. In marked contrast, efforts to attract graduate teachers proved highly rewarding. A crucial factor in the success of this work was the ability of the missionary lobby to secure from the Department of Education recognition of service in mission schools for incremental purposes. This concession, won in 1961, led to a dramatic increase in the numbers of arts, science, commerce and agricultural science graduates recruited by the M.M.S. Most graduate teachers worked in Nigeria, where they contracted for three-year terms. Salaries, which were paid by the Nigerian government, often compared favourably with those available at home. Moreover, teachers returning home from Africa had little difficulty in finding employment. In the years 1961-66 the M.M.S. was instrumental in filling 101 teaching posts. Comparable statistics for subsequent years are unavailable, but records show that between 1967 and 1973 the society processed 154 inquiries from teaching graduates. The flow of teachers to Nigeria eventually dried up in the years after 1973 with the Africanisation of the education system.

While the M.M.S. was to remain the most active recruiting agent for doctors and graduate teachers in the 1950s and 1960s, there existed other channels. Staff were also recruited directly by missionary societies, by overseas governments and by international relief and development agencies. No studies are available on the numbers recruited through these channels. But accounts from missionaries suggest that while significant numbers of Irish graduate teachers were employed directly, the response from the medical profession was restrained.

Nor did the M.M.S. represent either the first or the only attempt to organise Catholic members of the medical profession for missionary work. Towards the close of 1918 Fr Conway of the Maynooth Mission to China told an audience of medical students at University College, Cork (which included Anna Dengel) of plans to establish an 'Irish Medical Missionary Society'. Some months later (in January 1919) a meeting of eminent doctors in Dublin framed a resolution declaring that 'the formation of an Irish Medical Mission to China is desirable and that steps be now taken to gain the approval of the ecclesiastical authority'. Although this meeting was addressed by Lady Moloney (standing in for Fr Blowick), there can be no doubt that what was at issue was the establishment of a lay association of medical professionals and not a religious body. The scheme was therefore quite separate from that which later issued in the Sisters of St Columban. In the event, Archbishop William Walsh of Dublin refused permission, informing the chairman of the 'Doctors' Committee', Sir Andrew Horne, that 'New undertakings must wait for some more favourable time.'

There also exists evidence of plans to establish a lay medical missionary society in University College, Dublin, in 1939, modelled on one of the earliest and by far the most successful of the continental lay agencies, the Würzburg Institute in Germany.[47] But the time was unpropitious. The difficulty in dispatching personnel to the missions in wartime had led the M.M.S. to suspend its activities for the duration. And it is likely that similar difficulties caused the Dublin scheme to be abandoned. Had it succeeded, there is little doubt that the Irish contribution to medical missions would have been greatly enhanced. The Würzburg Institute had been founded in 1922 by Mgr Becker, a former missionary in India. Its members contracted to spend ten years on the missions and received postgraduate training at the renowned Julius Hospital in Würzburg before dispatch overseas. From 1952 the institute had its own 300-bed hospital in the city, which provided further opportunities for postgraduate training and for reintegrating staff who had completed mission assignments. Moreover, candidates received a thorough religious formation during their studies and dedicated themselves in a formal ceremony to the missionary apostolate before induction as members of the association. The Würzburg Institute, therefore, was able to provide medical personnel who were highly motivated, well qualified, and committed to spending long periods in the field. It was also able to address effectively the problem of reintegrating returning doctors which had proved such an obstacle in Ireland. The C.U.A.M.M. institute, founded in Padua in 1950, was another continental lay association whose members received a religious formation and pledged themselves to at least six years' service. This agency deployed newly registered doctors in hospitals where there was ample supervision by senior staff. In 1973 members of the institute obtained recognition from the Italian government for time spent overseas. Irish missionary bishops, unable to maintain an adequate supply from home, turned to these and other continental agencies for assistance to supplement the work of Irish religious and lay medical missionaries.

A new phase in the recruitment of lay Irish medical personnel was inaugurated in the mid-1970s with the establishment of the semi-state Agency for Personal Service Overseas (APSO) and a number of Irish development agencies, most notably Concern and Goal. In line with guidelines laid down by international agencies such as the World Health Council, the main thrust of Ireland's contemporary contribution is on primary health care and prevention, a fact which accounts for the extensive deployment of volunteer nurses. Nonetheless, the Irish agencies in particular also provide well-equipped medical teams for emergency relief. Finally, medical schools in Cork, Galway and Dublin (the Royal College of Surgeons) have developed programmes for the deployment of students in developing countries (mainly in Africa) during summer vacations. The purpose of these initiatives is to create an awareness of the deficiencies in health care and to encourage those who participate to consider more substantial commitments after they qualify.

ELEVEN

Laity and the Missionary Movement

I

FROM the earliest stages laity participated in the work of the modern Irish missionary movement, operating on a variety of levels and according to a model which remained relatively unchanged until recent decades. During the course of the nineteenth century the provision of financial support, mediated through the Association for the Propagation of the Faith and other mission-aid societies,[1] or given in response to direct appeals from bishops and missionaries, was the principal form of involvement. Throughout most of the twentieth century too the numerous clerical and religious societies which engaged in mission depended largely for their survival upon the financial contributions of Irish laity.[2] Given the depressed state of Ireland's economy up to the 1960s, this response was truly remarkable and provides clear testimony to the missionary movement's popular base.

Within the ranks of the lay contributors there were always those who wished to play a more active role. From the second decade of the twentieth century, when missionary magazines began to be published, these assumed responsibilities for promotion and circulation, devoting extraordinary energy and dedication to their task. In addition, the more highly motivated lay supporters became leaders of 'missionary circles' and other special groups established for the purpose of meeting the ever-increasing demands for revenue. These same people were also to be found in the groups of 'apostolic workers' which made vestments and supplied sacred vessels and other liturgical *matériel* for the missions. It should be noted that in all cases the structure of this lay activity was determined by the missionary agencies or mission-aid societies. The various systems of promotion were devised by priests and religious designated by their institutes, while the 'apostolic work' groups were established by the A.P.F.

From the movement's inception laity also served on the mission-fields. Among those who went overseas was the sister of Bishop

Griffith, Margaret, who accompanied her brother to Cape Town in 1838 and spent much of the remainder of her life teaching in South Africa. Laity were also present in the small groups of missionaries who went to India during the nineteenth century. In the early decades of the twentieth century notable lay missionaries included Dr Evelyn Connolly and Marie Plunkett, both recruited by Mother Kevin for East Africa, and their contemporaries, Agnes Ryan, Marie Martin and Elizabeth Ryan, who laboured for a period in West Africa. Perhaps the most remarkable Irish lay missionary in the pre-Conciliar era was Edel Quinn, who worked as an envoy of the Legion of Mary in East Africa during the 1930s.

But the scale of lay participation was small. Church documents on mission were hardly encouraging. Benedict XV in his apostolic letter *Maximum illud* (1919) mentioned the mission catechist only to exclude him from the work of catechesis. 'A diligent missionary', he wrote, 'will not leave the duties of explaining Christian doctrine to each catechist but must reserve this department to himself . . . as the most important portion of his task.'[3] Apart from this fleeting reference to the mission catechist—who in any case was unlikely to be an expatriate—the letter made no other reference to lay activity in the mission-field. Pius XI in his encyclical *Rerum ecclesia* (1926) acknowledged that catechists might instruct catechumens, but added that while catechists might be expatriates, they should be 'preferably . . . natives'.[4] Beyond this he had nothing to offer the lay person anxious to go to the mission-field. Instead he made it clear that the principal contribution of the mission-minded lay person was to be made at home through 'prayer for the missions and the conversion of heathens' and through participation in the work of the various funding agencies.[5]

This reluctance to allow laity a meaningful role in the field was the consequence of an impoverishment which had begun with the growth of clericalism and sacerdotalism in the Apostolic period and which had been sealed in the Middle Ages. The 'squelching of the charismatic gifts'[6] given by the Holy Spirit to the baptised, and the appropriation of the 'appointed ministries' to the clergy, effectively emasculated those who were not ordained. Laity came to be regarded as the subjects of ministry conducted by those in orders rather than ministers in their own right.[7] At most they might contribute to the Church's mission by *assisting* clergy in the liturgy or in the work of catechesis.

The accelerated growth of secularism from the latter half of the nineteenth century provided the background for a rejuvenated theology of laity which was actively promoted by the *magisterium* (the Church's teaching authority) from the late 1920s onwards. Focusing on the Church's mission *within society*, laity were urged to assist the hierarchy in the sanctification of the 'temporal order' by the application of Christian principles in their homes, in their professions, in social and cultural affairs, in literature and scholarship, and in public life.[8] They continued to be called upon to assist in 'the preparation of children for Confirmation and First Communion, and of the sick for Viaticum and Extreme Unction; in teaching catechism, in liturgical matters and in Church music'.[9] But the priority, according to the new model, was to be given to service of society rather than service of the ecclesial community. Efforts to develop a model of the lay apostolate predicated on greater autonomy and the priority of strictly pastoral activities attracted considerable suspicion from the clerical establishment. In Ireland the Legion of Mary was one such movement which in the minds of many clergy would have been better advised to confine its activities to infusing the 'temporal order' with Christian values under the strict supervision of the hierarchy.[10]

The application of the 'temporal' model to mission occurred in the early 1930s with the expansion of educational and health-care apostolates. Laity were encouraged to participate as teachers, nurses or doctors, while those who professed an interest in other, more formally pastoral tasks were usually urged to pursue religious or clerical vocations. The scale of lay involvement during this period was also restricted by practical considerations. Lack of financial resources to house and maintain lay personnel, as well as a scarcity of trained professionals, were the main inhibiting factors.

The great expansion of lay participation in the field came in the post-war period and occurred largely in the African theatre. The British authorities, for a variety of reasons,[11] increased spending on post-primary education and health care and sought partnership with missionary churches to provide the services. Bishops took full advantage of the grants available and conducted intensive recruitment campaigns in Ireland, especially for teaching personnel. The increasing numbers of arts and science graduates emerging from the universities facilitated their task. Although exact figures are not available, it is probable that between 1950 and 1970 in excess of 800

Irish laity went overseas serving three-year tours, mainly as teachers in secondary schools.[12] Although attractive salaries were on offer, a thorough screening of prospective volunteers ensured that those accepted were highly motivated young men and women, anxious to make a contribution to the Church's missionary effort. Testimony from bishops responsible for the management of mission education during this period provides overwhelming evidence to the generosity and effectiveness of the volunteers. Efforts to recruit for medical work have been discussed in Chapter 10. Although the numbers of Irish medical personnel were small, the quality of their contribution, often made in circumstances of great hardship, was of the highest order.

During most of this period it must be stressed that lay missionaries continued to be cast in the role of *auxiliaries* to the hierarchy in the sanctification of the 'temporal order'. Those who may have cherished an opportunity to engage in pastoral activity or those who would have preferred a less dependent status were inhibited by the entrenchment of the 'temporal' model and the thrust of mission policy. Mission policy remained firmly committed to the development of education and health care and left little latitude for formal pastoral contributions. As for models of lay mission, the theological insights of the late 1920s were further developed in the encyclical letters *Evangelii praecones* (1951) and *Princeps pastorum* (1959). But the new directives applied more to the laity of mission lands than to expatriate volunteers, and in the final analysis they amounted to proposals for new methods rather than new orientations. Laity were urged to collective action through the establishment of associations, clubs and sodalities, but the context for this and other recommended activities remained firmly rooted in the 'temporal order'; moreover, all such endeavour was to be conducted under the close supervision of the hierarchy.[13]

It would be inaccurate to assert that *all* lay missionaries confined themselves to the professional tasks for which they were recruited. The role of laity as catechists had been emphasised repeatedly in church documents since *Rerum ecclesia*, and lay teachers and nurses willing to engage in catechesis were encouraged. However, such work was ancillary to their professional tasks and could never be conducted on a large scale. Lay missionaries also participated in the establishment and direction of apostolic organisations such as the Legion of Mary, the Society of St Vincent de Paul and the Y.C.W. The Legion of Mary, a movement which proved of inestimable value to the work of evangelisation, was widely employed by missionaries both in Asia and Africa, although it did not fit easily within the traditional model of the lay apostolate.[14] Introduced by priests and religious who had observed its success in Ireland, its *modus operandi* proved eminently suited to communities in mission territories. Legionary envoys like Edel Quinn in Africa and Alfie Lamb in South America provided another, more direct channel of extension. But only a handful of envoys were deployed; and, because of the heavy schedules imposed on teachers, nurses and medical staff, the scale of expatriate lay involvement in the promotion of Legionary and allied activity was destined to remain severely restricted.

One lay missionary who was far from satisfied with her dependent status was Edwina Gateley, an Englishwoman who took up teaching duties with a religious congregation in East Africa in 1964. Although the Volunteer Missionary Movement which she later founded cannot be regarded as a product of the Irish movement, it was not without its influence. For it was soon extended to Ireland and provided an important outlet for laity who felt called to make an independent contribution to missions. In her book *Psalms of a Laywoman* (1981) Gateley described her frustration at the limitations of the prevailing model:

> I spent my first year teaching postulants and sisters belonging to an African congregation. But I soon discovered it was not easy to be a lay missionary in a Church that tended to see mission only in terms of priests and sisters. I was simply a 'volunteer' *helping* the missions rather than being an intrinsic and full member of the missionary activity of the Church. . . . I soon realized that it was not my calling to work within a religious structure into which I did not quite fit.[15]

Her first efforts to found an independent lay missionary movement won little favour with English ecclesiastics, who regarded the initiative as premature.[16] However, her advocacy coincided with a radical development in the Church's understanding of laity, first signalled in the writings of theologians such as Yves Congar and Karl Rahner and formally articulated in the Vatican Council's Constitution on the Church (*Lumen gentium*, 1964) and the Decree on the Apostolate of Lay People (*Apostolicum actuositatem*, 1965). At the heart of this new understanding was the concept of a distinct lay vocation to mission within the Church. Gateley's initiative also coincided with changing circumstances in many of the developing countries in the post-colonial era, which provided a wider range of challenges for laity willing to engage in mission.

Bishops in Africa, South America and the Far East, with few exceptions, and also the missionary bodies, readily accepted the implications of the Council's teaching on laity. Practical support from St Joseph's Missionary Society, Mill Hill, enabled Gateley to launch the Volunteer Missionary Movement (V.M.M.) in 1969. Bishops welcomed the movement's missionaries into their jurisdictions, and within the space of five years over 300 volunteer missionaries were deployed on temporary assignment in more than a dozen countries in Africa, South America and the Far East. By the end of the decade the number had increased to over 500 located in twenty-six countries throughout the world.[17] The formal extension of the movement to Ireland occurred in 1972.

The Viatores Christi, an indigenous Irish organisation, predated the V.M.M. by seven years. Although there were (and remain) important resemblances between the two movements, there is no evidence to suggest a causal relationship. The circumstances which brought the Irish movement into being were very different from those which attended the birth of the V.M.M. The Viatores developed out of an experience of lay pastoral work in England conducted during the summer of 1958 by members of the Legion of Mary drawn from University College, Dublin, Trinity College (Dublin University) and the National College of Art.[18] The expansion of the summer project in the following two years led the group to consider involving lay graduates destined for overseas assignments in similar work. Meetings were held for these at which it was suggested they should 'dedicate their time and talent inside and outside of normal work hours to an exercise of full Christian responsibility',[19] and orientation courses for those interested in this concept were provided.

By the end of 1962 several members of the original group had departed for three-year overseas assignments. By that time too, in the absence of any other available model, it was found necessary to entrust the planning and organisation of the movement to newly established praesidia of the Legion of Mary. The departure of a group of missionaries for Latin America in the same year (a project inspired by the Pope's appeal for missions to that region) signalled a further development, since hitherto the direction of the lay outreach had been towards Africa. Although this did not quite amount to a shift in the centre of gravity of lay mission, it was the beginning of an important adjustment. Moreover, the inclusion of tradesmen in the group was significant in that it emphasised 'that the lay apostolate overseas was for *all,* not just for those with access to higher education'.[20] Two years later, in 1964, a formal constitution was drawn up and the movement adopted the name of Viatores Christi (Travellers for Christ). Its rapid expansion throughout Ireland and into England in the early 1970s was clear testimony to the existence of a deep reservoir of committed laity willing to join in the Church's missionary enterprise. In 1976, recognising that the scope of the Viatores' apostolate was wider than its own, and believing also that the movement was now viable, the Legion of Mary decided to sever its links. Subsequent developments were to show the wisdom of this decision. By 1986 the movement was still growing and had some 128 members serving overseas: 72 in Africa, 35 in the Americas, 16 in Asia, and 5 in Europe.[21]

II

Practical experience in the field by Viatores and V.M.M. members produced a philosophy of the missionary apostolate which was predicated on three important insights. In the first place, both movements were insistent that the lay apostolate constituted a distinct vocation within the Church. The implication of this view was that lay missionaries could no longer be regarded as *auxiliaries* working under the supervision of episcopal/clerical authority. The relationship they sought to promote was one of *co-operation* with bishops, priests, religious and local laity in the service of local churches, through activities which were proper to lay missionaries. There is little doubt that in formulating this position the Viatores and V.M.M. were influenced by the ecclesiology of Vatican II. *Lumen gentium* called on lay people 'to carry out, for their own part, the mission of the whole Christian people in the Church and in the World';[22] while *Apostolicum actuositatem* asserted that 'The laity . . . have . . . their own assignments in the mission of the whole People of God.' Furthermore, bishops and priests were exhorted to 'remember that the right and duty of exercising the apostolate are *common to all the faithful*' [my italics] and were urged to 'work as brothers with the laity in the Church and for the Church'.[23]

In the second place, both movements sought for lay missionaries the exercise of a 'full Christian responsibility' or, in Edwina Gateley's words, an 'intrinsic and full member[ship] of the missionary activity of the Church'. The implication here was that, in addition to its apostolate in the 'temporal order', laity should be admitted to a substantial exercise of ministry *within* the ecclesial community. The Council, however, was reluctant to recover the Pauline theology of 'inspired ministry' which had provided much of the basis for lay pastoral activity in the Early Church and which had been obscured over the centuries. *Lumen gentium* emphasised that 'the normal sphere of the ministry of the laity' was 'the secular as opposed to the inner ecclesiastical life of the Church'.[24] *Apostolicum actuositatem*, it is true, acknowledged a 'diversity of ministry' in the prosecution of the Church's mission to its members and the world. But in its application of this insight to laity there was a failure to invoke those gifts and charisms conferred by the Holy Spirit in baptism.[25] The proposal that laity might be admitted to some 'appointed ministries' (official ministries) *by way of exception*[26] was poor compensation for this omission. Nor was there anything innovative in the *Ad gentes* (Decree on Missions, 1965) exhortation that laity should continue to assist the hierarchy in parochial and diocesan activity and in pro-moting various forms of the lay apostolate.[27] Recognition by the *magisterium* for the view on ministry which had been current among Viatores and V.M.M. members since the early days of both move-ments came belatedly in 1976 with the publication of Paul VI's apostolic exhortation *Evangelii nuntiandi*. Paragraph 73 of that document—arguably the most impressive of modern statements on mission—asserted that

> The active presence of the laity in temporal affairs is of the greatest importance. We must not, however, overlook or neglect another aspect: the laity must realise that they have been called, or are being called, to co-operate with their pastors in the service of the ecclesial community, to extend and invigorate it by the *exercise of different kinds of ministries* according to the grace and charism which the Lord has been pleased to bestow on them [my italics].

In the third place, both movements regarded the distinction, made over the centuries, between the 'temporal' and the 'spiritual' orders as a false dichotomy. In particular they reacted strongly against the tendency to view the work of lay Christian professionals as less significant for 'building up the kingdom' than that of clerics and religious and those involved in 'direct' forms of pastoral ministry. Offering a holistic vision both of the world and the Christian mission, they stressed that each level of created reality needs to be addressed with equal vigour and without qualitative distinction.[28] This particular vision of mission emerged not from any theoretical exercise in theology but from experience in the field. Employed mainly in the exercise of their professional skills, lay missionaries were forced to reflect deeply on the factors which differentiated them from other professionals whose motivations were unrelated to Christian concerns. The crucial insight which emerged was the reality that in virtue of the gift of faith the lay missionary consciously co-operates in the redemptive work of Christ, a work which embraces the totality of creation. The Council's Constitution on the Church and the Decree on Laity acknowledged the authenticity of this vision, first articulated in Romans 8:18–25. Paul spoke eloquently of the whole of creation groaning towards fulfilment (redemption). The Council Fathers, applying the Pauline insight to the laity, offered the following statement:

> God's plan for the world is that men should work together to restore the temporal sphere of things and to develop it unceasingly. For the Lord wishes to spread His Kingdom by means of the laity also, a kingdom of truth and life, a kingdom of holiness and grace, a kingdom of justice, love, and peace. In this kingdom, creation itself will be delivered out of slavery to corruption and into the freedom of the glory of the sons of God.[29]

The Council, in addressing the quality of apostolic contributions, while asserting a diversity of functions, also made it clear that in no sense could the role of laity be considered less valuable than that of clergy and religious:

> Although by Christ's will some are established as teachers, dispensers of the mysteries and pastors for the others, there remains, nevertheless, a true equality between all with regard to the dignity and to the activity which is common to all the faithful in the building up of the Body of Christ. . . . And so amid variety all will bear witness to the wonderful unity in the

Body of Christ; this very diversity of graces, of ministries and of works gathers the sons of God into one, for 'all these things are the work of the one and the same Spirit'.[30]

III

In considering the role of laity in the Irish missionary movement, it is essential for the historian to determine the precise status of those bodies established in recent decades which are commonly called 'development agencies'. These are agencies which, through a variety of strategies and in a spirit of co-operation, seek to address the economic and social problems of the developing nations in the interests of justice and peace and as a token of human solidarity. The principal Irish agencies currently committed to development are Gorta, Concern, Trócaire, Christian Aid (the agency of the British and Irish Council of Churches), the Methodist Development and Relief Agency, the Agency for Personal Service Overseas (APSO), the State Agencies Development Co-operation Organisation (DEVCO), Higher Education for Development Co-operation (HEDCO), the Confederation of Non-Governmental Organisations for Overseas Development (CON-GOOD) and Goal.[31] The question at issue here is whether any or all of these agencies can be claimed for the missionary movement. The theologian will have no difficulty in replying in the affirmative because the work of all patently responds to the social, economic and political demands of the Gospel, elaborated in the documents of Vatican II, Paul VI's encyclical *Populorum progressio* (1967), the apostolic exhortation *Evangelii nuntiandi* (1976), the Synod of Bishops' document *Justice in the World* (1971), the encyclical *Redemptoris Missio* (1990) and in theological writings on the subject of liberation. The historian, however, can only make a similar claim if a clear continuity with the past is established. An analysis of the facts reveals elements of both continuity and discontinuity.

Before discussing this question in detail it should be stressed that 'development' action is not a wholly modern phenomenon. In fact much of the work undertaken by missionaries in the past was development-orientated in the sense that it made economic and social contributions to developing countries. In his analysis of a 1970 Irish Missionary Union[32] survey, Richard Quinn, author of *The*

Missionary Factor in Irish Aid Overseas, asserts that 60 per cent of the work undertaken by Ireland's 4,600 clerical and religious missionaries[33] in developing countries (of which education and training and health-related tasks accounted for 90 per cent) was 'development-orientated'.[34] No earlier parallel survey exists, but it is probable that from the late 1950s the percentages were something of the same order. It is true that there was no *formal* development philosophy underpinning this enterprise. Although humanitarian considerations were always a factor, health care and education were undertaken primarily as a means of spreading Church influence. Yet, whatever the motivation, the effect of such activity was to enhance economic opportunities and to assist the creation of a social infrastructure favourable to development.

There are good grounds, too, for challenging the assertion made by some development theorists that missionaries tended to treat the symptoms rather than the causes of underdevelopment. For the provision of educational facilities, especially, was to have profound political and, ultimately, structural repercussions. In British colonial possessions the process which led to independence was significantly advanced by the emergence of a mission-educated cadre imbued with a strong sense of self-worth, a belief in their own capacities and a desire to be free.[35] It is true that the achievement of political self-determination by no means guaranteed the elimination of underdevelopment. But it was an essential first step along that road. Mission education was provided by Christian churches of all denominations and by missionaries of many nationalities. But because of the scale of their commitment to schools, Irish missionaries can be credited with playing an important part in this process.

Action for justice and human rights, integral to development theory, also forms part of the history of the modern Irish missionary movement. Irish members of the Holy Ghost Congregation, working in West Africa at the turn of the nineteenth century, played an active part in the campaign against slavery. Missionary sisters, both in Africa and the Far East, worked resolutely to upgrade the status of women in societies where they suffered discrimination. In 1915-17 Irish priests in Liberia risked their lives in defence of tribesmen against undisciplined government forces and made repeated (often successful) representations on their behalf for equitable treatment.[36] In China, at great personal cost,[37] Irish missionaries opposed tyranny in many forms and sought to uphold the right to religious freedom.

Development theorists of some schools portray missionaries as collaborators in colonial exploitation and perpetrators of underdevelopment.[38] Historians agree that missionaries did play an important role in the colonisation of Africa, while noting that the first resistance movements were led by Christians. But most *Irish* missionaries came to Africa after the colonial era had begun. Nor should the nature of their collaboration necessarily be characterised as exploitative. Collaboration in the provision of education and health care was rarely regarded as subversive by Africans. The clearest evidence of this was the willingness of African governments to accept the presence of missionaries in the post-independence era. Irish missionaries, too, cannot easily be accused of promoting colonial objectives in the classroom. On the contrary, such a practice would have been repugnant to the vast majority, given the Irish Catholic historical experience of oppression.

In the post-Vatican II era the Church participated in the formulation of modern development theory through papal encyclicals and exhortations like *Populorum progressio, Octogesima adveniens, Evangelii nuntiandi, Redemptoris Missio* and the synodal document, *Justice in the World.* The radical orientation of 'liberation' theology occurred largely in the South American theatre and was pioneered by theologians, missionaries and bishops from that region.[39] Irish missionaries, it must be said, have been involved more in the application than the formulation of the Christian development model, although there are some notable exceptions (Dorr, Lovett, Kirby, MacDonagh, O'Halloran, Healy/Reynolds).[40] Initiatives by missionaries in Africa and Asia to establish crafts centres, agricultural co-operatives, village water schemes, credit unions and artisan training programmes, aimed at improving the economic circumstances of impoverished farmers and city-dwellers and at fostering local skills, date from the late 1940s. Although such initiatives remained peripheral to the main thrust of mission policy until after Vatican II, they did at least signify the beginning of a movement away from the paternalism of the past and an acknowledgment of a more authentic model of development based on co-operation.

Today, in Africa, South and Central America and Asia, Irish missionaries are active in the promotion of social justice and human rights. Perhaps the most effective of the techniques employed is the animation of 'small Christian communities' (sometimes called 'basic Christian communities'). These are groups which acknowledge the holistic nature of the Christian vision which they act to promote among the wider community. Irish missionary bodies, too, are in the front line of the struggle against famine, working closely with secular development agencies, local communities and governments in providing emergency aid, development aid and technical assistance. Finally, Irish missionary bodies form part of a growing lobby in the developed world for a fundamental readjustment in the relationship between North and South.

There are some obvious contra-indications to claims of continuity between many of the recently established development agencies and Ireland's historic missionary movement. Currently, as in the past, all the missionary bodies rely for their maintenance on the private subscriptions of Catholics or on grants from Catholic funding agencies. A number of the development agencies, in contrast, are the product of government initiatives and are partly state-funded; they are also directed by government-appointed councils. APSO (1974), DEVCO (1975) and HEDCO (1978) can be regarded as semi-state bodies implementing public policy towards development co-operation. Although Gorta (1965) draws the balance of its funds from private subscription, the manner of its constitution and the shape of its governing structure suggest that it too can be regarded as an instrument of public policy.[41]

There can be little doubt that the Church has exercised an influence on the evolution of government policy towards development. Missionary bodies, both individually and collectively, have done much over the years to create an awareness of social and economic needs in developing countries and in highlighting justice and peace issues. The Irish Church, through official statements and the activities of its own development agency (Trócaire, founded in 1973), has played its part in this process of conscientisation. But there are other influences at work which also have made a significant impact. The Charter of the United Nations (1945) called for the promotion of 'international co-operation in the social, economic, cultural, educational and health fields, and assisting in the realisation of human rights and fundamental freedoms for all without distinction as to race, sex, language or religion'. Responding through its Multilateral Aid Programme, inaugurated in 1974, the Irish state has participated in the work of the specialised agencies established by the United Nations to achieve these objectives, including the

U.N. Development Programme (U.N.D.P.), the U.N. Children's Fund (UNICEF) and the U.N. High Commission for Refugees (U.N.H.C.R.). The initiative which led to the establishment of Gorta was prompted by an international campaign against hunger launched by the United Nations' Food and Agriculture Organisation (F.A.O.) in the early 1960s.[42] Furthermore, the Irish government's Bilateral Aid Programme (1974) (which provides some 40 per cent of DEVCO's budget) was inaugurated in response to the U.N. General Assembly's adoption of an 'Official Development Aid' target of 0.7 per cent of Gross National Product.[43] Membership of the European Economic Community also has exercised an influence on government policy. The growth of Irish state-sponsored development agencies and programmes, therefore, must be seen as the product of local and international influences, both religious and secular. Thus, in the final analysis, the involvement of the state in development agencies is only a contra-indication of continuity with the missionary past to the extent that such action has been motivated by external secular influences.

Yet there are factors other than state participation which differentiate modern development agencies from the missionary bodies. The non-denominational status of many development agencies signifies a fundamental break with the past in terms of ideological motivation. Many of those engaged in missionary activity may regard the work of the agencies as an authentic expression of Gospel values. Yet there are also those (often within the agencies) who would see the development movement as something quite distinct, originating in social and economic concerns and the demands of natural justice. For such persons neither the profession of religious faith nor the extension of the Church are integral or even relevant. Moreover, they regard the work of Christian missionaries as valuable only to the extent that it furthers the elimination of poverty and the promotion of justice. In short, while the Irish Church subscribes fully to the aims and objectives of the development agencies and is itself engaged in their validation (through Trócaire), the agencies, by and large, remain indifferent to an area of concern which remains central to missionary activity, namely the implantation of indigenous churches. This is perhaps the most important area of discontinuity with the past.

Trócaire can clearly be regarded as a continuation of the Irish Catholic missionary outreach, since it was inspired by a stated desire to respond to those needs in developing countries articulated in the encyclical *Populorum progressio.*[44] Equally, Christian Aid and the Methodist Development and Relief Agency represent new dimensions of the Protestant churches' missionary movement. Elements of continuity with the past are also to be found in the fact that some of those engaged in the establishment of Concern were already experienced missionaries. These were men and women who saw the need for a specialised agency to provide emergency aid and rehabilitation programmes for peoples affected by famine and natural disasters in Africa and Asia. Another clear linkage with the missionary movement has been the placement of missionaries and clerical/religious personnel on the controlling councils of Gorta and APSO.

In conclusion, it is evident that there exists a high level of practical co-operation between the development agencies, whatever their provenance, and those bodies which would describe themselves as 'missionary'. The agencies make considerable use of the infrastructure established over the years by the missionary bodies, and also furnish human and financial resources for projects undertaken by churches which accord with their own development aims. Their sponsorship of lay missionaries, most notably Viatores and V.M.M. members, is substantial. Moreover, as already mentioned, the government-sponsored agencies appoint missionaries (who act in an individual capacity) to their ruling councils. The missionary bodies, for their part, rely increasingly upon the agencies for advice, support and assistance in the implementation of their own development strategies. In the last analysis, therefore, while the case for continuity with the past is incomplete, there exists today a clear community of purpose towards development between the churches and the semi-state and independent agencies.

PART FOUR

The Irish Movement:
Self-Propagation, Style
and Structure

TWELVE

Communicating the Message:
The Role of the
Missionary Magazine[1]

I

THE earlier chapters of this book have described how the great release of religious energy, evident in Ireland from the close of penal times, was harnessed for the benefit of 'non-Christian missions'. The process was gradual, even laborious, but by the second decade of the twentieth century a coherent Irish movement directed towards non-Christian peoples, mainly in Africa and the Far East, had been created and was quickly gathering momentum. Thereafter the task for those engaged in propagating missions was to sustain and heighten interest among the general public so that the movement would be adequately funded and staffed. The delivery of talks by returned missionaries, often illustrated by the slide-lantern, was one of a variety of techniques used to stimulate interest. Another was the insertion of articles or 'reports from the missions' in the *Irish Catholic*, the *Universe*, the *Catholic Times*, the *Tablet* and other Catholic newspapers and journals which circulated in Ireland at this period. But the most effective means of communicating with the public was the 'missionary magazine' produced directly by the missionary bodies.

The prototype for this particular genre of literature was the *Annals* of the Association for the Propagation of the Faith. From its first issue in 1823 this journal became a highly successful instrument of missionary propaganda on the continent, while its English-language edition, available from 1839, made a similar impact in Ireland, England and Scotland. The Church Missionary Society's *Gleaner*, which first saw the light of day in 1838, was the first of many journals and broadsheets published by Protestant missionary societies in England and Scotland. Written in a style similar to that of the *Annals*, these were to enjoy wide popularity among Anglican and Evangelical Protestants throughout the British Isles. The purpose of such literature was less to provide a critical analysis of the work of mission than to edify, loosen purse-strings, and to promote recruitment. And although technical articles, dealing with the methods of evangelisation, were occasionally included, such material invariably had a promotional context.

The Irish movement, drawing on existing Catholic and Protestant models, wasted little time before producing its own literature. The first magazine to go into print was the S.M.A.'s *African Missionary* in 1914, followed in 1918 by the *Far East*, the organ of the newly founded Maynooth Mission to China, and the C.S.Sp.'s *Missionary Annals*, which first appeared under a different title in May 1919. The *Far East* and *Missionary Annals* were monthlies; six issues of the *African Missionary* were published annually. Although exact figures are not available, it is probable that by 1930 the cumulative circulation of these three journals was in the region of 130,000 copies per issue.[2] The journal of St Patrick's Missionary Society, *Africa*, was first published in January 1939 and soon built up a substantial list of subscribers. Other magazines circulating in Ireland were the English edition of the *Missions Catholiques* (successor to the *Annals* from 1930) and the publications of the Mill Hill (English) and Maryknoll (U.S.A.) missionary societies. Each of the congregations of missionary sisters published its own periodical; and although these were not included in the research for this chapter, a cursory glance suggests that they were of the same variety as the others and that conclusions drawn below can also be applied confidently to them.

II

The appeal to Irish Catholics carried in the pages of the missionary magazines was a mixture of argument and exhortation, persuasion and encouragement. It was directed as much to the imagination as to the intellect. And it was made with skill and ingenuity. In the early years perhaps the most striking feature was the capacity of the magazines to harness often contradictory forms of non-religious idealism for the missionary movement. Specifically the magazines set out to show that political and cultural idealism, although worthy and commendable, can never satisfy the human spirit; while the pursuit of religious aspirations, representing the highest form of idealism alone provides true fulfilment.

During the period 1914-18 the world was convulsed in a war between the strongest nations, fought for economic and military hegemony in Europe and for imperial supremacy in Asia and Africa. In Ireland Catholics were generally opposed to conscription, yet tens of thousands joined in the conflict. The missionary magazines, reflecting on the war, suggested that spiritual conquest alone merited such gallantry and self-sacrifice. As the fighting ceased and the magnitude of the calamity which had occurred became apparent, the missionary propagandists spoke more plainly. They stressed that a war waged for temporal possessions was bound to lead to catastrophe and that the only struggle worthy of the sacrifices borne by the peoples of Europe was the 'battle' for Christ's kingdom. They added that since Ireland had emerged relatively unscathed from the Great War, she was now in a position to 'go on the offensive'.[3] It should be emphasised that there was no rejection of the martial orthodoxy as such. To have called it into question would have been to cast aspersions on those who had suffered and died in the war. What was suggested was that the spirit of conquest and the sacrifices endured in its name had been misdirected. Dr Edward Leen, C.S.Sp., addressing a congress of students at Dalgan Park, Shrule, in June 1919 made this patently clear. In a paper entitled 'Ireland's Destiny' he wrote:

> There is something natural in the spirit of conquest. . . . This tendency being natural is good if rightly directed. . . . Ireland was certainly aggressive from the sixth to the tenth century. But its aggression was not to extend its own political influence, but to enlarge the boundaries of Christ's kingdom.[4]

But there were other historical developments nearer home which were to present the movement's literary propagandists with an even greater challenge. From 1916 the minds of many Irishmen gradually began to shift from preoccupation with worldwide events to the struggle for freedom in Ireland. The missionary magazines detected the change of mood and sought to interpret it for the benefit of the movement. The imaginative link between Irish freedom and Irish Catholicism had already been forged by nationalists such as Pearse and Plunkett. But the advocates of the missionary movement gave it a new dimension by extending it to include those 'fighting the battle for Christ in Africa and Asia'. Freedom, it was argued, was the object for which the nationalists were fighting. Freedom of a spiritual order—a higher freedom—was the object of the 'warriors' on the missions. Thus a common objective, a common idealism, differing only in degree, was at the root of both struggles.[5]

Endorsements of the link between missionary enterprise and the national struggle were eagerly sought after and widely publicised. In November 1921 *Missionary Annals* described, under the title of 'A Great Day in Carrig on Shannon in aid of the Irish African Missions', how Commandant Seán McKeown (Mac Eoin) presided over the function, and quoted extracts from his address, which stressed the affinity between the national and missionary movements.[6] At Christmas of the same year the *Far East* gave headlines to the opening of the annual Columban Bazaar by none other than Mrs Pearse, mother of the nationalist leaders executed in 1916. It was commented that it was

> surely significant to see the noble mother of the Pearses opening such a function, showing how deep the Missions have taken root in the national life, or rather that the national and missionary spirit have their origin in one common source—the spirit of sacrifice for the splendid things of God.[7]

As the fight for independence gave way to civil war the missionary magazines were quick to sense the disillusionment spreading throughout the country; and in the same way as they had interpreted the disenchantment in the wake of the Great War they now analysed the new national mood. The theme most frequently stressed was that despite the Civil War and the humiliation which it brought, one aspect of the 'old idealism' remained untarnished, namely the Faith. Although divided, Ireland had not turned her back on God. It was implied that by greater preoccupation with the work of spreading the Faith abroad, Ireland could best emerge from the ashes of civil strife and rid herself of the bitterness it had engendered.[8] The 'war for Christ in Africa and Asia', it was suggested, was a struggle in which all Irishmen, whatever their political persuasion, could unite.

III

The ability of the missionary magazines to confront the constantly changing articulations of nationalism and to relate them to the missionary cause was, by any standards, a signal achievement. The contradictory concepts of 'conquest' and 'freedom' which twentieth-century nationalism strangely canonised were both embraced and successfully translated into spiritual and missionary terms. National euphoria was put into perspective, and disillusionment was reinterpreted. But in many other more subtle and ingenious ways mission literature captured the spirit of the times and conveyed a sense of belonging, relevancy and modernity—a spirit which was bound to appeal.

One method was the adoption by the magazines of the terminology of warfare in presenting the missionary movement. Before the Great War men were obsessed with matters military. Popular novels were written about military inventions, guns, ships, dirigibles and aeroplanes; strategy and tactics became subjects of common conversation. In using military terminology to describe the missionary movement and its adherents, the magazines were able to address their readership in a language which was readily understood. An article in the *African Missionary* in 1917 entitled 'Killed in Action' recounted the death of a missionary priest who 'gave up his life in the trenches of West Africa'.[9] God was frequently described as the 'Great Commander'; the missionaries were 'His troops'.[10] And just as the armies had their marching songs and martial poetry, the missionary institutes produced their own stirring anthems and verses.[11] The task of winning adherents to the missionary life was expressed in military terms. Deaths were described as 'war casualties'. Reports from the missions were described as 'News from the Front'. Much was made of the question of logistics, particularly after the breakdown in the German lines of communication in the latter months of the war. The 'Notes Column' of the *African Missionary* for January 1920 offered the following cautionary piece:

> After brilliant conquests . . . a first-class military power has crumbled and disappeared. Why? The idolised chief of the vanquished hosts sums up the cause in one caustic phrase: 'because of the collapse of the home front'. Such a catastrophe should furnish food for thought to every soldier and we officers and soldiers of Christ may ask ourselves is all well with our mission pioneer forces on the mission fronts? For the valiant army of missionaries can hope for victory only as long as the home front stands firm.[12]

The language and imagery of 'heroism' and 'self-sacrifice' was used to great effect. During the Great War propagandists on both sides had sought to harness the energies of the populace by accounts of feats of valour and daring. Special awards, such as the Victoria Cross, the Croix de Guerre and the Iron Cross, were distributed to the most valiant. Similarly, during the Irish struggle for independence the language of heroism was used to inspire greater effort. Ballads and songs were composed about ambushes and about those who died in the war. The Pearse brothers, James Connolly, Seán Treacy and Kevin Barry were extolled in verse and song as exemplars because of their selfless devotion to their country. Figures like Michael Collins and Eamon de Valera became folk heroes. The promoters of the missionary movement were quick to find their own heroes and to describe their deeds in the same idiom. Fr Daniel O'Sullivan, who died prematurely in Sierra Leone, was presented as a 'hero and martyr, giving his life for the sublimest of causes'.[13] The death of Fr Joseph O'Leary in China was hailed as a martyrdom. Fr William Shine's tragic death after six weeks in Liberia was described as 'a sacrifice worthy of the highest admiration'.[14] In order to underscore the heroic nature of the missionary's work, Africa was described repeatedly as 'the White Man's Grave' and statistics of the frightening mortality rate were published.

Departure ceremonies for those bound for the missions gave ample opportunity for stressing the heroic nature of the missionary's life. A piece written on the departure of a group of missionaries for Africa in 1922 reads as follows:

> We in Ireland today who live in a period of heroism and self-sacrifice appreciate the grand motive which urged these five young apostles to deny themselves home comforts and Irish surroundings to bring to the benighted African negroes a foretaste of the joys of heaven.[15]

Poetry and hymns written in the heroic mode were, as has been mentioned, an essential part of the appeal. The S.M.A.'s 'Go Forth For Life, O Dearest Brothers' was a classic in the genre. The death of a young missionary, Fr O'Hara, in 1921 prompted a poem entitled 'Voices from the Grave'. A very popular offering was the poem 'Sons of Erin':

> Sons of Erin, brave and true,
> God has work for you to do,
> Sweet and thrilling, strong and clear,
> Comes the call to heart and ear,

Go ye forth all danger braving,
Souls of men for Jesus saving.[16]

Not only did the magazines promote dead heroes, there were also
the living ones. Bishops Shanahan (C.S.Sp.), Galvin (Maynooth
Mission to China) and Broderick (S.M.A.) were all (justly) extolled
as heroic and inspirational figures.

Another powerful source of appeal was the use of statistics. Since
the Franco-Prussian War of 1870 people had come to appreciate the
value of statistics as a means of influencing public opinion. During
the Great War statistical analysis proved a powerful psychological
instrument in stimulating greater national effort and in undermining
the confidence of the enemy. As the conflict developed into a war of
attrition scientific examination of human and material reserves, as
well as of industrial capacity and agricultural output, provided
political and military leaders with an accurate estimate of the war's
progress. As an instrument of propaganda in wartime, inaccuracies
in the arrangement of statistics were carefully contrived. The
missionary magazines did not have to manipulate the figures in
order to make statistics a telling weapon in their crusade. The facts
spoke for themselves, showing the immensity of the task and the
scarcity of resources to fulfil it.[17]

A further method used by the magazines to promote the movement was the association of contemporary mission enterprise with
the 'Golden Age of Irish Civilisation' and specifically with its
missionary content. It was emphasised that the modern movement
was a revival of the ancient missionary tradition, and some articles
and editorials went so far as to claim that a continuity had been
maintained down through the centuries.[18] Historically there was no
basis for the latter assertion, since the early medieval movement
failed to survive beyond the ninth century. Moreover, the modern
missionary impulse was very different in character from the
medieval[19] and was by no means indigenous in its origins. The missionary propagandists, however, can hardly be blamed for inaccuracies relating to the movement's origins, since little effort had been
made to document its early history.

The appeal to the spirit of adventure was another constant
feature of mission literature. The missionary vocation was presented
as an undertaking requiring considerable daring and courage, capable
of gratifying the most adventurous of natures. Excerpts from

missionary letters describing voyages of exploration and encounters with fascinating cultures were published in the *Irish Catholic* from the turn of the century. The missionary magazines took up these themes with relish. The second issue of the *African Missionary* told its readers that

> There is yet much of the old beauty of adventure on the missions. . . . There is yet adventure of the old sort. . . . Men are still attracted by the double fascination of travel and religion.[20]

Articles with such titles as 'First Impressions of Sierra Leone', 'A First Journey to the Bush', 'Christmas in Nairobi', 'The Call of China' and 'Journey up the Great Yangtse River' were all written so as to excite the adventurous and stir them to action.

Closely allied to this was the appeal to romanticism. Undoubtedly romanticism had been one of the major factors in generating the French missionary revival of the nineteenth century. Chateaubriand's *Génie de Christianisme*, which idealised mission life, was a powerful influence and initiated a literary genre which was widely popular among new generations of Catholics tired of the arid rationalism of Voltaire and his fellow-Encyclopaedists. The Irish missionary magazines adopted a similar perspective. The missionary was presented as a romantic figure, filled with the Holy Spirit, shrouded in a halo of light, carrying the joyous message of salvation to 'pagans' eager for the Faith. Africa was portrayed in word and in pictorial design as a continent covered by a glowing haze shot through with shards of light—resembling the 'faerie-land' of Spenser's *Faerie Queene*. Its inhabitants were characterised as benevolent and kind, filled above all else with a longing for the light of Christ. The phrases 'Dark Continent' and 'benighted Africa', employed frequently in romantic passages, were not intended as pejorative. Africa's 'darkness' was neither hostile nor despairing; rather it was full of mystery and, above all, full of expectancy for the coming dawn of Christianity.[21]

Those preparing for the missionary life were also depicted in highly charged romantic language. A reception ceremony for novices in the C.S.Sp.'s Blackrock College is described as follows:

> Thirteen missionaries of the future stepped out of the ranks of their fellow students and offered their young lives for the evangelization of Africa. . . . For many a month preceding

their youthful oblation they had mingled with the other students of the College. . . . They played on the same football grounds, frequented the same lecture halls, but all the while the whisper of God's Angel was growing louder and louder in their ears. . . . The voices of little African children are wafted to them 'o'er the seas' as of old the voices of the Irish were borne to St Patrick in his Gallic retreat.[22]

Poems in the romantic mode were frequently published. 'The Novice' by M. A. Lee contained such lines as: 'trample me underfoot / In the fierce winepress of Thy Love'.[23] 'Will a Boy Say No to the Call?', printed in the *Far East*, possessed a strong romantic flavour.[24]

As for the vitally important area of spiritual motivation, the missionary magazines used a variety of arguments, the most common being the *obligation* on all Catholics to respond to Christ's command 'Go ye therefore, teach all nations.' This injunction, readers were told, was more than a counsel, more than an ideal—it was in fact a solemn and sacred precept which *must* be obeyed at the peril of one's soul. Naturally not everyone was expected to become an active missionary, but all were bound to contribute in some degree to the missionary effort, if not by joining the 'ranks of the missionary army', then by supporting it from at home. This message was emphasised repeatedly to the reading public.[25]

Occasionally, in their efforts to motivate Irish Catholics, missionary writers invoked the prospect of certain damnation for those in non-Christian lands who died without baptism. These sombre pronouncements reflected a particular interpretation given by certain neo-scholastic theologians to the teaching that 'outside the Church there is no salvation' (*extra ecclesia nulla salus*), an interpretation which remained influential until the second half of the twentieth century. Church teaching on the matter was somewhat obscure, but it never gave official sanction to the restrictive neo-scholastic construction. Clarification finally came in Vatican II's Constitution on the Church (*Lumen gentium*, 1964). While reiterating the teaching that outside the Church there can be no salvation, this key Conciliar statement declared that non-Catholic Christians, members of non-Christian religions and even those who belong to no religion but live according to the light of conscience, all must be considered linked to the Church and so can be saved.[26] It must be said that few writers in missionary magazines made the explicit claim that baptism was necessary for salvation, although instances can be found; but this thinking was implicit in much of what they wrote. Significantly, no mention was made of the 'escape clauses' devised by the more cautious neo-scholastic theologians, such as the concept of 'baptism of desire'. An example of an explicit claim for the absolute necessity of baptism is to be found in a card offered for sale by the *African Missionary* to its subscribers. The legend on the card reads:

> Twenty millions die each year without baptism. Is baptism necessary for salvation? 'Baptism is necessary for salvation, for without it we cannot enter the kingdom of heaven' (John 3:5). Pray every day that some soul may be saved from hell.[27]

There were other appeals based on a sounder theology of salvation. The magazines declared that God so wished for the salvation of His creatures that He became man and died on the Cross; the duty of the Church, in the scheme of salvation, was to bring to fulfilment Christ's work on earth. The missionary movement, it was said, presented Irish men and women with the opportunity of bringing the sacrifice of Calvary to the most abandoned souls. There were in fact two elements to this appeal: firstly, that Christ had died for *all*; and secondly, that God requires His Church to *share* in the work of redemption by bringing the Gospel to the ends of the earth.[28] Missionary magazines also frequently asserted that the missionary life was a certain way of saving one's soul. In an epoch when much was made of the dangers of the 'world' the missionary life was singled out as perhaps the surest way to salvation.[29]

The idea of blood-sacrifice, which had influenced some of the leaders of the 1916 Rising, surfaced frequently in the catalogue of reasons why young men and women should embrace the missionary vocation. Tertullian's maxim 'The blood of martyrs is the seed of new Christians' re-echoed across the pages of the missionary magazines. Fr Francis McGovern, who died shortly after his arrival in Liberia, was hailed as 'Our Latest Martyr' and a source of strength for the future.[30] Shortly after the news of Fr William Shine's death reached Cork in 1914 the *African Missionary* declared:

> Hence if Africa must be converted, life must be sacrificed. Call it folly if you will, but so must it be. . . . Thus in this 'far foreign field' will the holocaust of life assure for millions unborn a faith permanent and pure as the faith of the Gael.[31]

Finally, the threat to 'pagan souls' from the 'heresy' of Protestantism and the 'abomination' of Islam was offered as ample and appropriate motivation for missionary action. Readers were informed that there was in existence a desperate scramble between the religions in Africa and Asia and that the Catholics, late into the field, had much headway to make up. Islam was considered the greatest threat:

> The free and easy morality which is preached and practised by the sons of the Prophet falls in with the inclinations of the Blacks. . . . A native who has become a Mohamedan can scarcely ever be converted. . . . The low position of woman which exists in African society is endorsed by Islam.

Such were the main conclusions of a lengthy inquiry into Islam by the *African Missionary* in 1914.[32] Fr John Lupton, a frequent contributor, wrote that 'Instead of being a half-way house, Mohamedanism is one of the most serious obstacles the foreign missionary has to face in Africa.'[33] 'Mohamedanism is more in the nature of a perversion than a conversion,' stated an editorial in *Missionary Annals*.[34]

Protestantism was presented as less dangerous but nonetheless to be reckoned with. 'We are forcibly struck', wrote Fr James McGettigan, S.M.A., in 1915, 'by the efforts displayed by our separated brethren in propagating their tenets. . . . They have, at the peril of their lives, penetrated into the darkest regions of darkest Africa.'[35] A book by Fr Frederick Schwager (of the Society of the Divine Word) on Protestant missionary activity was reviewed in great detail by McGettigan. According to Schwager, the key to the successes of the Protestant missionary movement was its excellent organisation, the zeal of its missionaries, the ready availability of funds, and its 'easy morality'.[36] Fr John Blowick, the co-founder of the Maynooth Mission to China, made much of the Protestant threat. 'The destiny of China', he said, 'may be decided within the next fifty years. Protestantism is flooding her cities with its emissaries. The battlelines are drawn.'[37]

Such perceptions of Islam and Protestantism, characteristic of the pre-ecumenical era, were based less on sound theology than upon ignorance and fear. The Vatican II Decree on Missions (*Ad gentes*, 1965) and Paul VI's apostolic exhortation *Evangelii nuntiandi* (1976) made it clear that Protestantism and Islam represent authentic spiritual impulses and called for dialogue between Catholicism and all Christian and non-Christian churches and religions.

IV

Although the missionary magazines directed their material to a general readership and were essentially popular publications, attempts were made, particularly in the earlier years, also to cater for well-educated Catholics. Intellectually rigorous presentations of the theological arguments for mission were published. Critically sound statistical analyses of missionary resources and their deployment appeared from time to time. Well-argued cases were presented to show that the missionary movement was no passing fashion but a durable reality and that its principles of operation were scientific.[38] The bearing of political and historical circumstances on missionary work was discussed. Articles on mission methodology were commonplace. Fr Thomas Broderick, who was later to become Bishop of Western Nigeria, wrote regularly on the value of the Catholic school as an instrument of evangelisation. He highlighted the benevolent attitude of the colonial authorities in British Africa towards mission education, and also the receptivity of Africans to education on account of its economic benefits. Bishop Shanahan, Vicar Apostolic of Southern Nigeria, was another frequent contributor on this topic.[39] The catechist system too was scrutinised in articles which stressed the catechist's ability to communicate directly and intimately with his people, and which encouraged the expectation that from his ranks would come the indigenous clergy of the future.[40]

The scientific or intellectual approach formed part and parcel of the content of the missionary magazines from the earliest publications until the early 1940s, when it gradually vanishes from view. In 1918 the *African Missionary* apologised for the scarcity of 'serious missionary matter' because of postal difficulties experienced during the previous year. A promise for the inclusion of a larger proportion of 'technical articles' was fulfilled as soon as the Great War had ended. Excellent articles were written on the problems arising from African marriage custom, on African culture and the problems of missionary adaptation. In 1919 the editor of the *African Missionary* decried the lack of appropriate handbooks dealing with the conduct of mission and made an unfavourable comparison between the Catholic and Protestant approaches:

> Every local Protestant missionary society pursues some definite line of work, studies some field and by means of this systematic

> study each member is saturated by the facts concerning the topography, climate, customs, language and history of the peoples concerned.[41]

This was indeed refreshing self-criticism and contrasted sharply with the complacency which developed in later decades. Even more refreshing was Mgr Broderick's call for co-operation and a pooling of information between the heads of the various missions:

> We in Western Nigeria look forward to the day when the heads and representatives of all West Coast missions will meet to compare notes, and methods, to discuss all important questions such as the catechumenate, central training schools and colleges, a Catholic printing press, catechists and a native clergy.[42]

To the discerning mind contemplating a missionary career the emphasis on a critical approach was an earnest that missionaries were progressive and professional. Unfortunately, as the movement developed and as competitiveness between the missionary institutes for funds and recruits came to dominate, less energy was devoted to a serious study of missionary topics; and the co-operation which Broderick had urged was never to materialise. The damaging effect of such neglect was obscured by the abundance of missionary vocations and by the spectacle of widespread activity on the mission-fields; it only became evident in the late 1960s and early 1970s when the rate of entry into missionary institutes dropped sharply and when deficiencies in the emerging missionary churches began to appear. Vocation directors suddenly found themselves required to provide well-reasoned arguments for missionary work and were unable to turn to a serious mission literature for answers. Similarly, missionaries in the field were faced with problems as to their role in a rapidly changing environment and had nowhere to turn to for guidance.

This chapter has attempted to analyse the techniques employed by the mission propagandists which proved so successful in attracting recruits to the movement. It must be stated, however, that such techniques alone could never account for the large influx of personnel. Without the existence of a religious milieu favourable to the cause of missions, such propaganda could never have succeeded. It must also be stated that over the years there was always a percentage of recruits who entered missionary seminaries and novitiates for reasons unconnected with the missionary movement. Some chose a missionary career because of lack of job and educational opportunities and because of the esteem which attached to religious vocation. In some instances parental and peer-group pressure played a role. It should be noted, however, that the average seminary course lasted for a period of not less than seven years, and during that period a very thorough monitoring of each candidate's progress took place. In the case of missionary sisterhoods and brotherhoods, final profession followed a lengthy period of probation. It is probably true that a proportion of those who entered from motives unconnected with the missionary movement did in fact escape the notice of their superiors and subsequently came to grief on the missions; but because of the extremely rigorous vetting process, the number must have been very small. In many cases those who entered because of sociological or economic pressures acquired a new and more authentic motivation during their years of training. It is naturally impossible to give statistics for the number of those entering missionary institutes with inappropriate motivation. However, those engaged in the direction of seminaries and novitiates, and who thus had their fingers on the pulse of the movement, appear not to have rated the matter of much importance.

In conclusion, the most striking feature in the attempts to motivate Irish Catholics towards missionary commitment was the manner in which the missionary magazines related the movement to contemporary political and cultural preoccupations. The missionary was consistently presented as a man of his time, living out in their fullest expression the virtues of the ethos. At the heart of missionary propaganda was the message that to be missionary was to be modern.

THIRTEEN

Style and Structure
of the Irish Missionary Movement

THE 'style of performance' of the Irish missionary in the field and the structural organisation or 'shape' of the Irish movement are topics each of which could form the subject-matter of a separate book. To treat them together in a single chapter underlines the character of this book as an introductory survey. At the same time the modern Irish missionary movement *was* a coherent reality in which motivation, organisation and performance were well integrated. The structure of the movement, which centred on institutions devoted exclusively to the work of missions, was ideally suited to the complexity of the missionary task. It ensured a singlemindedness which was essential for the success of the work, a capacity to secure and supply bridgeheads in non-Christian territories and thereafter to consolidate and to expand the scope of the work. Moreover, since most of the institutes were modern creations (whether indigenous or continental in origin), they were able to evolve a style of activity in the field unencumbered by traditionalism. The structure was also eminently suited to the task of harnessing the great surge of interest in non-Christian missions among Irish Catholics, providing opportunities for commitment which ranged from service overseas as priests, religious or laity to participation in the provision of material resources and the dissemination of promotional literature. Nonetheless, the Irish movement was not without its shortcomings. Originating in the early decades of the twentieth century, its methods of promotion did not always keep pace with the changing complexion of Irish society, which in the latter part of the century saw widening cultural horizons as well as the emergence of a better-educated population. Not all the features borrowed from the continental movement were helpful. For example, the spirit of competitiveness between institutes was an inheritance of doubtful value. Nor, in the conduct of missions, did the movement's methods always respond to changing needs. In this regard one may instance a tardiness in embracing wholeheartedly the models of 'human development' and 'liberation' proposed by the Second Vatican Council. Finally, its organisational structure, which was so admirably suited to conditions in the first half of the century, was slow to adapt to new circumstances in more recent times when human and material resources began to diminish. Such shortcomings were perhaps inevitable in a movement already in existence for over half a century, capable of developing beneficial traditions but susceptible also to the dangers of traditionalism.

I

The distinctive style of the Irish movement emerges from comparisons with its continental counterpart. The following reflections are based on comparative studies conducted on Irish and French missionaries in Africa. The validity of the conclusions for other missionary theatres remains to be tested.

It is known that when French agencies first came to Ireland to recruit for their missions in British African territories they entertained a very low estimate of the missionary capacity of the Irish. It is very likely that had there been a possibility of procuring English-speaking missionaries elsewhere, they would have avoided Ireland. Clearly the reputation of the Irish as the Church's foremost missionaries in the period extending from the sixth to the ninth centuries carried no weight with figures such as François Libermann, founder of the C.S.Sp. and one of the leading lights of the continental movement. He declared that the Irish as a race lacked that 'spirit of generosity' which made good missionaries.[1] More telling criticisms came from French S.M.A. missionaries who had worked alongside Irish priests for a brief period in South Africa. According to these, the Irish lacked apostolic zeal and were given to 'softness' and worldliness. One recorded the following indictment of his Irish colleagues:

> The Irish priest eats his steak, drinks his punch and occupies himself only with his exiled fellow-countrymen; and of course he does not scruple to accept money from the Association for the Propagation of the Faith. Such is his so-called ministry. The Cape of Good Hope has been lost to the Church by the Irish.[2]

Mgr Melchior de Marion Bresillac, a member of the Paris Foreign Mission Society (M.E.P.), wrote of Irish colleagues working in India:

Really can you be happy with the results of the Irishmen's apostolic efforts in India? Is it not heart-breaking to see the way they treat the poor black Christians? They are very good at publishing newspapers in English, preaching in English, establishing English schools and orphanages for the children of Irish soldiers. But what are they doing for the black people? They don't even know the language! . . . Have they even got the kind of temperament needed for evangelization in these countries? Maybe their temperament is the most inappropriate of all for such work.[3]

He added that Bishop Fennelly, Vicar Apostolic of Madras, 'is not at all favourable to the idea of a Native Clergy—not any more, I think, than Bishop Carew of Calcutta'.[4] In addition to these comments, there were reports emanating from continental sources that Irish C.S.Sp. priests had abandoned their stations in West Africa without due cause.[5] Criticisms by the French were perhaps to be expected, given the seniority of French agencies in the work of non-Christian missions. More alarming, however, was the fact that the low estimate of the Irish was shared by leading officials at Propaganda Fide, the agency responsible for the Church's missionary activity. In the 1890s it was being said at Rome that the Irish were 'temperamentally unsuited' for non-Christian missionary work.[6]

What can be said of these unfavourable assessments? In most cases they were unwarranted or, where there was some foundation, the verdict was over-harsh. Libermann, writing in the 1840s, pronounced his judgment after representatives of his institute seeking recruits in Ireland had been rebuffed.[7] He may also have been influenced by reports on the colonial clergy—some of whom were Irish—which questioned their commitment to fight slavery.[8] In fact he had no practical experience of Irish missionaries. Mgr Bresillac, who first made his remarks in 1845, was uneasy with the special position enjoyed by Irish missionaries in India and specifically the government's formal recognition of Bishop Fennelly as 'leader of the Roman Catholic Community'. Although elements of his criticisms may have had substance—notably his comments relating to the acquisition of local languages—he made no concession to the lack of a modern Irish missionary tradition. With regard to Irish secular priests in South Africa, the S.M.A. experience there in the late 1870s had been unhappy, to say the least.[9] A number of the French priests assigned to this mission were either disaffected confrères critical of the society's leadership, or priests whose health had failed to withstand the rigours of the West African coast; in addition, most of them lacked a knowledge of English, essential for an effective ministry in South Africa. They made little impact and eventually were withdrawn when the leader of the group abandoned his post in 1882 and (reputedly) embraced Protestantism. At best, criticism of the Irish by such men must be regarded as unreliable. As for the reports from West Africa concerning Irish Holy Ghost missionaries, which dated from the 1880s, it is true that, of the handful of priests and brothers who went there, some withdrew prematurely; but in most cases there were good reasons, mainly relating to ill-health. In fact the majority of the Irish proved themselves resourceful and effective. Some, like James Browne, John O'Gorman and Joseph Shanahan, established reputations which are still intact among the Catholics of Sierra Leone and Southern Nigeria. Finally, it must be said that most of Propaganda Fide's information about the Irish came from prejudiced sources, from S.M.A. and C.S.Sp. headquarters in Lyons and Paris.

If the French had no love for the Irish, the sentiment was reciprocated. Irish missionaries in West Africa tended to resent the patronising attitude of the French (they found the Alsatians more congenial) and were often highly critical of French missionary lifestyles and work practices. Some dissatisfaction also surfaced in China. Fr Joseph O'Leary wrote of his French colleagues in 1914:

> [They] are splendid, of course, but they are very conservative. They are gentlemen to their fingertips, but they will legislate on the number of buttons on a man's soutane or the number of hairs in his beard. They are 'gone mad' on rubrics.[10]

Some of these complaints by Irish missionaries were valid; but others had their roots in insecurity or inexperience.

In the final analysis, the difference between the Irish and the French related to matters of technique rather than to missionary zeal. In Africa the French missionary, as a rule, sought to identify closely with his flock, eating local food, living in the native 'compound', and employing the local remedies against disease; nor was he always anxious to leave his mission for furlough in Europe. For this he was to pay a high price. In the period 1848-1900 the average life-span among French C.S.Sp. and S.M.A personnel was 32.7 years;

the majority were 26 years of age on reaching Africa. During the same period British traders living according to European standards, and taking regular vacations outside the tropics, often managed to live normal life-spans.[11]

Irish missionaries from the outset rejected the French model of missionary lifestyle. They imported foodstuffs from Europe and only ate local food to supplement their diet or when nothing else was available. They built their houses of brick or cement blocks, situated them on hills to avail of the breeze, introduced modern water-filtering equipment, used mosquito nets, and made use of prophylactics against malaria. They also returned to Ireland at relatively regular intervals to regather their strength.[12] In short, they lived or attempted to live according to European standards, and for this reason survived much longer than their continental counterparts. The French despised what they described as the Irish 'softness' and desire for '*la vie confortable*'; but in time the frightening mortality statistics forced them to adopt similar standards.[13]

In the work of building up the Church the Irish were renowned for evangelisation through the medium of education; they also gained a reputation for constructing solid chapels and churches. Yet in terms of evangelising methods or work practices, the French were generally more progressive. The Irish (with some notable exceptions, including Bishop Shanahan in Southern Nigeria) engaged in education not as a *planned strategy* but because they worked mainly in the British colonies, where missionaries were expected to supply educational needs. In the French colonies education was secularised from 1903. Yet the French preoccupation with evangelising technique predated the prohibition on missionary education. From the very start French and continental missionaries appreciated the importance of learning local languages—the Irish rarely did—and of developing the indigenous missionary potential. The well-trained catechist who in practice evangelised many more Africans than the European was largely the creation of French and Alsatian missionaries. French missionaries, too, engaged in anthropological study (even before that science was properly recognised), compiling *coutumier*s or compendiums of local customs and basing their evangelising methods on the findings. In Africa it was the White Fathers, founded by Cardinal Lavigerie in 1868, who were to lead in the field of apostolic technique, approaching their task with a professionalism which was not to be surpassed. Not only did they adapt the presentation of Christianity to local religious experience, not only were their catechists far better trained than any others, but the White Fathers were first in the field of social development. But what the Irish lacked in technique they made up for in numbers. Already by 1957 there were more Irish priests deployed in Africa and Asia than Italians, Germans or Spanish, and there was evidence that Dutch and Belgian totals were being gradually overhauled. In Africa too, by this time, there were more Irish sisters in the field than Dutch, Italian or Spanish, while French and Belgian totals were already within range. In relative terms (*per capita* of Catholic population), the Irish were to outstrip all the European mission-sending countries by the early 1960s; and in absolute terms, by the 1970s Irish totals were among the highest in Europe.[14]

II

Part of the explanation for the difference between Irish and French missionaries in approach to lifestyle lay in the spirituality which animated the missionaries. During the nineteenth century the French ascetical school of the seventeenth century, which had been founded by Pierre de Bérulle and was closely linked to the Jesuit school, again came to enjoy wide popularity on the continent. Other forms of asceticism were also revived and new strands introduced. Most of the important sixteenth- and seventeenth-century ascetical treatises were reissued and ran into numerous editions. The works of Alphonsus Rodriguez, Ignatius Loyola, St Teresa of Avila, Guillère, de Ravignan, Surin, Scaramelli and Saint-Juré were widely read. The result was a rigid, uncompromising ascetical spirituality which placed a premium on obedience, expiation, self-sacrifice, detachment and supremacy of will over other faculties. Jesuit, Lazarist and M.E.P. missionaries in the Far East, deeply influenced by this spirituality, saw abandonment of home and country as integral to the missionary commitment. For them the chosen country of mission became their true home; and this contributed in no small measure to their dedication in learning its language and studying its culture, and also to their reluctance to return to Europe. Nineteenth-century continental missionaries in Africa, the Far East, Oceania and North America tended to exhibit similar attitudes.

While no adequate study of the spirituality of Irish missionaries exists, it is clear that they were never influenced to the same extent by the prevailing continental version. It is true that most Irish missionaries belonging to continental institutes were exposed to the ascetical model during their period of training. However, in practice their spirituality tended to be based more on a devotional model, centred on a strong Eucharistic piety and on veneration of the Blessed Virgin and the saints.[15] Those aspects of the ascetical model which formed part of their spiritual motivation for mission, notably the spirit of self-sacrifice and the willingness to embrace exile, were tempered by dictates of another kind—by a profound love of country, an unease with external (non-Irish) sources of authority, and a keen solicitude for physical survival. These traits owed much to Ireland's distant and more recent historical past. The centuries-old experience of oppression, which had produced a resistance to authority in Ireland, generated in Africa a certain suspicion of continental superiors and an unwillingness to accept unquestioningly the continental approach to the conduct of mission. The dreadful toll on human life exacted by the Famine left its mark in a reluctance to carry too far the glorification of missionary deaths and a determination to take every measure available to preserve life. The cultural movement and the stirring of nationalist sentiment, within a community which was already tight-knit, produced a sense of national and cultural identity not easily given up. Not surprisingly, neither the idea of total abandonment of home and country nor the tendency to over-identify with the people they served ever featured to any great extent in the Irish approach to missions.

Whether, in their attitude towards Africans, Irish missionaries were influenced to any significant degree by nineteenth-century racial theories which denigrated the Negro and proclaimed the superiority of the white race is doubtful. Lamin Sanneh, in his history of West African Christianity,[16] notes that 'Catholic missionaries, unlike their Protestant counterparts, did not move quickly to train an indigenous priesthood' and adds that the 'conspicuous concentration of power in white missionary hands tended to suggest and confirm the view that the Catholic Church was indifferent to genuine African aspirations'. But he does not conclude from this that Catholic missionaries doubted the capacity of Africans to make good priests, or that they deliberately set out to suppress Africans. Rather he attributes the slow progress towards indigenisation to 'the nature of the Church and its historical circumstances'. More tellingly, Elizabeth Isichei, in her study of the Igbo priest Michael

Tansi[17] refers to 'the curious conviction of [Irish] expatriate mission-aries that a genuine Christian needs six generations of Christian ancestors' and the opinion that while African clergy might do well under close supervision, their capacity to remain celibate and to administer their parishes honestly when left to themselves was at least in doubt. She mentions too a prohibition on Africans against joining religious congregations and the 'readiness with which [highly motivated] seminarians were sent away', often because of 'academic failures'.

What is to be said of the points raised by these African scholars? The fact was that the Catholic Church required of candidates for priesthood a higher standard of education than did the Protestant churches, and, given the inadequacy of second-level educational facilities, this was certainly an important factor in inhibiting the emergence of a cadre of African clergy. Nor, in terms of intellectual formation, were African seminarians treated more harshly than their counterparts in Europe, since uniform requirements had been long since established, and applied rigorously, by the Holy See. By the same token, the dismissal of aspirants during their long and arduous course of training, because of academic weakness (and also for reasons which nowadays appear relatively trivial), was a feature of seminary life in all continents. In Africa, however, the problems of seminarians were compounded by social and economic factors, most notably by the pressure to abandon their studies in order to support indigent families. The prohibition on joining religious congregations, it appears likely, had little to do with the question of suitability or a refusal to admit blacks into white communities. Rather it derived from the priority given to the creation of secular (diocesan) clergy for the building up of an indigenous Church. The comment that the emergence of 'genuine Christians' could only be expected after generations of missionary endeavour (made by Mgr Joseph Shanahan in a letter to the *Annals* of the Association of the Propagation of the Faith in 1917) reflected Shanahan's perception of the strength of traditional religious culture which he had observed since his arrival in Nigeria in 1902. Its implications were not inherently racial or racist. In the event, strong Catholic com-munities capable of producing a self-propagating Church were to develop in the second half of the century. As to the misgivings concerning the capacity of Africans to remain celibate and to administer church property with probity, while individuals may have been prejudiced, it would be wrong to ascribe such sentiments to the vast majority of missionaries and their bishops. (Since 1976 this author has conducted extensive interviews with 34 Irish missionary priests (including four bishops), some of whom commenced work in West Africa in the late 1920s, and many of whom went there in the 1930s and early 1940s. All shared a strong commitment to the development of indigenous clergy, describing ways in which they 'fostered vocations'. Among the difficulties which were freely acknowledged as inhibiting the growth of an African clergy were social, cultural and economic pressures, weakness of second-level education in the pre-war period, the lack of a tradition of African clergy, and the fact that it took time for robust Christian communities to develop. Although celibacy was perceived as presenting a problem to those who might otherwise have offered themselves for priesthood, this was not in any way to be construed as an indication that the African was somehow 'weaker' than the European in such matters. As one bishop explained, 'Marriage was an integral and very important aspect of native culture. The Africans simply could not understand why their children should not get married.' The suitability of Africans for priesthood, and, specifically, their capacity to discharge the priestly functions with integrity, was not an issue. Where lapses were known to have occurred they were attributed (as they would be in Ireland) to poor admission procedures by seminaries, inadequate formation, or subsequent lack of support, rather than to any innate defect in the 'African character'.) Finally, the fact that the missionaries held over-tightly to the reins of control did not necessary mean that they were indifferent to African aspirations. It did mean that they had a different schedule for the fulfilment of these aspirations than the one conceived by some African Christians. Both schedules proved to be inaccurate. Africans were capable of assuming responsibility sooner than the missionaries believed but somewhat later than they themselves may have wished. What is important here, however, is to stress that from an early stage the policy pursued by Irish missionaries (which in large measure they had inherited from their continental predecessors and was strongly urged by Propaganda Fide) was predicated upon a belief that Africans *were* capable of being educated to the highest standards, would in time be able to assume the responsibility of priesthood and religious vocation, and eventually the leadership roles in their own churches. In the principal theatres of mission the establishment of seminaries for the education of indigenous clergy was given a high priority. In the few instances where such institutes were lacking it was scarcity of resources rather than racial prejudice or lack of commitment which was responsible; and in such cases candidates for priesthood were usually sent to seminaries in adjoining countries (or jurisdictions) until such time as facilities could be provided locally.

It must be stated that Irish missionaries came late to Africa, and their attitude to the conduct of mission was shaped not only by their own historical and cultural backgrounds but also by the hard-earned lessons of their continental predecessors. One notable feature of continental missionary spirituality was the perception of pioneering as a sacrificial act in which missionaries must be prepared to die in order that the mission might prosper. This was an adaptation to the missionary context of Tertullian's renowned maxim 'The blood of martyrs is the seed of new Christians', which in turn drew upon the Johannine text 'Unless the grain of wheat falls into the earth and dies, it remains alone; but if it dies, it beareth much fruit' (John 12:24). The invocation of Tertullian's maxim was calculated not only to inspire heroic dedication but also to give meaning to the deaths of young missionaries so prevalent in the nineteenth century. But it could also be easily distorted, producing in the impressionable a disregard for common prudence, a slackness in taking precautions against disease and climate, and even a self-fulfilling wish for death. For those entrusted with the direction of missionaries it could provide an easy rationalisation for catastrophes which might otherwise have been avoided. That such distortions occurred from time to time and contributed to the extremely high mortality among missionaries, there can be little doubt. One striking example which merits description was the case of the Company of Mary (S.M.M.), which staffed a mission in the West African Republic of Liberia in the years 1902-4.[18]

Although forewarned of the dangers, from the outset the S.M.M. expedition exhibited a reckless attitude to the climate and tropical disease. Working out of doors in the heat of the day, rejecting the offer of European-style accommodation and refusing the ministrations of a resident European doctor when priests fell ill, the missionaries set themselves on a course which was bound to result in fatalities. The attitude of mind which could permit such folly was articulated in the death-bed declaration of the first to die, Fr Le Goff. He exclaimed: 'The mission needs a victim. I am prepared to be that victim and am thankful to have been found worthy for the role.'[19] That his confrères shared this attitude is evident from letters sent to Europe describing the incident. Fr Sarré, the superior, made much of Le Goff 's disturbing pronouncement in his report to his superiors, clearly subscribing to the view that the success of the mission required missionary deaths. After Le Goff 's death, despite a full report on the circumstances furnished to S.M.M. superiors by the Dutch consul in Monrovia, there was no reappraisal of Sarré's capacity to lead. Instead from S.M.M. headquarters in France came letters of encouragement in which the motif of 'blood-sacrifice' was seen as ample justification for the tragedy. The S.M.M Superior General relayed the comment of a high-ranking cardinal attached to Propaganda Fide (Cardinal Vives el Tuto) that Le Goff's death 'was God's sign of blessing on the mission'. According to the Cardinal, 'The confrère who died became a martyr and has been given the sacred task of watching over the future of the mission.'[20] The Superior General himself felt that if Le Goff's death was presented in terms of heroic sacrifice, it would appeal to the young and secure recruits for the congregation. In view of the circumstances which precipitated the tragedy, such remarks were dangerously close to an endorsement of the unhealthy missionary spirituality which characterised the expedition. The subsequent course of the mission followed a pattern similar to that of the early weeks. Fr Sarré eventually died en route to Europe, while the remaining members of the party, some dangerously close to death, abandoned the mission and returned to France.

There can be little doubt that the attitudes which contributed to the failure in Monrovia were by no means isolated. It was noticeable that while premature missionary deaths in the early years of the movement were frequently explained in terms of 'blood-sacrifice' and were welcomed as tokens of future progress, by the first decade of the twentieth century such comment was scrupulously avoided in the promotional literature of the major missionary societies.[21] The reason for this change was to discourage the fatalism of those who saw early death as their certain destiny and who may have been disposed to assist the process by neglecting to take sensible precautions. Irish missionaries, who in the early years worked alongside continental confrères, were well aware of the danger of such attitudes. It is true that in the literature produced by the Irish movement there were frequent references to Tertullian's maxim and the idea of 'blood-sacrifice'. Doubtless the popularity of such themes in Ireland owed much to their use by the leaders of the 1916 Easter Rising. But while they may have been good for home consumption and helpful in promoting the movement, there is no evidence that they were ever allowed to influence behaviour on the missions. On the contrary, while believing that the death of young missionaries brought special graces to the mission and would ultimately be rewarded, Irish missionaries took every precaution to avoid such occurrences. Those who took charge of the Liberian mission after the S.M.M. débâcle learned from the mistakes of their predecessors. More generally, in the various theatres of West Africa entrusted to Irish missionaries, reports by local superiors to their headquarters in Ireland presented premature missionary deaths first and foremost as tragic occurrences, and every effort was made to identify the probable causes and to adopt measures which would prevent reoccurrences. One striking example which illustrates this solicitude for survival occurred in 1937 when two Irish missionaries recently assigned to Northern Nigeria fell victim to yellow fever. In the following year scientists at the University of Dublin produced a serum against the fever which required the quarantine of subjects for a period of some weeks. Irish missionaries were among the first to take advantage of this yet untried vaccine against a disease which over the years had accounted for such a high proportion of missionary deaths.[22] This willingness to submit to any remedy likely to improve prospects of survival, despite the illness and discomfort involved, was characteristic. In the event, a more satisfactory serum was soon produced, and the dreaded yellow fever no longer posed a threat.

III

In terms of its structure and organisation at home, if not in the manner of its conduct abroad, the Irish movement was less distinctive. Indeed, the influence of continental models and attitudes was pervasive. One beneficial continental borrowing was the model of the agency dedicated exclusively to missions and whose members belonged to the agency rather than to the missionary jurisdiction in which they worked. This, as has been mentioned, not only made for singularity of purpose, but it also ensured adequate resources of funds and personnel as well as proper care for those forced to return from the mission through illness.

A less fortunate inheritance from the continent was the spirit of competitiveness, which quickly took root within the Irish movement. At least in part, this was responsible for a proliferation of seminaries and novitiates all offering much the same type of training. It was responsible too for the spectacle of vocation directors tugging likely candidates in the direction of their particular institute. It contributed also to making fund-raising increasingly complicated and wearying as each institute sought to secure its share of the funds available. Such unnecessary duplication of effort had the effect of keeping many missionaries in Ireland who could have been usefully deployed abroad. And there were other equally serious consequences for the movement. Experience gained on the missions was never pooled between the missionary bodies; instead discussions on technique rarely went beyond the bounds of the individual institute. The absence of a serious journal dealing with missionary matters was a further reflection of the prevailing competitive spirit. Nor was any effort made to develop a theology of mission based on an Irish experience of overseas ministry among non-Christian peoples. In short, everything was subordinated to maintaining the competitiveness of the individual institute.

Only a firm hierarchical involvement could have prevented this regrettable situation from arising. Propaganda Fide could never have provided the necessary focus, because its energies were dissipated in grappling with a missionary movement of worldwide proportions. And in any case, far from intervening, Propaganda seemed almost to welcome and promote rivalry between missionary bodies.[23] Had the hierarchy assumed a supervisory responsibility from the outset, a strategy might have emerged which would have encouraged institutes to work *for* rather than against or in isolation from each other. Zimmermann had attached great importance to creating formal links with the Irish Church, and to this end had involved individual members of the hierarchy intimately in the affairs of his institute. In the case of the five indigenous institutes formed between 1916 and 1937, the hierarchy as a body stood back from any formal involvement. Nor is it certain that such participation would always have been welcomed, either by the missionary agencies or by Propaganda Fide. At least one member of the hierarchy saw the necessity of creating structures to link the missionary movement with the Church in Ireland. When St Patrick's Missionary Society was founded Bishop Matthew Cullen of Kildare and

Leighlin, in whose diocese the institute was established, suggested to Propaganda that Diocesan Consultors should be appointed to assist in the administration. However, the terms of their appointment were much too weak, and they had ceased to exercise their function long before they were dispensed with at the General Chapter of 1944.[24] In general, however, the role of bishops in the affairs of the Irish agencies was limited to encouragement and approval, the granting of permissions to recruit and raise funds within their dioceses, and, in most cases, a willingness to release priests who wished to join the movement. Their relationship with the Irish branches of continental missionary agencies was of much the same variety, although in some specific instances it tended to be remote and even disapproving. Lacking a competent, overriding authority to give cohesion, it was hardly surprising, therefore, that the Irish movement should develop into an unwieldy instrument.

There were some tentative attempts to coordinate the movement's activities. The establishment of a Mission Service Centre in 1959 was a significant development. The Centre, located in Dublin, provided a wide range of practical support services. Nonetheless it was only in recent decades, with the sharp contraction of resources, that the structural weaknesses of the movement were finally addressed. In 1970 when the consequences of competitiveness could no longer be ignored, and influenced also by the Conciliar call for co-operation and co-responsibility in the work of mission, the Irish missionary institutes and agencies with missionary commitments (some sixty-two in all) came together with the hierarchy to form the Irish Missionary Union, with a view to co-ordinating missionary endeavour and restoring the missionary movement to the Irish Church. Among the benefits which followed this development were measures to regularise the process of admission to dioceses for purposes of promotion and recruitment. Structures were also put in place for the discussion of the important issues affecting the movement and for articulating a common position. Nonetheless, efforts to establish a national missionary institute for the training of candidates and for in-service training have been only partially rewarded. Although a missionary institute has recently been established, missionaries continue to be trained at a variety of centres. Moreover, although the Irish Missionary Union has published excellent statistical surveys on the movement's resources and also issues a bulletin, there is as yet no serious national journal dealing with missionary issues.

FOURTEEN

Epilogue: Towards the Future

IT is said that historians make unreliable prophets. Yet in times of uncertainty they are frequently called upon to perform that function and rarely resist the temptation. No one will dispute that historical perspective can greatly assist understanding of the present. It is evident too that there are elements of continuity between past, present and future, while seeds of the future are always contained in the present. By a discerning illumination of present realities history may therefore provide modest indications of things to come. Thus it can be of service to those who seek to mould the future, as well as helping those who have difficulty in confronting the present.

Since the late 1950s, and especially following the Vatican Council, the structure of the Church's missionary movement, as well as the theory and practice of missionary activity, have been undergoing a gradual transformation, and it is becoming evident that a watershed is approaching. The shape of the future remains unclear. However, the analysis of current developments offered in the following pages suggests that missionary enterprise in the twenty-first century may well be conducted as energetically as in the past. At the same time, as a consequence of the shift presently taking place in Christianity's centre of gravity from North to South, the geographical focus of 'primary proclamation' to non-Christians inevitably will change. For the same reasons the provenance of missionary resources also seems set to change; clerical and religious missionaries will be increasingly drawn from the new churches of the southern hemisphere, compensating in some measure for a declining supply of human resources from the northern churches. The pattern in the northern churches, of course, is not one of uniform decline. For example, the Church in Poland is currently experiencing an upsurge in vocations to priesthood and religious life, and there is a growing interest too in the work of missions. It would be premature to conclude that this augurs a more general resurgence in Eastern Europe. Nonetheless, there can be little doubt now that the systematic persecution of Christians and the suppression of churches has failed to achieve its purpose, not only in Poland but in the other countries and communities subjected to communist rule. What is certain, however, is the continuing decline in vocations in Europe's liberal democracies which traditionally furnished the bulk of missionary personnel.

The enhanced understanding of the Church's 'Mission' emerging since the Second Vatican Council, too, will have important repercussions for the future. The Mission of the Church, as expressed in the theological idiom of the Council, is to gather humanity as a 'people' into the 'Kingdom of God'. This 'Kingdom and the 'people' which form it, according to the Council, subsist in the Catholic Church. But it also extends to members of other churches, of other religions and even to the non-religious living lives of integrity, although these categories lack the fullness of participation enjoyed by Catholics. Declaring that the Church is 'missionary' by its very nature, the Council imposed on all Catholics responsibility for the fulfilment of its Mission. The Council emphasised that there are many different ways in which this responsibility may be discharged. For instance, pastoral care of professing Christians is distinguished from missionary enterprise, the latter being a 'special activity' which takes place on the frontier between belief and unbelief and which is specifically addressed to those not yet incorporated into the Catholic community. Paul VI in *Evangelii nuntiandi* (1976) extended this frontier to include also those who are already baptised but 'live lives entirely divorced from Christianity', those who have 'a certain measure of faith but know little even of its fundamental principles', and 'intellectuals who feel that they need to approach Jesus Christ from a different standpoint from that which was taught them in their childhood days'.[1] The most recent encyclical on missions, *Redemptoris Missio* (1990) situates the frontier between belief and unbelief especially in the South and East and chiefly in Asia. It also largely reserves the re-evangelisation of baptised who abandon the Church to a new category of evangelisation distinct from 'missionary evangelisation'. The significance of this adjustment is explored in Appendix C. Nonetheless, it can confidently be said that missionaries will continue to be concerned with extending the visible Church and facilitating those who seek participation in the Church's sacramental life. They will be concerned too with the recovery of Christians, especially in the young Churches of the South and East, who have abandoned their faith for whatever reason, or who are alienated through ignorance of its principles. Finally, they will also now enter into dialogue with other religions and with the non-religious who may not be ready to embrace membership of the Catholic Church, affirming them in their response to God's grace however it is mediated.

The Council also declared that in gathering together God's 'people', the Church must address itself not simply to individuals but to human society whose structure it seeks to transform according to the principles of the Gospel. Those undertaking missionary enterprise, therefore, will be increasingly engaged in action for justice, peace and liberation and other activities which bear on the structural transformation of human society. They will also be in the vanguard of the Church's efforts to combat hunger, poverty and human distress, so that the 'Kingdom of God', which embraces humankind in its totality, may be made manifest in the present and give hope for the future. Moreover, missionaries will be concerned with the evangelisation of human culture, restoring the transcendent dimension to the world of communications, art, literature, philosophy and science. In the future too, greater lay participation in missionary enterprise will be assured, not only because of the Council's heightened valuation of laity within the Church but also because of the great diversity of missionary tasks which require attention.

The General Roman Catholic Missionary Movement

I

Effectively until the eve of the Second Vatican Council missionary enterprise was conducted much as it had been since the early nineteenth-century revival: it took place mainly in the southern hemisphere and was spearheaded by priests and religious from northern countries who gave lifelong commitment and were members of missionary institutes or religious orders. From the second decade of the twentieth century this professional core of permanent evangelising workers was assisted by small groups of diocesan volunteers on temporary assignment and, from the post-war period, by increasing numbers of laity, usually offering temporary commitment. Financial and material resources were gathered from Catholics in mission-sending countries by the various missionary societies, or by international aid societies approved by the Holy See. The motivation for mission was the same as it always had been since Apostolic times. Missionaries went forth in response to Christ's command 'Go therefore and make disciples of all nations, baptising them in the name of the Father and of the Son and of the Holy Spirit' (Matt. 28:19). In practice this command was most commonly construed as an injunction to establish the Catholic Church through-out the world. Responsibility for this *implantatio ecclesiae* was confided by the Holy See to the various institutes and orders com-mitted to mission, from which individual members were selected to rule as vicars apostolic or bishops. In church law this conferral of jurisdiction, termed the *jus commissionis*, gave the institutes and those appointed to positions of authority exclusive charge (under the Holy See) of designated mission territories. Missionary method centred on catechesis, the administration of sacraments, and the formation of indigenous catechists, clergy and religious. From an early stage the provision of schooling and health care were recognised as important ancillary techniques. Although motivated in part by humanitarian considerations, these and other techniques which promoted social and economic advancement were valued primarily as means of attracting adherents to Catholicism.

In the immediate aftermath of the Second World War, which caused significant disruption of missions, Roman Catholic enterprise quickly regained its momentum, and for a period it appeared that the upheaval was to have no far-reaching consequences. By the early 1950s, however, a very different picture had begun to emerge as the post-war order took more definite shape. The emergence of inde-pendence movements in many colonial territories raised questions about the future of expatriate missionaries. The rising tide of com-munism in Asia threatened the very existence of organised religion. In Africa an expanding Islam seemed set to undermine missionary achievements accomplished over a century and a half.

Paradoxically, the post-war era also witnessed a marked expansion of the so-called 'missionary churches'. Sometimes changed political circumstances assisted this expansion. For instance, colonial powers preparing to disengage but anxious to maintain their influence frequently made generous resources available for education and health care. Missionary churches were to benefit substantially from such policies. However, even in countries where political conditions were unfavourable, missions tended to thrive, suggesting that the phenomenon of post-war growth was essentially a token of the missionary movement's maturation. At the same time it was becom-ing increasingly evident that the movement would have to respond to the changing conditions for the conduct of the apostolate if progress was to be maintained. In regions where communist influ-ence was in the ascendant time was rapidly running out for

expatriate missionaries. In other regions the exploitation of opportunities for evangelisation was being hampered by an insufficiency
of personnel.

Reacting to the various challenges of the post-war era, the Holy See
breathed new life into a centuries-old policy, which had previously
been applied unevenly (because of resistance from missionaries),[2] of
appointing indigenous bishops to vacant jurisdictions whenever
suitable candidates could be found. Moreover, missionaries in the
field, now without much urging, were encouraged to intensify the
training of indigenous clergy, religious and lay catechists. Such measures were intended to make missionary churches self-propagating
and capable of surviving the expulsion of expatriate missionaries or
the onset of persecution. But indigenisation could not be accomplished overnight. Other steps would have to be taken which would
have a more immediate effect in making the most of existing opportunities for evangelisation and in preparing missionary churches for
an uncertain future. One obvious measure would be an injection of
fresh personnel, provided that new sources of supply could be found.

Pius XII's encyclical *Fidei donum* (1957) was designed for just
such a purpose. Although Catholic theology and the *magisterium*
(the Church's teaching authority) had always acknowledged that
implantation of the Church was the concern of the whole Church
and pre-eminently that of bishops in virtue of their position as
successors of the Apostles,[3] for centuries the exercise of this responsibility had been given over to Propaganda Fide and the missionary
agencies subject to that Congregation. *Fidei donum*, which was produced against a background of a shortage of evangelising workers in
Africa and the growing influence of Islam, called for more active
collaboration from the universal Church. Specifically it reminded
bishops that their mandate extended beyond their dioceses to
embrace the Church's universal apostolic mission and urged them
to 'a new ardour for the missionary activity of the Church throughout the world'.[4] The Second Vatican Council took up these themes,
declaring that 'the Church on earth is by its very nature missionary',[5] drawing attention to 'the express command [to evangelise all
nations] which the order of bishops inherited from the Apostles',[6]
and exhorting bishops everywhere to 'come to the aid of the
missions by every means in their power'.[7] Thus was the traditional
jus commissionis (formerly residing in the missionary agencies until
transfer to individual bishops on the erection of national hierarchies)

effectively abrogated in favour of a more general and far-reaching commission to the universal Church and its leaders.

II

In the early stages these efforts to harness wider support for missions met with a disappointing response. By 1964 it was estimated that at most 300 priests had gone on mission under the title of *Fidei donum*.[8] Part of the problem lay in the thrust of the Church's efforts to secure additional personnel. Although Pius XII had affirmed that the whole Church was responsible for missions, his appeal, made specifically on behalf of Africa, was directed to the older-established churches of the North. It was the Vatican Council which was first to propose the work of missions to more recently established churches. Its decree on missionary activity called upon 'local priests' of the 'young churches' to 'eagerly offer themselves to the bishops for missionary work in distant and abandoned areas of their own or other dioceses' (*missio ad intra*); it also urged the young churches 'to take part in the universal Mission of the Church as soon as possible and [to] send missionaries to preach the Gospel throughout the whole world' (*missio ad extra*).[9]

It is probable that many of the Council Fathers regarded these as prophetic declarations relating to developments which would take place in the distant future. In the event, the Council's exhortation was to prove timely. The primary tactical objective of missionary effort, since the establishment of Propaganda Fide in 1622 and more especially since the nineteenth-century revival, had been the development of indigenous clergy. In the decades following the Council the patient labour of generations of missionaries began to bear fruit in a manner which astonished even the most experienced observers. So marked were the signs of growth, especially among churches in Africa and Asia, that from the late 1960s it became clear that collaboration in the work of missions was soon destined to become truly universal and, indeed, that in the longer term missionaries from these younger churches might shoulder the greater burden of responsibility.

For the post-Conciliar papacy, keenly aware of disturbing trends in the older-established churches of the North and their implications for the future of missionary enterprise, the cultivation of a missionary outlook in the younger churches became an important priority. Drawing on the theological and pastoral insights of the

Council, in addresses delivered during pastoral visits to Africa and Asia and Latin America, Paul VI and John Paul II encouraged local churches to assume responsibility for missions in their own continents and urged the dispatch of missionaries to other continents.

The response to such exhortations and the Council's appeal has been especially striking in Africa and Asia.[10] In Africa three recently established missionary institutes are already engaged in *missio ad intra* and are currently preparing for activity further afield. In addition, some fourteen international institutes and orders, as well as a handful of indigenous institutes originally founded for local apostolates, are training African members for service of the universal Church. In Asia the Philippines Church, which represents more than 60 per cent of the continent's Catholics, has established its own missionary institute (although yet far from flourishing); and several international agencies are now actively involved in the formation and deployment of Filipino missionaries. The Korean Church too has its own missionary society in an early stage of development, while in India several societies, some international and others founded locally, have had flourishing missions to non-Christians in the subcontinent for some time and are now attempting a wider apostolate.[11] In Thailand, where there are only a quarter of a million Catholics, a missionary society has been established by the bishops as recently as 1989. Meanwhile *Fidei donum* missionaries from India and the Philippines and from a number of Latin American countries continue to be deployed in increasing numbers in other continents, chiefly Africa. Although churches in Mexico, Columbia and Brazil have had a tradition of missionary work overseas predating the Council by some decades, the years since the publication of *Ad gentes* have witnessed an upsurge of interest throughout Latin America. Few can doubt that a strong missionary movement is now germinating and that the influence already exercised on the universal Church by this creative region will be greatly extended in the future.

III

No less important for the future than the structural changes just described will be the impact of recent theological insights. A discussion of these theological developments, not always easily accessible, will require some forbearance on the part of the reader. Vatican II's understanding of Mission was the product of a process of thought, study and testing which had originated in the 1930s and which was directed towards a consideration of the Church's *nature*. Those engaged in the process[12] at the outset had found the ecclesiology bequeathed by neo-scholasticism deficient in its scriptural reference, as well as too heavily influenced by an inherited, almost hostile, anthropology. Such inadequacies produced an image of the Church which was strongly juridical, static, and pervaded by that dualism which set spirit against flesh, soul against body, Church against World, and took insufficient count of Christ's victory over sin in all its manifestations. At the risk of caricature, it was an image of a visible institution, founded once and for all by Jesus Christ, in which individuals were incorporated by baptism, and whose task was to proclaim Christ's message accurately, uniformly and with authority, so that truth might prevail over falsehood, good over evil, and the Kingdom of God over the Kingdom of the World. The purpose of missionary enterprise within this scheme of things was to implant the Church in regions which had never heard the Christian message. This was to be accomplished by proclamation of the truths of the Faith, so that those who listened might be baptised and thereafter subscribe to the Church's dogmatic and moral teachings, submit to its discipline and authority, participate in its liturgy and sacramental life, and engage in its approved spiritual and social apostolates.

Pius XII's encyclical *Mystici corporis* (1943) sought to deepen the understanding of the Church's inner nature through the exploration of scriptural models. His invocation of the Pauline analogy of body to express the unity of the Church in Christ illustrated the capacity of this approach to yield up treasure. Nonetheless, the Pauline analogy illuminated an attribute rather than the essential nature of the Church. And it was the Second Vatican Council which was to draw from scripture the richest insights. *Lumen gentium* characterised the Church as a 'people called by God' for the purpose of embodying and bringing to fulfilment the 'kingdom of salvation' promised in the Old Testament and preached by Christ.[13] In short, the Church was revealed as the 'new People of Israel', and so part of the history of salvation; its declared Mission was to 'proclaim and establish among all peoples the Kingdom of God of which she is on earth the seed and the beginning'.[14]

Here was a dynamic image of a pilgrim people but also a messianic people (and therefore a missionary people) moving through history under the guidance of the Holy Spirit, as 'a sign and instrument [sacrament] of communion with God and of unity with all men [salvation]'.[15] Existing therefore as the 'sacrament of salvation',[16] the Church could no longer be said to stand against or apart from the World despite the reality of sinfulness. On the contrary, Christians were urged to emulate Christ in cherishing 'a feeling of deep solidarity with the human race and its history'.[17] Other religions were to be recognised as 'related to the people of God'[18] and containing much that is 'true and holy'.[19] And while continuing to 'proclaim Christ who is the way, the truth and the life', Christians were now 'to enter into discussion and collaboration with members of other religions',[20] a process of dialogue which the Council recognised as mutually enriching. Finally, the Council made it clear that nothing which exists can be excluded from the Church's Mission, since all things—'the whole human family and everything which envelops it'[21]—are redeemed in Christ.[22]

These seminal ideas formed the basis for the doctrinal principles outlined in the opening chapter of the Council's decree on missionary activity. *Ad gentes* declared that 'the Church is by its very nature missionary', since it is called to bring to fulfilment Christ's Mission 'according to the Father's plan' and under the guidance of the Holy Spirit.[23] The Church's missionary nature therefore derives from its Mission, which is 'to gather together [humankind], not merely singly, but as a people sharing in the life of Christ'.[24] The decree also asserted that this 'gathering together of the human family embraces such elements as the transformation of human culture, society, and 'the various worldly goods which bear the mark both of man's sin and God's blessing',[25] so that all things may finally be restored in Christ.[26]

Ad gentes's translation of these inspiring doctrinal principles into a pastoral methodology of Mission was at times tentative and unimaginative. For example, a more forthright acknowledgment extending the geographical focus of missions beyond the traditional boundaries of the southern hemisphere would appear to have been warranted both by theological principle and the analysis of contemporary history offered in the Constitution on the Church in the Modern World (*Gaudium et spes*, 1965). Clearly the recovery of those alienated from Christ, especially in the northern hemisphere, was now a matter of some urgency and, indeed, merited recognition as the proper work of 'those engaged in gathering together people who had never heard of Christ', namely 'missionaries'; while the transformation of society and culture was manifestly also a matter of global concern. Again, the decree's discussion of 'human develop-ment'—a critical strategy in the Council's approach to the transfor-mation of sinful society—left many key questions unanswered. Christians were urged 'to interest themselves, and to collaborate with others, in the right ordering of society and economic affairs'.[27] In addition, they were 'to share in the efforts of those peoples who, in fighting against famine, ignorance and disease, are striving to bring about better living conditions and bring about peace in the world'. However, there was no serious attempt to explore such activities in the context of political action. No less important was the failure to address the question of violence, an omission which was to nurture ambiguity. Moreover, the decree's remarks would have gained greater force had they been directed to local churches rather than to individual 'Christians'. Also there was no great encouragement for Christians to 'leadership' in tackling the re-ordering of society and pressing social problems.

Underlying the decree's approach to the methodology of Mission and specifically that aspect called 'missionary enterprise' there was perhaps a concern that an older model which had served the Church well should not be seen to be discarded. Yet if any such concern existed, it was quite unnecessary, since the central elements of traditional theory of missionary enterprise, far from being replaced or superseded, were in fact enhanced and strengthened by the Council. For instance, the pre-Conciliar image of 'conversion' as 'incorporation through baptism into the mystery of the Church' received added meaning from Conciliar ecclesiology. *Lumen gentium*'s assertion that the mystery of the Church is revealed in Christ bore the implication that the fundamental conversion is to the person of Christ. *Ad gentes* stated this plainly in its declaration that 'Everyone ought to be converted to Christ.' Yet it also declared that 'Everyone ought to become incorporated by baptism into the Church which is Christ's body.'[28] The burden of the Council's teaching, therefore was that those who are joined to the visible structure of the Church by baptism and thereafter participate in the Church's sacramental life present the most complete expression of conversion to Christ.

Ad gentes's failure to develop adequately the theme of 'human development' elaborated principally in *Gaudium et spes* was under-standable. Although the Church had always been engaged in works of human development, such strategies had never been satisfactorily integrated into the theology of Mission. It was inevitable that although the position had now changed, it would take time before the full implications of the formal commitment became apparent. With regard to the validity of re-evangelisation as an appropriate object of missionary enterprise, there may have been a fear that a formal commission would promote confusion in missionary ranks and might lead to a dissipation of energy.

Yet despite its shortcomings, *Ad gentes* offered missionaries much food for thought on the conduct of their apostolate. To the decree's persistent emphasis that all apostolic activity is a continuation of Christ's Mission was added the corollary that Christ must be regarded as the *model* for every undertaking. The decree devoted considerable attention to describing the manner in which Christ approached his Mission while on earth. It noted that he had 'committed himself to the particular social and cultural circumstances of the men among whom he lived', entering into their lives and identifying with their concerns. Those entrusted with implantation of the Church were urged to 'walk the road Christ himself walked, a way of poverty and obedience, of service and self-sacrifice, even of death'.[29] They were told that

> As Christ went about all the towns and villages healing every sickness and infirmity . . . so the Church, through its children, joins itself with men of every condition, but especially with the poor and afflicted, and willingly spends herself for them. It shares their joys and sorrows, it is familiar with the hopes and problems of life, it suffers with them in the anguish of death . . . and it wishes to enter into fraternal dialogue with those who are working for peace, and to bring them the peace and light of the Gospel.[30]

In short, the Council reminded the Church that conversion to Christ, hearing the good news of salvation, breaking the bread of life, having sins forgiven, all are only meaningful to the extent that they produce a Christ-like commitment to the suffering, the oppressed and the poor of this world.

No less important in terms of the methodology of missionary enterprise among non-Christians, though of another category, was the decree's reference to 'inculturation'. Just as a seed planted requires a congenial environment if it is to flourish, *Ad gentes* declared, so the implantation of the Church will best succeed if it is rooted in the traditions, philosophy and culture of those it seeks to evangelise.

Every effort, therefore, must be made to reconcile Christianity with the philosophy, wisdom, customs, concept of life and social structures of non-Christians so that the faith can be fully explained, fully understood and made fully incarnate.[31]

Undoubtedly one of the Council's most signal achievements was its restoration of missionary enterprise to its roots in the Mission of the Church. Up to the opening decades of the twentieth century the term 'missionary' was rarely used in writings on 'the Church'. Missionary enterprise tended to be regarded as a special concern of a select group of Christians rather than a preoccupation of the universal Church. This attitude persisted more or less down to the Second Vatican Council. For example, while in Ireland most church leaders facilitated the work of missionary societies, few felt any great responsibility for developing the missionary movement, and still less took part in its direction. The declaration by Vatican II that 'the Church on earth is by its very nature missionary' was greeted with enthusiasm by missionaries who saw it as a means of harnessing greater support from their churches of origin. Yet its significance was to be more far-reaching, relating not just to support but to responsibility—and, in the final analysis, to *responsibility for the Mission of the Church*, of which missionary activity was merely one expression.

The fundamental obligation, deriving from the 'missionary nature' of the Church, according to the Council, was 'to proclaim the faith and salvation which comes from Christ';[32] and this was to be discharged through the evangelisation of non-Christians in every culture, through work for Christian unity, and through the pastoral care of those already baptised.[33] Moreover, the Council explained that 'The differences in this activity of the Church [just described] do not flow from the inner nature of that Mission itself, but from the circumstances in which it is exercised.'[34] In other words, the aim of missionary activity directed towards non-Christians (i.e. missionary enterprise) is no different from that of pastoral care of the faithful, these activities having for their purpose the fulfilment of the Mission of the Church. At the same time the Council, in *Ad gentes*, emphasised that there was a close connection between these activities. For example, it described division between Christians as 'injurious to the holy work of preaching the Gospel to every creature' because it impairs the value of Christian witness.[35]

IV

Paul VI's apostolic exhortation *Evangelii nuntiandi*, published in 1976 and prompted by the deliberations of the third Synod of Bishops held two years earlier,[36] provided an integrated presentation of the Church's Mission. It is true that the various aspects of the Church's Mission had already been discussed in Conciliar documents, but attempts to draw the threads together had never quite succeeded. *Ad gentes*, which, as has been shown, went a long way towards achieving this objective, fell short because of its (necessary) concentration on one particular element of the Church's Mission—namely apostolic enterprise among non-Christians—also its lack of an adequate terminology and its tendency to use the existing terminology loosely (especially its use of the term 'missionary').[37] *Evangelii nuntiandi* not only treated all elements of the Church's Mission in the same document, but it provided a comprehensive description of each, showing also how they are interrelated. Imprecision was avoided by invoking the concept of 'evangelisation' as the most apt expression of the Church's Mission. At its core evangelisation is to be understood as 'the carrying forth of the good news to every sector of the human race so that by its inherent strength it may enter into the hearts of men and renew the human race.'[38] This in turn requires 'the conversion both of the individual consciences of men and their collective conscience, all the activities in which they are engaged and, finally, their lives and the whole environment which surrounds them'.[39] Evangelisation therefore 'goes to the very centre and roots of life, impregnating the culture and the whole way of life of man'.[40] As such it is a 'complex, rich and dynamic reality', comprising many elements all of which must be taken into account if the concept is to be properly understood.[41] In presenting the elements of evangelisation, *Evangelii nuntiandi* (drawing on *Ad gentes*) distinguished between primary proclamation of the Gospel among non-Christians and pastoral care of believing Christians, while at the same time asserting a close connection between both. However, whereas *Ad gentes* never adequately elucidated the connection, *Evangelii nuntiandi* explained that 'If the Church is to preserve the freshness, the ardour and the strength of her own work of preaching the Gospel, she must herself be continually evangelised.'[42] Pastoral evangelisation, therefore, was to be seen as laying the foundation for missionary enterprise since 'the man who had been [properly] evangelised becomes himself an evangeliser'.[43]

Again, while *Ad gentes* emphasised that the various activities of primary proclamation (i.e. missionary enterprise) 'are, for the most part, carried out in defined territories recognised by the Holy See (generally called missions)',[44] *Evangelii nuntiandi*, reflecting the concern of the synod, viewed primary proclamation in a wider perspective. Although acknowledging that 'this first primary proclamation will be directed primarily towards those who have never heard the good news of Jesus', it also stressed that 'it will always be needed nevertheless on account of the extent of dechristianisation today'.[45] Thus the global nature of primary proclamation emerges clearly, since it goes beyond those to whom the Gospel has never been preached to embrace baptised Christians who for various reasons become alienated or disaffected and abandon the profession or practice of their faith. Among the implications of this widening of the frontier between belief and unbelief is the recognition that Latin America and post-Christian Europe are now theatres of missionary evangelisation.[46]

Finally, benefiting from a decade of reflection and experience since the Council, *Evangelii nuntiandi* provided a penetrating analysis of the techniques of evangelisation. In its survey it dealt comprehensively with such topics as primary proclamation of the Gospel, the sacramental ministry, witness of life, ecumenism, basic communities, liberation and development, the question of violence, inculturation, the lay apostolate, the function of popular devotion, dialogue with other religions, catechetics, and the use of the mass media—subjects which (with few exceptions) preoccupied the Council but which of necessity were presented in a plurality of documents. Of particular relevance to missionaries was the treatment of human development and liberation. Since the Council these techniques had become prominent in those parts of Asia, South and Central America and East and Southern Africa where exploitation, poverty and oppression were endemic. *Evangelii nuntiandi* reflected a measure of concern that, in the pursuit of human development and liberation, Christians might lose sight of the fact that such techniques are ultimately directed towards 'salvation and eternal happiness in God'.[47] The extensive treatment of the question of violence reflected a similar fear of misinterpretation. On this topic *Evangelii nuntiandi* declared that 'The Church cannot accept any form of violence, and especially of armed violence—for this cannot be restrained when once it is unleashed—nor the death of any man as a method of liberation.'[48] Yet there is no diminution of the commitment to authentic human development and liberation first proclaimed at the Vatican Council and which was to form one of the major themes of Paul VI's pontificate;[49] for it is stated that

> Evangelisation will not be complete unless it constantly relates the Gospel to men's actual lives, personal and social. Accordingly, evangelisation must include an explicit message . . . concerning the rights and duties of the individual person and concerning family life, with peace, justice and progress. It must deliver a message, especially relevant and important in our age, about liberation.[50]

The Irish Missionary Movement

I

Since the early decades of the twentieth century Irish missionaries have featured prominently in apostolic enterprise among non-Christians. However, changes are now taking place in the structure of the Irish movement which are bound to affect its future contribution. In the first place, the numbers of clerical and religious missionaries, which had been steadily increasing since the 1920s, reaching a plateau in the mid-1970s, have now begun to diminish. Although the numerical strength still remains relatively stable, it is probable that the years ahead will register a substantial decrease.[51] The basis for this projection is the sustained shortfall in fresh personnel which shows no prospect of mitigation. In the years 1965-75 the number of Irish candidates entering missionary societies and congregations for men dropped by approximately half from class intakes recorded in the previous two decades; and figures for the 1980s show further, if less dramatic, reductions. Furthermore, the numbers of those persevering to priesthood or final profession stand at less than a third of entrants, in contrast to a proportion well in excess of two-thirds in the period before 1960. In the case of religious sisterhoods, the decline in numbers entering and receiving final profession is more marked. The result has been a sharp rise in the average age of missionaries over the past decade, producing a steady decline in the numbers of active personnel as older members reach retirement and are not replaced. This pattern seems set to continue.[52]

What are the implications of this changing profile for the structure of Irish missionary societies? It is said that any organisation whose age structure exceeds an average of 56 and whose intake falls below 1.5 per cent of its membership cannot hope to remain viable. Already several Irish missionary congregations or Irish branches of international institutes, especially those of women religious, have membership profiles which fall within these parameters. Yet in recent years many missionary bodies (both Irish and continental) have begun recruitment in the territories where they work. In the long term the success of such initiatives is likely to ensure the survival of most institutes, while greatly altering their complexion.

In the second place, in contrast to the growing crisis affecting religious and clerical vocations, the numbers of Irish laity who may be described as missionary[53] has remained relatively constant.[54] Yet there have been important adjustments in the relationship between lay and clerical/religious missionaries. Up to the mid-1960s laity were recruited by missionary agencies to assist in the work of evangelisation. In the past two decades, however, reflecting a desire for greater autonomy, a number of independent lay missionary bodies have been established. And while lay volunteers continue to be recruited by religious agencies, the bulk of those coming forward tend to offer their services to the independent lay organisations or to the non-denominational development agencies.

II

The question of dwindling numbers in clerical and religious missionary bodies has been the subject of much discussion in recent years.[55] The problem is not peculiar to Ireland (nor to missionary institutes) and in fact is more acute in other Western European countries, especially in France, Holland, Germany, England, and also in North America. An abundance of information on statistical trends is now available. However, attempts to analyse the cause of the decline or to face up to its implications, with some notable exceptions (Newman, Ó Murchú, Weafer/Breslin), have been generally disappointing and reflect perhaps an element of denial. A recent Pro Mundi Vita dossier on the subject, quoting a survey of young people in the U.S.A. and Canada, highlighted the Church's failure to encourage vocations as a key factor.[56] An article emanating from the Irish Church's national vocations agency, Response, reflecting on downward vocation trends in Ireland, takes a similar line. It traces the cause to a loss of confidence and self-esteem among those entrusted with the task of recruitment.[57]

But such analyses are based on the assumption that a plenitude of vocations still exists. There is growing evidence to suggest that this is no longer the case and that a more robust approach to the garnering of vocations may at best slow down the pace of decline. More deep-seated reasons for the current difficulties present themselves and cannot lightly be ignored. As early as 1966 Newman in his perceptive study 'Vocations in Ireland, 1966'[58] related the 'incipient decline' in vocations to the affluence and urbanisation produced by Ireland's recent programme of industrialisation. This, he suggested, had promoted a materialistic climate unfavourable to the cultivation of vocations. Weafer's survey on 'Change and Continuity in Irish Religion, 1974-84' drew attention to the 'gradual but persistent movement towards a secular society' (as demonstrated in the 1981 census).[59] There can be little doubt that the root causes of the decrease in vocations are to be found in the impact of changing social, economic and cultural patterns. One crucial factor in the erosion of Ireland's former near-theocratic consensus and the emergence of an increasingly secular society has been the communications revolution which has exposed the population to external cultural influences and value systems in a fashion never before experienced. Industrialisation and urbanisation have disrupted settled rural communities, substituting in their place a social and economic order in which religious values are constantly challenged. While attachment to Christian principles still remains remarkably strong, the underlying trend is towards a pluralist society based upon the model of developed capitalist nations in Europe and North America.

The implications of these developments for the Church's role in Irish society and for the state of religion are now becoming increasingly evident and bear forcefully on the question of recruitment. No longer does the Church's position as arbiter of both public and private morality remain unchallenged. By the same token, the Church's dominance of the secondary school sector and health-care services is much less evident. Religious practice has declined among the lower age groups, especially in urban areas, while reverence for priesthood and for religious life has diminished. In these circumstances, therefore, it is hardly surprising that fewer young people are prepared to embrace a religious vocation, or that parents are more cautious in offering encouragment. There are other factors at work which also must be taken into account in any explanation of the dearth of missionary vocations. The range of career options open to young people has increased and continues to do so despite the current lack of job opportunities at home. Moreover, the missionary movement, now in its eighth decade, lacks the freshness which made it so attractive during the early years of its existence. The growth of indigenous clergy and religious in many mission theatres has raised questions about the continuing need for European personnel; while Vatican II's rejection of the narrow neo-scholastic interpretation of *extra ecclesia nulla salus* has cast doubts on the necessity and urgency of missionary work conducted along traditional lines. For all these reasons, highly motivated Catholics tend to be more attracted by the prospect of contributing to the alleviation of famine and the remedying of injustice than to the baptising of non-Christians and the extension of the Church. Finally, the spirit of the age lends itself more to temporary commitment than to the lifelong dedication which religious vocation demands.

III

While the phenomenon of declining numbers tends to be ignored or, at best, is treated with a certain fatalism, the future for Irish clerical and religious missionaries in their traditional mission-fields remains a subject of lively debate in missionary circles. In many locations, especially Africa, but also in Asia and Central and South America, the local churches are becoming increasingly self-sufficient. Most bishops are now drawn from the ranks of the indigenous clergy, while almost everywhere numbers of clerical and religious vocations continue to increase. Missionaries who have witnessed these developments sometimes question whether they are still needed. It is probable also that such questioning has been influenced by the fact that conditions for missionary work in many developing countries have become more difficult. For example, missionaries are no longer responsible for the direction of the Church but are cast in the role of auxiliaries, or at most collaborators. Not only have they now to come to terms with this change of status, but they have to learn how to collaborate effectively with indigenous bishops and clergy. Moreover, in an atmosphere where developing countries are more openly assertive of their independence, the climate is less favourable to the presence of expatriates.

Yet it is doubtful whether the new churches have reached a stage of development where missionaries are no longer needed. Certainly this would appear to be the view of the leaders of these churches, now overwhelmingly indigenous, who in most instances remain anxious to retain the services of European missionaries. A salutary reminder of the danger of premature withdrawal is provided by the experience of the early modern missionary movement. When European missionaries abandoned their missions at the end of the eighteenth century, in the wake of the French Revolution, much of the patient work of generations was undone because the local churches were insufficiently formed. Although it is unlikely today that a withdrawal of missionaries would precipitate a crisis of the same magnitude (on account of the resources of local personnel), its effect would be nonetheless damaging. It is true that when missionaries were expelled in large numbers from Eastern Nigeria during the Nigerian Civil War the Church quickly went from strength to strength. But the case of Eastern Nigeria was exceptional, the mission being at that time among the most advanced in Africa, with significant numbers of local priests, religious and seminarians drawn from a virtually homogeneous tribal grouping which was strongly Christian. In the generality of cases, however, local churches established by missionaries over the past century continue to rely on outside assistance for particular requirements. Missionaries are frequently called upon to co-operate in the education and formation of priests and religious because of an insufficiency of suitably qualified local personnel. In regions where the resources of local clergy are fully concentrated in supplying the pastoral care of Christians, missionaries provide a means of reaching out to those yet untouched by the Gospel. In this regard they play an important role in proclaiming the Gospel among the large populations of rural inhabitants, migrants and refugees who have gravitated to cities during the last quarter-century and who often live on the fringes of society. Increasingly, too, missionaries are engaged in transmitting their experience of Mission to the young churches, training those who were in the past the object of missionary evangelisation to be themselves missionary. Again, in virtue of their expertise in such matters, expatriate missionaries are helpful to local churches in the training of lay leaders, the animation of laity and the preparation of catechists. Finally, missionaries are well equipped to undertake specialist tasks such as the conduct of dialogue with Islam, other Christian religions and the non-religious.

In conclusion, as has been mentioned at the outset of this chapter, Christianity is currently experiencing a shift in its centre of gravity from the northern to the southern hemisphere. This transformation is the latest and perhaps the most far-reaching of a series which has taken place down through history. The first was the transplanting of Christianity from Palestine to the Greek world; the second was its extension westerwards which in time produced the great medieval Church of Western Europe. Just as Irish missionaries laid the groundwork for the great medieval religious revival after the Dark Ages, so now in the modern era, along with their continental counterparts, they have been responsible for the implantation of the Gospel in the southern hemisphere; and it is likely that a resurgence of Christianity in the developed world is destined to be accomplished through missionary activity conducted by the young churches of the South. Herein lies the importance of the contemporary Irish missionary contribution and its continuing relevance for the future.

Appendices

APPENDIX A
Religious Institutes with Missionary Commitments in the Nineteenth Century

The following tables show the growth of religious institutes for priests, brothers and nuns during the nineteenth century. Those marked with an asterisk were founded solely for missionary activity. The tables also indicate, where possible, the date at which other institutes assumed missionary commitments.

Table 1: New Religious Institutes for Men, 1805–95

Date	Name	Founder	Missions	Numbers
1805	Prêtres du S. Coeur (Picpuciens)	P. Coudrin	1825: S. America, Oceania	800 (1947)
1816	Oblats de Marie Immaculée	E. de Mazenod	1836: Oceania	1,200 (1922)
1817	Petits Frères de Marie	M. Champagnat	Africa, America Australia	11,000 (1946)
1817	Frères de l'Instruction Chrétienne	J.-M. de Lammenais	Africa, America	2,000 (1900)
1817	Marianists	C. Cheminade	Asia, Africa, Oceania	1,900 (1930)
1821	Frères du S. Coeur	P. Coindre	N. America	900 (1946)
1822	Soc. de Marie de Lyon (Marists)	P. Colin	1836: Oceania	1,200 (1922)
1835	Clercs de St Viateur	L. Querbes	N. America	1,500 (1946)
1841	Prêtres du S. Coeur	M. Garicoits	Palestine, Asia	200 (1946)
1841	*Cong. du S. Coeur de Marie	F. M. Libermann	Africa	n.a.
1848	*Cong. du St-Esprit et du Coeur Immaculé de Marie (C.S.Sp.) *formed through fusion of the institutes founded in 1703 and 1841*	F. M. Libermann	Africa	2,500 (1946)
1850	*Pontificio Instituto Missioni Estere (P.I.M.E., Milan)	Mgr Ramazzotti	Asia, Oceania	850 (1980)
1851	Assomptionnistes	P. d'Alzon	1863: mission literature	900 (1946)

Date	Name	Founder	Missions	Numbers
1854	*Missionnaires du S. Coeur d'Issoudun (M.S.C.)	P. Chevalier	S. America	900 (1946)
1856	*Missions Africaines de Lyon (S.M.A.)	M. de Marion Bresillac	Africa	1,600 (1946)
1856	Cong. des Prêtres du S. Sacrement	P. Eymard	N. & S. America	500 (1946)
1862	*Les Missionnaires du Coeur Immaculé de Marie (Scheut)	T. Verbist	Asia	n.a.
1866	*St Josephs Missionary Soc. (Mill Hill)	H. Vaughan	Africa, Asia, U.S.A.	250 (1920)
1866	*Cong. de Fils du S. Coeur de l'Afrique (Verona Fathers)	Mgr Comboni	Africa	n.a.
1868	*Pères Blancs	Card. Lavigerie	Africa	n.a.
1873	Oblats de St François	A. Brisson	Africa, Australia	600 (1946)
1875	*Soc. of Divine Word	A. Janssen	Asia, Africa, Oceania	n.a.
1877	Prêtres du S. Coeur	P. Dehon	Africa, Madagascar	600 (1946)
1879	Pères de Sallette	P. de Bruillard	Madagascar	n.a.
1880	*Cong. of Marianhill	F. Pfanner	S. Africa, Australia	n.a.
1895	*Institut de St François-Xavier pour les Missions	Mgr Conforti	Asia	n.a.

Table 2: New Institutes of Women Religious, 1800–89

Date	Name	Founder	Missions	Numbers
1800	Dames du S. Coeur	M. Sophie Barat	Africa, Australia	200 (1946)
1806	*Soeurs de St Joseph de Cluny	M. Javouhey	French colonies	4,000 (1946)
1816	Soeurs de la St Famille de Villefranche	E. de Rodat	Education	1,500 (1946)
1816	Soeurs de St Joseph de Lyon	Card. Fesch	Education	2,000 (1946)
1829	Soeurs du Bon-Pasteur	M. Pelletier	Filles repenties	10,000 (1946)
1833	Soeurs de St Joseph de l'Apparition	E. de Viator	Africa, Australia	641 (1930)
1841	Petites Soeurs des Pauvres	J. Jugan	Care of destitute	n.a.
1850	*Soeurs de l'Immaculée Conception de Castres	M. Villeneuve	Africa	74 (1930)

Date	Name	Founder	Missions	Numbers
1854	Franciscaines de Calais	C. Duchenne	Care of sick/poor, education (Africa, S. America)	900 (1946)
1856	Soeurs Auxiliatrices du Purgatoire	Mlle de Monthiver	Care of sick/poor	n.a.
1861	*Religieuses de N. Dame de Lyon	P. Jardin E. Barbier	Africa	600 (1946)
1869	*Soeurs de N. Dame de l'Afrique	Card. Lavigerie	Africa	700 (1946)
1871	*Franciscaines de Ste Marie	P. Chrysostome	India	n.a.
1876	*Soeurs de N. Dame des Apôtres	A. Planque	Africa	n.a.
1877	*Franciscaines Missionnaires Connaisses de Marie	H. de Chappotin	China	10,000 (1963)
1882	Filles de N. Dame du Sacré Coeur	P. Chevalier	New Guinea	n.a.
1889	*Missionary Sisters, Servants of the Holy Spirit	A. Janssen	Asia, Africa, Oceania	4,500 (1964)

There were at least ten other communities founded during this period.

APPENDIX B

Canon 489: *Maternity Training for Missionary Sisters* (Instruction, S. Cong. Prop. Fid., 11 Feb. 1936), *Acta Apostolicae Sedis*, xxviii, 208.

An Instruction by the S. Congregation of Propaganda is as follows: It has been the constant and sedulous practice of this S. Congregation to adapt the character of the apostolate to the varying necessities of times and places. At the present time many Ordinaries of Missions have of their own accord represented to the Holy See the necessity of providing more suitable assistance for the welfare of mothers and infants. In certain districts of Africa some tribes are daily decreasing and will be brought to extinction unless they are helped by more efficacious care of the lives of mothers and infants. In other places children but a few days old are dying in large numbers. . . . The civil authorities and the non-Catholic sects in these parts are turning their minds and attention earnestly to this matter. Some governments refuse to admit Sisters to hospital service unless they are fully qualified nurses. Societies for the care of mothers and children have already been formed in some places through private initiative, and it is necessary, as soon as possible, to co-ordinate these and give them a definite discipline.

Accordingly, this S. Congregation . . . considers it opportune to issue the following regulations and instructions.

It is earnestly desired that new Congregations of Sisters be founded to devote themselves, with the necessary precautions, to the care of mothers and infants who are in danger. It will also be pleasing . . . if, in the religious institutes already existing, there be groups of Sisters who will apply themselves to the aforesaid work.

This provision, however, is subject to the following conditions:

(a) It is not necessary that all religious women should take up every kind of nursing. They may have subject to them native laywomen who are duly accredited nurses, and who are joined by the institute in a common life and spirit.

(b) No Sister can be obliged by her Superiors to take up the work of midwife, but it shall be for those Sisters only who freely choose to accept from their Superior this special work of missionary charity.

(c) These new duties require not only an adequate knowledge of medicine, but also special spiritual training. It is necessary, therefore, that Sisters should obtain public diplomas either in medicine or nursing; but especially they must be strengthened and safeguarded by special helps, which spiritual helps are to be determined by the Superiors. They must realise that the care of the sick involves a holy exercise of charity, and is meritorious; for, whilst they are relieving bodily pain, they are also preparing the soul for the grace of Redemption. It is well to recall the saying of St Francis de Sales, that charity is the watchful guardian of chastity.

(d) In order to obtain their diplomas, it is, of course, necessary that the Sisters attend Catholic nursing schools and universities, or, if these be wanting, then hospitals under Catholic management. If, however, they cannot attend Catholic nursing schools and universities, the Sisters may, with the permission of the S. Congregation, attend lay nursing schools. The candidates should frequent these hospitals in twos at least, and, as far as may be necessary, in modest lay dress; they must live in religious houses where they may have daily spiritual helps and safeguards.

(e) In the new institutes, however, which will apply themselves *ex professo* to this care of mothers and infants, the candidates should complete these university studies before they take their perpetual vows. In institutes already existing this regulation is to be borne in mind and, as far as the constitutions allow, is to be observed.

With regard to the practice of medicine or surgery by missionaries, this is regulated by the prescriptions of canon 139 of the Code of Canon Law and the indults which this S. Congregation is accustomed to grant.

Given at Rome from the S. Congregation of Propaganda, 11 Feb. 1936.

APPENDIX C

Redemptoris Missio – An Analysis

Redemptoris Missio, published in December 1990, was the first encyclical letter on missions to appear since the Vatican Council and honours explicitly the 25th anniversary of the Conciliar document, *Ad Gentes.* Its tone is decidedly optimistic. Reference is made to the dramatic 'collapse of oppressive ideologies and political systems', and to the growing consensus both in the non-Christian and traditionally Christian world on values and ideals which are profoundly Christian.[3] Its concluding lines declare that 'God is preparing a great springtime for Christianity', [86] and throughout there is the message that this is a time of new opportunity for missionary endeavour. In the final analysis this is a document which aims at preparing the Church in general, and its specialist missionary resources in particular, for the challenges of the twenty-first century.

While the thrust of the encyclical is optimistic and positive, it is, nonetheless, a document rooted firmly in the realities of present-day missionary endeavour. There is a frank acknowledgment of a weakening in the thrust of the Church's apostolate to non-Christians, [2] and an admission that the very rationale of this mission has been challenged. [4, 32, 36] There is a consciousness too of a certain confusion concerning the methodology of missions (or what is called 'the paths of mission'). *Redemptoris Missio* sets out to proclaim the continuing relevance and indeed the great urgency of mission 'ad gentes' (to non-Christians), invoking Church teaching, contemporary theology and historical necessity to make its case. It also clarifies at considerable length the 'paths of mission'. There is much more in this document, including chapters on missionary spirituality, on the role of the Holy Spirit, on the leaders and workers in the missionary apostolate (exclusively missionary societies are especially affirmed), and on the support organisations.

Much of *Redemptoris Missio* is in direct continuity with *Ad Gentes* and *Evangelii nuntiandi* (1976), expanding on the insights of these documents. However there are a number of notable new elements and new emphases. For example, Asia is given pride of place as a theatre for missions. Just as *Fidei Donum*, published by Piux XII in 1957, marked out Africa for special attention, *Redemptoris Missio* heralds the intensification of missions to the most populous of continents, 'towards which the Church's mission "ad gentes" ought to be chiefly directed . . .' [37] Again, there is an important adjustment in the categorisation of the Church's pastoral task (or Mission). Heretofore the Church's Mission was expressed as a twofold movement: the missionary evangelisation of people to whom the Gospel had never been preached (mission 'ad extra'); and the pastoral evangelisation of developed Christian communities (mission 'ad intra'). *Evangelii nuntiandi* also included in the first category those who had lost their faith, or whose faith was severely endangered. *Redemptoris Missio* offers a modified presentation. The Church's Mission, it is stated, expresses itself not only in the evangelisation of non-Christians and the pastoral care of Christians, but now also in a third category: in the 'new evangelisation' or 're-evangelisation' of the baptised who live in societies and cultures influenced by Gospel values, but 'have lost a living sense of the faith, or no longer consider themselves members of the Church, and live a life far-removed from Christ and his Gospel'. [33]

The encyclical also elaborates at length on a number of issues addressed in earlier documents on Mission, but which it suggests have not always been properly represented or given their appropriate importance. For example, the centrality of Christ to Kingdom, Church and Mission, is especially emphasised. [4–20] Christ is the kingdom to which all humanity is called and of which the Church is the sign and instrument. [9, 18] Mission, which is the gathering of humanity into the kingdom, begins and ends with the person of Christ and is accomplished through his Church. Consequently, 'founding new Churches' (plantatio ecclesia) is strongly affirmed, [18, 20, 48, 49], as is Baptism into the institutional Church, where alone Christ can be encountered in his fullness. [46, 47] The continuing relevance of territorial criteria when speaking about mission 'ad gentes' is also stressed, [37] and in this context, as has been mentioned, the continent of Asia is given priority. In terms of the methodology of missions to non-Christians, primary proclamation (of the person of Christ) is given pride of place over all other 'paths of mission'. [44] Finally, there is an affirmation of the ultimately transcendent nature of the missionary task, as opposed to any interpretation which would reduce the Christian message to a form of human wisdom. [11] Human development, liberation, work for the underprivileged, the poor, refugees, migrants, alleviation of suffering and want, all must ultimately lead beyond the horizontal dimensions of the material human world, to the transcendent. Liberation from human oppression is linked to (and must issue in) liberation from sin. The alleviation of hunger for food is linked to (and must ultimately address) hunger for God. Material development is linked to (and must ultimately address) humanity's spiritual development. [14, 17, 20]

At first sight it might appear that *Redemptoris Missio* represents a certain retrenchment on *Ad Gentes* and *Evangelii nuntiandi*. Indeed the encyclical has already been the subject of some sharp criticism. It has been suggested that its perspective is uncritically Eurocentric, and fails to reflect the great diversity and richness of a truly universal Church; that it regards missionary endeavour as a 'one-way' process; that its tone is overly assertive; that its model of mission is one of the past, a 'regression to pre-conciliar thinking'; that it has an undue emphasis on institutions; that it does not take sufficiently into account what Karl Rahner has called the 'Third Theological Age of Church History'; that it 'fails in scope and vision'; that it contains the false assumption that 'the Church', the 'Gospel', or 'Christianity' are available 'in some culturally disembodied form'. [Patrick Kalilombe, *Catholic International*, 2, 6, 296; John Wijngaards, *The Tablet*, 9 February 1991, 180–181; Aylward Shorter, *Ibid*, 179; see Brian Hearne, cited in *I.M.U. Report*, July-August 1991, 4]

Space does not allow us to examine these criticisms in any detail. What must be said is that all the elements which made *Ad Gentes* and *Evangelii nuntiandi* so exciting and innovative are to be found in the new encyclical. Ecumenism, Dialogue with other Religions, Inculturation, Liberation, Human Development, the formation of 'small' or 'basic' communities, are all re-affirmed as vital 'paths of mission'. The fact that the treatment of some of these 'paths' strikes a note of caution does not detract from their importance as instruments of missionary evangelisation. Again, affirming the continuing legitimacy of territorial criteria when defining the mission 'ad gentes' should not be construed as a return to pre-conciliar thinking. On the contrary *Redemptoris Missio* also writes at length on the sociological and cultural boundaries of missionary endeavour, providing new insights and directives. [37] For example, the encyclical mentions the need to concentrate on 'big cities, where new customs and styles of living arise together with new forms of culture and communications'. Mentioned too are the young. 'How do we bring the message of Christ to non-Christian young people who represent the future of entire continents . . . ?' Migrants and refugees are also singled out as constituting new sociological frontiers of the mission 'ad gentes'. As for the cultural frontiers, the encyclical (borrowing from St Paul) writes about the several forms of the Areopagus of the modern age which the mission 'ad gentes' must address. 'The first Areopagus . . . is the world of communications'. And it is not enough merely 'to use the media simply to spread the Christian message and the Church's authentic teaching', but missionaries must also seek 'to integrate that teaching into the new culture' created by modern communications. Other forms of the modern Areopagus to which the Church's missionary activity ought to be directed are, for example, 'commitment to peace, development and the liberation of peoples, especially those of minorities; the advancement of women and children, safeguarding the created world' – all areas 'which need to be illuminated with the light of the Gospel'. [37]

As for the suggestion that the encyclical is Eurocentric and fails to acknowledge the role of the Younger Churches, the following extracts (selected from several) suggest otherwise, emphasising as they do the universality of the missionary charism and the need for reciprocity in Mission: 'Every Church, even one made up of recent converts, is missionary by its very nature, and is both evangelised and evangelising'. [49] 'All the particular Churches, both young and old, are called to give and to receive in the context of the universal mission, and none should be closed to the needs of others . . .' [85]

A more substantial criticism is that the new categorisation of the Church's pastoral task does not correspond to the historical situation it seeks to address. It is true that the encyclical is careful to note that the boundaries between the mission 'ad gentes', pastoral evangelisation and the new evangelisation (or re-evangelisation) cannot easily be drawn. [34] But even with this important qualification the encyclical does maintain the existence of three distinct 'situations' for which three distinct categories of response are required. Herein lies the problem. One American commentator, writing of the U.S.A. as a country with Christian roots, raises the question: 'whether we have become in many sectors a people who need a proclamation which is closer to an initial proclamation as would be the approach in the mission "ad gentes" rather than a new evangelisation'? (Mary Motte, *Catholic International*, 2, 6, 295). The same could be said in relation to many of the major

Western democracies where, it may be argued, initial proclamation rather than re-evangelisation is the more appropriate. Another writer makes much the same point, commenting: 'The repeated attempts to distinguish between the "initial" proclamation of the Gospel among non-Christian peoples and the re-evangelisation of Europe are a sign that the extent of secularisation in the West is not fully appreciated' (Nazir Ali, ibid, 298) In short, the question must be raised whether *Redemptoris Missio's* reading of history is accurate, and this will certainly be a point of discussion for the future.

There is a suggestion too that the encyclical's introduction of an additional category of evangelisation is essentially an attempt to shore up the leaking barque of the mission 'ad gentes' (understood in the traditional sense of missions conducted by missionaries primarily from the Northern hemisphere to non-Christians largely in the Southern hemisphere). [Kalilombe, op.cit. 296] Is the idea of 'new evangelisation', or 're-evangelisation', a device to sharpen the focus of mission 'ad gentes', a focus which has been somewhat clouded in the two most recent documents on mission, *Ad Gentes* and *Evangelii nuntiandi*? Undoubtedly the assertion in these documents that the frontiers of mission to non-Christians could now be found in the heartland of the traditional mission-sending countries [EN. 52], was calculated to diminish the association of missions with geographical displacement, with the abandonment of home and country for a foreign land for the sake of the Gospel. Nonetheless it would be wrong to represent the inclusion of the new category as contrived. In fact the encyclical goes to considerable lengths to make its case for a 'third situation', a third category, which requires a distinct response from the Church. Whatever one's view on the validity of this case, what is most obviously lacking is an adequate description of the response. What precisely does 'new evangelisation', or re-evangelisation' mean? How is it different from 'initial evangelisation'?

It is true that the tone of this encyclical is assertive, overly assertive at times. Perhaps there is also an undue emphasis on institutions, and a tendency to affirm strongly some processes and concepts associated with pre-conciliar missionary endeavour. Its introduction of a new category of evangelisation ('re-evangelisation') may seem unnecessary. Yet it would be wrong to regard this encyclical as a reversal of conciliar and post-conciliar trends. One of its main objectives is to encourage and to exhort those currently engaged in missions and the Church at large. The 'meditative' tone which characterised documents like *Evangelii nuntiandi* would not serve this purpose. At the same time all the essential elements of recent documents on Mission are to be found and there are several important new theological and pastoral insights. One suspects that in the long term this encyclical will be best remembered as the document which made Asia the primary focus of missionary activity.

Notes and References

The following abbreviations are used in the references.

A.A.	*Apostolicum actuositatem* (Decree on the Apostolate of Lay People, 1965)
A.G.	*Ad gentes* (Decree on Missions, 1965)
A.I.P.	Archives of the Irish Province of the Congregation of the Holy Ghost
A.M.	*The African Missionary*
A.M.S.C.	Archives of the Missionary Sisters of St Columban
Corish, *Ir. Catholicism*	P. J. Corish (ed.), *A History of Irish Catholicism* (Dublin 1967-72)
E.N.	*Evangelii nuntiandi* (apostolic exhortation, 1976)
F.E.	*The Far East*
G.S.	*Gaudium et spes* (Constitution on the Church in the Modern World, 1965)
I.E.R.	*Irish Ecclesiastical Record*
L.G.	*Lumen gentium* (Constitution on the Church, 1964)
M.A.	*Missionary Annals*
M.R.	*Missionary Record of the Holy Ghost*

Introduction (pp. 1–10)

1. In particular the contribution of women has been neglected, and this is reflected in the uneven scope of the current study.

2. Melchior de Marion Bresillac to the S. Congregation of Propaganda Fide, 4 Jan. 1856 (cited in Jean Bonfils (ed.), *Marion Bresillac: Mission Documents* (Paris 1986), 138). The writings and utterances of those engaged in the movement were full of similar expressions.

3. Until recently the term 'pagan missions' has been used widely to describe missions to the unevangelised. Currently the terms 'non-Christian missions' or 'primary evangelisation' are preferred.

4. The Holy See organises its mission territories into prefectures, ruled by prefects apostolic, and, when progress has been accomplished, into vicariates, ruled by vicars apostolic who bear the rank of titular bishop. The final stage of development is the constitution of the episcopacy, with bishops named after the dioceses over which they rule. The term 'jurisdiction', as used in this book, refers to the various divisions of ecclesiastical administration, e.g. prefectures, vicariates and dioceses.

5. In this study the term 'institute' denotes any of three types of religious organisation, namely 'orders', 'congregations' or 'societies'.

6. In church law the process of formal attachment to a jurisdiction is called 'incardination'. 'Excardination' denotes the process of release.

7. Bede McGregor, 'Commentary on *Evangelii nuntiandi*', *Doctrine and Life*, Special Issue (Mar.–Apr. 1977), 53.

8. The concept of the 'Kingdom of God' is foreshadowed in the Old Testament and was explicitly formulated in the New Testament. It signifies the establishment of 'God's reign' on earth, both in the present (principally through the Church) and at the end of time. Essentially it is a metaphor for the existential and the eschatological dimensions of salvation.

9. See n. 6 above.

10. See pp. 179–87 below.

11. The motivation of the early medieval movement was quite different from that of its modern counterpart. It was rooted in a particular form of monastic spirituality which valued exile as a form of asceticism; see ch. 12, n. 19.

12. *Irish Missionary Union Brochure* (Dublin 1972), 134.

13. E. M. Hogan, 'The Modern Irish Missionary Movement', *Ireland Today*, no. 1026 (Mar. 1986), 7.

14. See p. 138 below.

15. E. M. Hogan, 'African Conversion to Roman Catholicism', *African Ecclesial Review*, xxiv, 2 (Apr. 1982), 71-80.

16. Ireland's concern is exceptional in two respects. The contribution to voluntary aid agencies is the highest *per capita* within the European Community. Also Ireland's contribution in terms of personnel deployed in Third World countries is relatively higher than that of its E.E.C. partners. Against this, Ireland's 'official development assistance' (state assistance) is currently at a rate of 0.16 per cent of G.N.P. (the percentage recommended by the United Nations is 0.7) and is the lowest in the E.E.C. (Information provided by Seán J. Healy, Justice and Peace Desk, Conference of Major Religious Superiors, Dublin) (See also pp. 136–40 below)

17. Patrick Kelly, 'A Man of Ideas', *Far East,* Oct. 1972, 9; 'The Modern Irish Missionary Movement', *Herder Correspondence*, iv (1967), 204ff; Thomas Ronayne, 'A Tour through the Vicariate of Southern Nigeria', *I.E.R.*, 5th ser., xviii (1921), 4; C. M. Cooke, 'Irish Diocesan Priests in Southern Nigeria, 1920-42' (M.A. thesis, University College, Cork, 1971), 50; Xavier Carty, *Irish Missionaries* (Dublin 1970), 4ff, 51; J. A. Kielt, 'The Maynooth Mission to China', *I.E.R.*, 5th ser., cvi (1966), 193-204; cf. Joseph McGlade, 'The Missions: Africa and the Orient' in Corish, *Ir. Catholicism*, v (1967), 2-3; Cyril Hally, 'A Hundred Years of Irish Missionary Effort', *The Furrow*, xxii (1971), 335. It must be remarked that most of the foregoing make brief references to the work of the 'foreign' institutes before 1916, but attach minimal significance; they are usually described as 'having kept the flame alive'. Hally goes against the general trend in dating the movement to the arrival of Fr Joseph Shanahan in Nigeria in 1902.

18. See E. M. Hogan, 'The Motivation of the Modern Irish Missionary Movement, 1912-39', *Journal of Religion in Africa*, x, 3 (1979), 165; cf. E. M. Hogan, 'The Society of African Missions in Ireland, 1877-1916' (M.A. thesis, University College, Cork, 1973), 58, 64, 66, 84-5, 96.

Chapter 1: The Irish Church after Catholic Emancipation (pp. 13-19)

1. See Louis Paul-Dubois, *Contemporary Ireland* (Dublin 1908), 477.
2. The scale of the growth in Church cadres is indicated in the following table compiled from issues of the *Irish Catholic Directory*. Since the series displays minor differences in classification, it has been impossible to produce fully accurate figures, but the general trend emerges clearly.

Year	Churches	Parishes	Parish priests	Curates	Regulars	Religious houses nuns	priests	brothers	Total clergy
1839	n.a.	1,010	976	1,195	n.a.	n.a.	n.a.	n.a.	n.a.
1849	2,205	1,036	983	1,366	301	140	n.a.	n.a.	2,552
1859	2,284	1,053	986	1,407	465	220	n.a.	n.a.	2,925
1869	2,341	1,072	989	1,690	371	208	77	84	2,997
1879	2,378	1,086	998	1,747	439	260	78	97	3,171
1889	2,382	1,087	1,013	1,895	542	303	86	103	3,374
1899	2,434	1,090	1,010	1,869	557	341	84	122	3,438
1909	2,465	1,112	1,039	1,976	600	407	91	140	3,610

   Cf. Donal Kerr, 'The Early Nineteenth Century' in Michael Maher (ed.), *Irish Spirituality* (Dublin 1985), 135; P. J. Corish, *The Irish Catholic Experience* (Dublin 1985), 159ff, 199.

3. E. R. Norman, *The Catholic Church and Ireland in the Age of Rebellion, 1859-73* (London 1965), 15; cf. P. J. Gannon, 'A Study of Religious Statistics in Ireland', *I.E.R.*, 5th ser., xvii (1921), 144; Jeremiah Newman, 'The Priests of Ireland', ibid., 5th ser., xcviii (1962), 6.
4. P. J. Corish, 'Catholic Ireland', *I.E.R.*, 5th ser., cii (1964), 201; Norman, op. cit., 15; Paul-Dubois, op. cit., 413.
5. Eugene O'Riordan, 'The Religious Question in the Early Irish National Schools' (Ph.D. thesis, Boston College, 1970), 286.
6. The Irish Universities Act of 1908 marked the decline of the controversy (see Norman Atkinson, *Irish Education* (Dublin 1969), 128-31); in relation to secondary education see J. King, *Religious Education in Ireland* (Dublin 1970), 8.
7. George O'Brien, 'New Light on Emigration', *Studies*, xxx (1941), 23; E. J. Coyne, 'Irish Population Problems', *Studies*, xliii (1954), 153; see also Kevin Condon, *The Missionary College of All Hallows, 1842-91* (Dublin 1986), 81.
8. *All Hallows Annual, 1953-54*, 22.
9. Ibid.
10. See Condon, op. cit., 223-5.
11. Laws against religious freedom also applied in the British colonies, although the process of relaxation occurred somewhat earlier than in the British Isles (see M. Boucher, 'Ex Glande Quercus: Bishop Griffith at the Cape', *Historia*, ii, 4 (Dec. 1966), 245, 247-8; 'Bishop John England to the Central Council of the A.P.F.', *Annals*, x (1838), 16).

12. Condon, op. cit. 26.
13. John Monaghan, *Records relating to the Diocese of Ardagh and Clonmacnois* (Dublin 1886), 328-33.
14. These details were supplied to the author by the archivists of the various congregations of sisters.
15. These details were supplied to the author by the archivists of the various institutes of brothers.

Chapter 2: The Role of All Hallows College (pp. 20-24)

1. T. J. O'Donnell, 'Centenary of All Hallows College', *Studies*, xxxi (1942), 430; *All Hallows Annual, 1953-54*, 9; 'Bulletin of the Irish Province', Apr. 1958, 9 (Archives of the Irish Province of the Congregation of the Holy Ghost (henceforth A.I.P.)); 'Towards an Irish Foundation' (unsigned memoir) (ibid., Box 2, f. 2).
2. See Kevin Condon, *The Missionary College of All Hallows, 1842-91* (Dublin 1986), 290-320.
3. Ibid., 20.
4. 'Prospectus for a College' (All Hallows College, Dublin, Archive, 38/2, K^2).
5. Ibid.
6. Ibid.
7. Condon, op. cit., 21.
8. Ibid., 44.
9. Ibid., 46.
10. Ibid., 22, 34.
11. Entries in the Minute Book of the Association for the Propagation of the Faith (A.P.F.), Dublin, show that the matter of founding a missionary college was considered a matter of some urgency. At a special meeting of the management committee held on 14 February 1842, chaired by Dr Yore, it was resolved that 'the establishment of a College for the education of Priests for the Foreign Missions would be of the first advantage to Religion and well calculated to assist this Society in its efforts to propagate the Faith in Foreign Countries'. It was further resolved that this resolution should be transmitted to Archbishop Murray, President of the A.P.F., and that he 'be respectfully requested to aid us in these our views by procuring the sanction of His Holiness for the establishment of this College and at the same time be prayed to communicate as our President these proceedings to the Central Committees'. At a special meeting on 24 February 1842 'a communication was read from Rev. Mr Hand at present in Rome to His Grace Dr Murray . . . announcing the approbation of the Holy See to the establishment of a College in this country for the foreign missions'. (See Minute Book, Library of the Pontifical Aid Societies, Lower Rathmines Road, Dublin) Archbishop Murray believed that the rescript granted by Propaganda on 28 February authorised him and the Dublin clergy to establish the college and that the project would receive subventions from the

A.P.F.'s Central Committee at Paris. In fact it was Hand who was authorised by the rescript to found the college; and there was no guarantee of A.P.F. support. (See Condon, op. cit., 47-8) The misunderstanding and confusion was eventually cleared up after Hand's return in June, but it had generated a certain amount of ill-feeling which made Hand's task all the more difficult.

12. Condon, op. cit., 32.
13. Ibid., 33.
14. Ibid., 32.
15. Ibid., 89.

Chapter 3: The Irish Church and Non-Christian Missions, 1830-1880 (pp. 25-51)

1. Francis Finnegan, 'Irish Missionaries in Bengal', *I.E.R.*, 5th ser., xcix (1963), 159.
2. They were Dr William Kennedy, aged thirty-three, Fr Rabascall, a young French secular priest, and Fr O'Shea, who was drowned in a boating accident. For an account of the 'Calcutta Christian Brothers' see *The Christian Brothers Educational Record* (Dublin 1892), 68-83. The remnant of the foundation was received into the Irish Christian Brothers established in India from 1890.
3. Thomas Gavan Duffy, 'An Irish Missionary Episode', *I.E.R.*, 5th ser., xvii (1921), 465.
4. Joseph McGlade, 'The Missions: Africa and the Orient' in Corish, *Ir. Catholicism*, v (1967), 79.
5. Gavan Duffy, op. cit., 469
6. Ibid., 475.
7. Fr Joseph Colgan of St Joseph's Missionary Society succeeded Bishop Stephen Fennelly as Vicar Apostolic of Madras in 1882.
8. Finnegan, op. cit., 162ff; Gavan Duffy, op. cit., 465.
9. Gavan Duffy, op. cit., 475.
10. Twelve missionaries went from the college to Bengal between 1844 and 1858.
11. 'Bantu' is the term used by contemporary scholars to differentiate peoples of wholly African origin from those of mixed race. The work 'Bantu' refers to a group of languages which with slight variations is spoken by tribal Africans. The term 'kaffir', used from the eighteenth century, has been discarded chiefly because of its pejorative overtones.
12. G. S. Were, *A History of South Africa* (London 1974), 51.
13. For statistics on population see Monica Wilson and Leonard Thompson (ed.), *The Oxford History of South Africa*, ii (Oxford 1984), 1-5; cf. pp. 426-31.
14. 'The antecedents of the coloureds (or people of mixed race) were Africans, Indians, East Indian slaves, Cape Hottentots (Khoikhoi), Bushmen (San) and Europeans of many nationalities' (Alex Hepple, *South Africa: A Political and Economic History* (London 1966), 11).
15. G. S. Were (op. cit., 50) notes that there were some missionaires of the Dutch

Reformed Church who tried to convert non-whites and defend their rights, but adds that they 'formed an insignificant minority'.

16. See Hepple, op. cit., 25-6; cf. Were, op. cit., 49-50; Albert Nolan, 'The Political and Social Context' in Andrew Prior (ed.), *Catholics in Apartheid Society* (London 1982), 3-4; see also Wilson and Thompson, op. cit., i (1973), 267; M. J. Ashley, 'Features of Modernity: Missionaries and Education in South Africa, 1850-1900', *Journal of Theology for Southern Africa*, xxxviii (1982), 52-4.

17. See Janet Hodgson, 'Mission and Empire: A Case Study of the Convergent Ideologies in Nineteenth-Century Southern Africa', *Journal of Theology for Southern Africa*, xxxviii (1982), 35-6; John Selby, *A Short History of South Africa* (London 1974), 123.

18. Robert Lacour-Gayet, *A History of South Africa*, trans. (London 1977), 49; cf. Selby, op. cit., 123; Hepple, op. cit., 25-6.

19. Arthur Keppel-Jones, *South Africa* (London 1977), 59-60; Wilson and Thompson, op. cit., i, 258. During 1857 the Xhosa slaughtered large numbers of their cattle in the belief that the dead would rise and that a great hurricane would drive the white men back into the sea. In the event, tens of thousands of Xhosa perished in the famine which followed, while others moved into areas of settlement.

20. Wilson and Thompson, op. cit., ii, 105.

21. T. R. H. Davenport, *South Africa: A Modern History* (London 1977), 117.

22. Ibid.; cf. Ashley, op. cit., 52.

23. B. F. Doyle, 'South Africa' in Corish, *Ir. Catholicism*, vi (1971), 9-10.

24. For an account of the background to Griffith's appointment and the state of the Catholic Church in the Cape see *The Cape Diary of Bishop Patrick Raymond Griffith for the years 1837-39*, ed. J. B. Brain (South African Bishops' Conference, [Cape Town] 1988), 8ff ; see also W. E. Brown, *The Catholic Church in South Africa* (London 1960), 8.

25. *The Cape Diary of Bishop Griffith*, 124-5, 128-9, 152, 165, 170, 175, 198 and passim; cf. Brown, op. cit., 28.

26. Brown, op. cit., 26ff.

27. M. Boucher, 'Ex Glande Quercus: Bishop Griffith at the Cape', *Historia*, ii, 4 (Dec. 1966), 247-8, 250-1.

28. See *The Cape Diary of Bishop Griffith*, 107, 108n, 130.

29. Josef Metzler, 'Die Missionen in Südafrica und auf den Ostafrikanischen Inseln', *Sacrae Congregationis de Propaganda Fide Memoria Rerum*, iii, 1, ed. Josef Metzler (Rome 1973), 306.

30. The success of the mission would ultimately depend upon the cultivation of an indigenous clergy and strong Catholic laity. But means would also have to be made available to build up an impressive 'visible' structure of chapels and schools.

31. Brown, op. cit., 195; *Annals*, xix (1848), 159; *The Cape Diary of Bishop Griffith*, 146, 162-3.

15

32. *The Cape Diary of Bishop Griffith*, 201-2.

33. *Annals*, xix (1848), 159.

34. Metzler, op. cit., 306-7.

35. *Annals*, xxxix (1867), 468.

36. Ibid., 465-73.

37. Metzler, op. cit., 308ff.

38. Brigid Flanagan, 'Education: Policy and Practice' in Andrew Prior (ed.), *Catholics in Apartheid Society* (London 1982), 84.

39. See H. J. Russell, *Ireland's Nuns in Africa* (Irish News Ltd, Belfast n.d.), 80-1, 16; cf. Sr Patricia Langan, Assumption Sisters, Ballynahinch, to author, 4 June 1988.

40. See Wilson and Thompson, op. cit., ii, 105.

41. See Brown, op. cit., 194.

42. Ibid., 197.

43. Metzler, op. cit., 311ff.

44. Ibid., 317ff.

45. James O'Haire, *Recollections of Twelve Years' Residence as a Missionary Priest in the Western District of the Cape of Good Hope* (Dublin c. 1877), 12.

46. Brown, op. cit., 195.

47. O'Haire, op. cit., 40.

48. Patrick Gantly, 'History of the Society of African Missions, 1856-1900' (MS in preparation for publication), 42. The Jesuits established over thirty mission communities, known as 'reductions' (settlements), in Paraguay and Uruguay in the seventeenth and eighteenth centuries. These were quasi-theocratic communities in which Jesuits and Indians lived and worked together in virtual independence of the colonial power.

49. Ibid.; cf. *Annals*, xlvi (1874), 51.

50. Mother General to author, 17 June 1987.

51. E. M. Hogan, 'The Society of African Missions in Ireland, 1877-1916', (M.A. thesis, University College, Cork, 1973), 52-5.

52. T. J. Walsh, *Nano Nagle and the Presentation Sisters,* repr. (Kildare 1980), 347-8.

53. See Kevin Condon, *The Missionary College of All Hallows, 1842-91* (Dublin 1986), 89.

54. Mary Purcell, *The Story of the Vincentians* (Dublin 1973), 118-19.

55. Ibid., 128-31.

56. Fr Thomas Davitt, C.M., Provincial Archivist, to author, 25 Mar. 1988.

57. A. M. Canning, 'South America' in Corish, *Ir. Catholicism*, vi (1971), 19; cf. pp. 6, 9.

58. Ibid., 3, 10ff.

59. Ibid., 18.

60. The details for much of this section are compiled from answers to a short questionnaire (Q.H.) sent to all institutes of sisters involved in missionary work. See also 'Ireland's Missionaries, Ancient and Modern', *Pagan Missions*, Jan. 1931, 1-20; ibid., Jan. 1932, 17-20.

61. See pp. 27-30, 39, 41-3 above. For a detailed account of the Loreto mission to India see Mother Mary Colmcille, *First the Blade* (Calcutta 1968).

62. Nano Nagle founded the Sisters of the Presentation in 1775; in 1821 Frances Teresa Ball established the Loreto Sisters (an Irish foundation of the Institute of the Blessed Virgin Mary, originally founded by Mary Ward in the seventeenth century); and Catherine McAuley founded the Sisters of Mercy in 1831.

63. Q.H. Reply (henceforth Q.H.R.), 22 Apr. 1973; cf. *The Good Shepherd of Angers* (1970), nos 3 and 4.

64. Q.H.R., 11 Apr. 1973. They worked in Ceylon, South Africa and Basutoland; cf. *Annals*, 1 (1878), 77 (records of departure, 22 Oct. 1876, 23 Apr. 1877).

65. Q.H.R., 16 Apr. 1973.

66. Ibid., 13 Apr. 1973; cf. Joseph McGlade, 'The Missions: Africa and the Orient' in Corish, *Ir. Catholicism*, v (1967), 11 (11 Irish sisters of the congregation worked in India before 1900).

67. Q.H.R., 12 Apr. 1973.

68. The scale of this recruitment was significant. The *New York Herald* of 12 Sept. 1873 noted the arrival of 24 recruits for the order and stated that by the end of the month 26 more were expected.

69. For an excellent treatment of the Irish De La Salle Brothers see John Towey, *Irish De La Salle Brothers in Christian Education* (Dublin 1980).

Chapter 4: The Continental Missionary Impulse (pp. 55-61)

1. Encouraged by Cardinal Nicholas Wiseman, Fr Vaughan established a missionary seminary at Mill Hill in 1866. Five years later the first group of priests was assigned to missions among blacks in the U.S.A. By 1927 St Joseph's Missionary Society had 250 priests overseas serving in Madras, Kashmir, Uganda, Cameroons, Kenya Colony, Sarawak, North Borneo, New Zealand, the Philippines and the Belgian Congo. In the same year the Missionary Sisters of St Joseph, also founded by Bishop Vaughan, had a membership of 215. (See F. J. Bowen, *England and the Foreign Missionary Movement (1838-1928)* (London 1928), 12-14)

2. C. S. Phillips, *The Church in France, 1848-1907* (London 1936), 324; cf. A. Boulenger, *Histoire Generale de l'Église*, viii (Paris 1941), 348.

3. See Boulenger, op. cit., ix (1950), 946; Bernard de Vaulx, *Histoire des Missions Catholiques Françaises* (Paris 1951), 225.

4. A. Olichon, *Les Missions: Histoire de l'Expansion du Catholicisme dans le Monde* (Paris 1936), 327.

5. de Vaulx, op. cit., 227; Olichon, op. cit., 327.

6. Olichon, op. cit., 322ff.

7. See Henri Daniel-Rops, *Église des Revolutions* (Paris 1960), 741. In 1868 another periodical appeared, the weekly *Les Missions Catholiques*, with an Italian edition and monthly résumés in English, German, Spanish, Dutch and Hungarian. This was also to become an important literary source.

8. Ibid., 740.

9. Roger Aubert, *Le Pontificat de Pie IX* (Paris 1952), 117-18 (vol. xxi of *L'Histoire de l'Église depuis les origines jusqu'à nos jours* (Paris 1938), ed. A. Fliche Martin).

10. The point has been made in Hubert Jedin et al. (ed.), *History of the Church*, vii (London 1981), 204-5, that Gregory XVI 'generated no deep or lasting missionary efforts, either with regard to strategy or method' and that the achievements of his pontificate with regard to missions were forced on him by 'contemporary events' or resulted from pressure by missionaries in the field. Nevertheless, while it is true that Gregory was no innovator, this characterisation appears somewhat harsh, taking insufficient account of his responsiveness to the promptings of Propaganda Fide and his missionaries.

11. Henri Daniel-Rops, *Un Combat pour Dieu, 1870-1939* (Paris 1963), 639; Boulenger, op. cit., 946.

12. See Johannes Beckmann in Jedin et al., op. cit., viii (London 1981), 176.

13. See Henri Daniel-Rops, *The Church in an Age of Revolution* (London 1965), 455-6; see also Adolph Tanquery, *The Spiritual Life* (New York 1930), xliiiff The spirituality of the nineteenth century also contained a strong strain of 'mysticism', but the dominant trend was towards asceticism.

Chapter 5: The Impact of the Association for the Propagation of the Faith
(pp. 62-68)

1. In 1836 Ireland contributed 7,818 francs (£310); France 1,041,955 francs (£41,261); England 19,217 francs (£761); Scotland 430 francs (£17); Germany 3,209 francs (£127); Bavaria 17,558 francs (£695); Belgium 74,967 francs (£2,968); Prussia 12,644 francs (£501); Switzerland 25,089 francs (£991) (*Annals*, x (1838)).

   In 1852 Ireland contributed 221,020 francs (£8,755); France 2,706,565 francs (£107,180); Germany 25,532 francs (£1,011); North America 191,502 francs (£7,583); Belgium 321,990 francs (£12,751); England 72,910 francs (£2,887); Scotland 14,426 francs (£571); Prussia 322,553 francs (£12,773); Portugal 28,372 francs (£1,124); Low Countries 127,987 francs (£5,068); Spain 17,701 francs (£701) (ibid., xxv (1853)).

   In 1877 Ireland contributed 103,966 francs (£4,117); England and Scotland 47,634 francs (£1,876); France 4,301,753 francs (£170,349); Alsace-Lorraine 222,500 francs (£8,881); Belgium 384,450 francs (£15,224); Spain 4,546 francs (£180); Italy 290,488 francs (£11,503); Switzerland 53,263 francs (£2,109); Germany 374,363 francs (£14,825) (ibid., 1 (1878)).

   In 1887 Ireland contributed 160,863 francs (£6,370); England and Scotland 58,147 francs (£2,303); France 4,073,250 francs (£161,301); Alsace-Lorraine 286,285 francs (£11,337); Germany 404,377 francs

(£16,133); Hungary 4,745 francs (£188); Belgium 375,839 francs (£14,883); Spain 93,665 francs (£3,709); Italy 342,919 francs (£13,580); Switzerland 83,866 francs (£3,321) (ibid., lx (1888)).

2. See ibid., xii (1840), 290.

3. Minutes of the Standing Committee, 6 Apr. 1847 (Archives of Pontifical Aid Societies, Lower Rathmines Road, Dublin).

4. Ibid.

5. Ibid., 5 May 1842.

6. *Annals*, xxii (1859), 479.

7. For example, in 1852 the following dioceses benefited: Kildare and Leighlin 2,000 francs; Clonfert 10,000 francs; Cloyne 8,750 francs; Galway 5,000 francs; Killaloe 4,000 francs; Kilmacduagh and Kilfenora 7,000 francs; Tuam 4,000 francs; Derry 3,050 francs; Cork 9,000 francs; Killala 5,000 francs; Kerry 8,000 francs; Limerick 5,000 francs; Ross 3,000 francs; Waterford 3,000 francs. By 1878 the only beneficiary was the diocese of Ross (2,000 francs).

8. Minutes of the Standing Committee, 17 Nov. 1851.

9. Kevin Condon, *The Missionary College of All Hallows, 1842-91* (Dublin 1986), 162-5.

10. For details of publication, printing and distribution see Minutes of the Standing Committee, 18 Feb., 8 Apr., 23, 27 May, 29 July 1839, 23 Feb. 1854.

11. The following examples give some indication of the thrust of material in *Annals*.

    Vol. xii (1840): Asia and Far East (9 items (articles, surveys, reports)); Africa (1); North America (4 – dealing with missions to Indians).

    Vol. xxix (1857): Asia and Far East (28); Africa (4); Oceania (12 – dealing mostly with the Sandwich Islands, Tonga, South Sea Islands).

    Vol. xl (1868): Asia and Far East (10); Africa (4); North America (2); Antilles (3).

    Vol. xlvi (1874): Asia and Far East (12); Africa (7); America (3 – none from U.S.A.).

    Vol. lvi (1884): Asia and Far East (15); Africa (6); North America (1); Oceania (3 – on South Sea Islands).

12. Ibid., lvi (1884), 117.

13. Ibid., x (1838), 273ff.

14. Ibid., 266-71.

15. Ibid., xl (1868), 87.

16. Ibid., 89.

17. Ibid., xix (1848), 159.

18. See, e.g., Joseph Zimmermann, 'Memoir—1886', 3 (S.M.A. Provincial Archives, Cork, Pr. Ir. 6) (where Zimmermann attributes the support given to his institute by members of the Cork laity against local clerical opposition (among other factors) to their familiarity with the missionary work of the A.P.F.).

Chapter 6: The Congregation of the Holy Ghost and the Immaculate Heart of Mary, 1858-1920 (pp. 69-78)

1. The substance of this chapter has already appeared as 'The Congregation of the Holy Ghost and the Evolution of the Modern Irish Missionary Movement' in *Catholic Historical Review*, lxx, 1 (1984), 1-14. Permission to reproduce the material has been obtained.

2. See E. M. Hogan, *Catholic Missionaries and Liberia: A Study of Christian Enterprise in West Africa, 1842-1950* (Cork 1981), 42-5, 172-5; Patrick Gantly, 'History of the Society of African Missions, 1856-1900' (MS in preparation for publication), passim. For Propaganda's attitude see p. 171 above.

3. See pp. 49-51 above.

4. Ibid.

5. P. J. Corish, *The Irish Catholic Experience* (Dublin 1985), 159.

6. See ibid., 199.

7. Emmet Larkin, *The Roman Catholic Church and the Creation of the Modern Irish State, 1878-86* (Dublin 1975), 15, 88.

8. For profiles of the Congregation of the Holy Ghost and the Congregation of the Holy Heart of Mary see Henry Koren, *The Spiritans* (Pittsburgh 1958), 16ff.

9. The congregation's reputation for orthodoxy was already evident in 1737 when the Bishop of Verdun entrusted his seminary to the institute in an effort to purify it of Jansenism. During the years of the Revolution not a single priest educated by the Spiritans took the schismatic oath in France. Later the congregation refused to teach the Gallican Articles imposed on French seminaries in 1816.

10. Libermann's conclusions about the colonial clergy were based largely on reports from inexperienced young priests and the speeches of politicians who accused the Church of an unenlightened attitude towards slavery. He was to change his mind about the value of the colonial clergy during this period after he became Superior General of the Congregation of the Holy Ghost in 1848 and had access to the files dealing with its activity.

11. Libermann became the Superior General, while the greater proportion of the membership was drawn from his congregation; at the time of the 'fusion' the Spiritans (Holy Ghost Fathers) had only thirteen members, while Libermann brought with him thirty-four priests.

12. *Notes et Documents Relatifs à la Vie et à l'Oeuvre du Vénérable F. M. P. Libermann* (Paris 1933), iii, 206, 240; cf. vi, 545; Seán Farragher, *Père Leman: Educator and Missionary, 1826-80* (Dublin 1988), 86-7.

13. Nicholas Wiseman was appointed Pro-Vicar Apostolic of the London District in 1847, and Cardinal and first Archbishop of Westminster in 1850.

14. 'Bulletin of the Irish Province', Apr. 1958, 10 (A.I.P.).

15. Koren, op. cit., 180-91.

16. See Leman to Freyd, 2 July 1860, 'Bulletin of the Irish Province', Dec. 1959, 8 (A.I.P.).

17. See pp. 160-2 below.

18. Holley was only twenty-six years of age when he came to Ireland. He was sent because of his excellent command of English. He returned to France after a few months and accompanied Jules Leman, superior of the Irish foundation, to Dublin in October 1859. Holley's health quickly failed, and he died in France in 1861.

19. Moriarty had been a director of the Irish College, Paris, and had visited Libermann at Notre Dame du Gard. He was deeply impressed, as he later told Leman in 1860, and since that time had taken a special interest in the fortunes of the congregation.

20. The Holy Ghost Fathers were initially put in contact with Bishop O'Brien by the Vincentians, who had assumed charge of the Irish College, Paris, in 1858. An outspoken Ultramontane, O'Brien found himself much in sympathy with the congregation.

21. Seán Farragher, 'Account of the Early Days' (n.d.) (A.I.P., Box 2, f. 3).

22. R. F. Walker, 'The Centenary of the Holy Ghost Fathers in Ireland, 1860-1960', *Pagan Missions*, Spring 1960, 18ff.

23. Joseph Byrne, 'A Review of the History and Development of the Irish Province of the C.S.Sp.', 8 (A.I.P.).

24. Ibid.

25. J. T. Murphy (Irish Provincial), 'Schemes of Organisation of the Irish Province' (paper read at the provincial meeting, 3 Jan. 1911) (A.I.P., Box 2, f. 5); Cornelius O'Shea, 'Address of the Provincial to his Council', 13 Aug. 1915 (ibid.); Byrne, op. cit., 17-18.

26. Byrne, op. cit., 12-17.

27. On the completion of their secondary studies, students destined for the priesthood spent some years as prefects in the schools.

28. These conclusions are drawn from a survey of the lists of personnel in the C.S.Sp. *Bulletin*, 1860-1912. It was, of course, natural that larger numbers would leave during the earlier years of training. But the proportion of losses was much greater than could reasonably have been expected.

29. See Murphy, op. cit.; cf. Superior General to Irish Provincial Council, 13 Aug. 1915 (A.I.P., Box 2, f. 5).

30. These figures are approximate but give a faithful indication of the trend. They refer to the number of official assignments of Irish personnel as recorded in the C.S.Sp. *Bulletin*, 1860-93, and to statistics in 'Personnel' (A.I.P., Box 5, f. 1).

31. The arrival of Fr Joseph Shanahan in Southern Nigeria in 1902 marked the turning-point, but it took at least another three decades before sizeable Irish contingents were dispatched to Africa. (See J. P. Jordan, *Bishop Shanahan of Southern Nigeria* (Dublin 1949), 8ff)

32. 'Notices Biographiques', 406 (A.I.P.).

33. The column was entitled 'The Dark Continent'. It first appeared in the *Irish Catholic* on 26 Oct. 1895.

34. By 1960 the Congregation of the Holy Ghost was Ireland's largest missionary institute, with 496 priests overseas. The Irish province possessed a total of

636 priests in all. (See Jeremiah Newman, 'The Priests of Ireland', *I.E.R.*, 5th ser., xcviii (1962), 6) No statistics are available before Newman's survey, but it is probable that already by the 1940s the congregation was the largest of the mission-sending agencies.

Chapter 7: The Society of African Missions, 1878-1920 (pp. 79-88)
1. This chapter is based on E. M. Hogan, 'The Society of African Missions in Ireland, 1877-1916' (M.A. thesis, University College, Cork, 1973).
2. See pp. 40-1, 44 above.
3. E. M. Hogan, 'The Congregation of the Holy Ghost and the Evolution of the Modern Irish Missionary Movement', *Catholic Historical Review*, lxx, 1 (1984), 2.
4. The priests were supplied for the purpose of celebrating Mass in diocesan churches.
5. For a treatment of the Cork appointment see Emmet Larkin, *The Roman Catholic Church and the Creation of the Modern Irish State, 1878-86* (Dublin 1975), 207-12, 223-7, 232-4, cf. Mark Tierney, *Croke of Cashel* (Dublin 1976), 157-62.
6. O'Callaghan was appointed coadjutor to Bishop Delany in 1884. He became bishop of the diocese in 1886.
7. The Blake family had been one of the most prominent in Mayo and Galway ever since its arrival with de Burgo in the twelfth century. Llewellyn Blake served in the Connaught Rangers for some fifteen years before retiring in 1875. Marrying in that year, he received a large estate in Co. Galway from his mother, and ten years later, on her death, he inherited his father's fine estate at Ballinafad, Co. Mayo.
8. Michael Collins, Maurice Slattery and D. O'Connell, 'Memoir of Llewellyn Count Blake' (c. 1948), 23 (S.M.A. Archives, Cork).
9. Zimmermann eventually went to work for the society in Savannah and died there in 1921.

Chapter 8: The Maynooth Mission to China (pp. 91-97)
1. J. M. Fraser, 'Prospects of the Catholic Church in China', *I.E.R.*, 4th ser., xxx, (1911), 277ff.
2. *Far East* (henceforth *F.E.*), Jan. 1918, 13.
3. See Introduction, n. 6.
4. *F.E.*, Mar. 1918, 14.
5. Jeremiah Pigott, 'Maynooth, 1910-17, and the 1914 Concursus', *F.E.*, Oct. 1972, 5.
6. Fr Patrick Cleary, a young Professor of Moral Theology at Maynooth who joined the Columbans in 1918 and became a bishop in China, recalled the failure of the Maynooth Mission to India, which, he said, 'had foundered in a sea of indifference' ('Beginnings Remembered', *F.E.*, Oct. 1966).
7. See pp. 82ff above.

8. *F.E.*, Feb. 1918, 7.
9. The seminary was transferred to 'Dalgan Park', outside Navan, Co. Meath, in June 1941.
10. Michael O'Neill to author, 3 Feb. 1988; cf. *F.E.*, Nov. 1987.
11. 'Blowick's Account of the Early Days' (c. 1921-23) (Columban Central Raheny Archive, vol. i, 48).
12. Patrick Callan, 'Ambivalence towards the Saxon Shilling: The Attitudes of the Catholic Church in Ireland towards Enlistment during the First World War', *Archivium Hibernicum*, xli (1986), 107.
13. Michael O'Neill, '1916 and All That' (Columban Central History Archive, Dalgan Park, Co. Meath, code 1916, vol. i, 17).
14. See pp. 146-9 below.
15. O'Neill, op. cit, 17.

Chapter 9: Bishop Joseph Shanahan and the Foundation of St Patrick's Missionary Society (pp. 98-105)
1. This chapter relies mainly on C. M. Cooke, 'Irish Diocesan Priests in Southern Nigeria, 1920-42' (M.A. thesis, University College, Cork, 1971). Permission from the author to use this material has been obtained.
2. J. P. Jordan, *Bishop Shanahan of Southern Nigeria* (Dublin 1949; 2nd ed., 1971).
3. Mary Purcell, *To Africa With Love: The Biography of Mother Mary Martin* (Dublin 1987).
4. Cooke, op. cit., 53-4.
5. Ibid., 55ff.
6. Ibid., 58.
7. Jordan, op. cit. (2nd ed., 1971), 179-80.
8. Cooke, op. cit., 58.
9. Her amazing story has been told in C. M. Cooke, *Mary Charles Walker: The Nun of Calabar* (Dublin 1980).
10. Cooke, 'Irish Diocesan Priests in Southern Nigeria', 65ff.
11. Purcell, op. cit., 35-46.
12. Cooke, op. cit., 67ff.
13. Ibid., 92.
14. Fr Thomas Greenan to author, 14 Apr. 1988.

Chapter 10: The Development of Medical Missions (pp. 106-126)
1. 'Notes and Queries', *I.E.R.*, 5th ser., xlviii (1936), 427; 'Normae in Appro-bandis Novis Institutis', *Acta Apostolicae Sedis (A.A.S.)*, 1901; *Codicis Iuris Canonici* (Rome 1917), Canon 139. See Alberto Blat, *Commentarium Textus Codicis Iuris Canonici* (Rome 1921), 99; *A.A.S.*, 1921, xiii, 312; Catriona Clear, *Nuns in Nineteenth-Century Ireland* (Dublin 1987), 75.
2. See Sarah Summers, 'Women Energising Women', *The Medical Missionaries of Mary*, xlix, 2 (1987), 58-9.

3. T. L. Bouscaren, *The Canon Law Digest* (Officially Published Documents affecting the Code of Canon Law, 1933-42), ii (Milwaukee 1943), 153. See Appendix B for translation of text.

4. M. A. Mathis, 'Studies and Conferences', *Ecclesial Review*, xcv (1936), 71.

5. Katherine Burton, *According to the Pattern* (Toronto 1946), passim; cf. P*agan Missions*, Sept. 1931, 92ff; E. J. McCarthy, 'Catholic Medical Missions', *Far East*, Feb. 1918; Summers, op. cit., 58-62.

6. Nuns had played the principal role in medical care up to the time of the first prohibitions in the twelfth century (see *Catholic Encyclopaedia*, x (New York 1911), 142-3).

7. Dr McLaren had resided with the sisters during her studies at Montpellier.

8. For an account of her career see *Pagan Missions*, Sept. 1931, 92ff; see also Summers, op. cit., 59ff.

9. See Burton, op. cit., passim; M. M. McGinley, 'Mother Anna Dengel, M.D.— A Pioneer Medical Missionary', *Worldmission* (1980), 27ff; *Medical Mission Sisters News*, x (1980), 2; Monica M. McGinley to author, 25 Jan. 1988.

10. Burton and McGinley give different versions of the course of events at this point. According to McGinley, Anna Dengel considered joining the Franciscan Missionaries of Mary, with whom she had worked in Rawalpindi. Yet she had reservations because such a step would prevent her from continuing to practise surgery and obstetrics. On her way to America, according to McGinley, she made a retreat at Würzburg, Germany, where she was advised to establish her own community.

11. A. G. Cicognani, 28 Nov. 1935 (Archives of the S. Congregation for the Evangelisation of Peoples, Rome: Prot. di Propaganda, N. 4182/1935; R. 81/1); cf. 'Memorandum for His Eminence the Cardinal Prefect', prepared by Mgr Giuseppe Monticone (archivist at Propaganda), July 1935 (ibid., N. 2376/1935, 81/1).

12. Burton, op. cit., 215-16.

13. See Ralph Schran, *History of Medical Services in Nigeria* (Ibadan University Press 1971), 17ff.; cf. Sisters of Our Lady of Apostles, *Tidings*, Centenary Issue (Cork 1976), 38.

14. Sr M. Louis, *Love is the Answer* (Dublin 1964), 98.

15. Ibid.; cf. *Pagan Missions*, Sept. 1931, 92.

16. Sr M. Louis, op. cit., 100.

17. Mgr Francesco Mocchiutti (Archivist, Propaganda) to author, 14 Jan. 1988.

18. Burton, op. cit., 210-11.

19. 'Presentation Sisters' Medical Work in South India' (n.d.) (Presentation Archives, Cork); *Nano Nagle* (Matlock 1961), 24ff; cf. Clear, op. cit., 75 (quoting from *Mother Xavier Murphy* (Presentation Convent, Church Park, Madras 1974)).

20. Mary Purcell, *To Africa With Love: The Biography of Mother Mary Martin* (Dublin 1987), 32. (In the present study her baptismal name, Marie, is used

in preference to the name assumed on her religious profession (Sister Mary of the Incarnation).)

21. See Edward Fischer, *Maybe a Second Spring: The Story of the Missionary Sisters of St Columban in China* (New York 1983), 9; Purcell, op. cit., 29.

22. Purcell, op. cit., 29.

23. John Blowick to Lady Moloney, 19 Aug. 1918; Lady Moloney to John Blowick, 21 Aug. 1918 (Archives of the Missionary Sisters of St Columban (henceforth A.M.S.C.)).

24. Sr Rita Dooney (Archivist, Sisters of St Columban) to author, 14 July 1988; Joan Gumbrielle, *Far East*, Oct. 1972, 12; Patricia Sweeney, ibid., 15-16.

25. Paper read by Fr John Blowick at the Catholic Truth Society meeting, Mansion House, Dublin, Oct. 1917 (copy) (A.M.S.C.).

26. See Joan Gumbrielle, op. cit., 12.

27. John Blowick to Lady Moloney, 19 Aug. 1918 (A.M.S.C.). Blowick also wrote to Catholic medical mission headquarters in France, India, and the U.S.A. Much of the advice received was mistaken. (See Fischer, op. cit., 19)

28. Lady Moloney to John Blowick, 21 Aug. 1918 (A.M.S.C.); cf. Sr Rita Dooney to author, 18 Jan. 1988.

29. John Blowick to Charles Plater, S.J., 15 July 1919 (copy) (A.M.S.C.).

30. See pp. 100-1 above.

31. Marie Martin may have been under the impression that Shanahan agreed with her proposal to found a congregation exclusively dedicated to medical missions (see Marian Keaney, *They Brought the Good News* (Dublin 1980), 128). However, Shanahan envisaged a congregation which would engage in a variety of apostolates (see Purcell, op. cit., 38-9, also 34-5).

32. Purcell, op. cit., 55.

33. Statistics supplied to author by Medical Missionaries of Mary, Drogheda, 1988.

34. Statistics supplied by Holy Rosary Sisters, Dublin, 1988.

35. Statistics supplied by Sisters of St Columban, Co. Wicklow, 1988.

36. Statistics supplied by Sisters of Our Lady of Apostles, Cork, 1988.

37. Sr Philomena Jump, O.S.F., to author, 14 Mar. 1988. Currently the institute has 201 members, of whom 72 are trained for medical work.

38. An article in the *Journal of the Irish Medical Association*, 18 Dec. 1976 (quoted in the Annual General Report of the Medical Missionary Society, University College, Cork, 1976), described the problems as follows: 'The obstacles are clearcut. If he [the doctor] is in training for a speciality (including General Practice), he cannot afford to drop out of the "scheme" he is in, since he has no assurance that on his return a place will be available. If he is a Registrar, he must do his exams and wait to get a Senior Registrar's post. If he is a Senior Registrar, he must do the approved four years and join the rat-race for consultancy.... Thus the modern Irish medical "executive type" doctor has a career structure that constricts his personal liberty and choice.'

39. For information on the society see, *inter alia*, the Annual Reports and the Council Minute Books (Chaplain's Office, University College, Cork); cf. Jeremiah Foley, 'Medical Aid to the Missions' (text of a lecture delivered to a

medical conference in Rome, 1949—unpublished MS, in possession of Maurice Foley); Jeremiah Foley, 'The Irish Guild of St Luke, SS Cosmas and Damian' (unpublished address, 1947—in author's possession); a series of articles in *Studies*, xxxii (1943), 1-24. The author is also indebted to the following who provided written accounts of the society: Dr Robert F. O'Donoghue, 18 Dec. 1987; Dr Patrick Kiely, F.R.C.S., 20 Jan. 1988; Dr Eithne Conlan, 18 Nov. 1987; Rev. Dr James Good, 28 Nov. 1987; Fr Tom Riordan, 17 Dec. 1987.

40. See *First Annual Report of the M.M.S., 1945-46*, 3.
41. James Bastible, 'Nigeria Calling for Irish Doctors', *Studies*, xxxii (1943), 17.
42. A seat on the M.M.S. Council was reserved for the Chairman of the Guild.
43. The length of service required by the M.M.S. varied. From 1946 it was set at two periods of three years with one year's leave. From 1953 volunteers were expected to spend 'at least four years' overseas. From 1961 the length of service had diminished to a period of 'at least two years' (see *Annual Reports*, 1946, 1953 and 1961). From 1958 scholarships were confined to fourth- and final-year medical students (see ibid., 1958, 1959 and 1964).
44. Bursaries were established by the Congregation of the Holy Ghost, St Patrick's Missionary Society, the Society of African Missions and the White Fathers. Apostolic workers from the diocese of Meath also sponsored a scholarship.
45. See *Annual Report of the M.M.S., 1976*.
46. The statistics cited here and below are compiled from a study of the society's reports conducted by the author in January–April 1988.
47. Rev. Professor F. X. Martin, O.S.A., to author, 4 Feb. 1988.

Chapter 11: Laity and the Missionary Movement (pp. 127-141)

1. The Holy Childhood (now called the Society of Missionary Children) and the Society of St Peter the Apostle.
2. Supplemented in some cases by collections among American Catholics.
3. Raymond Hickey (ed.), *Modern Missionary Documents and Africa* (Dublin 1982), 39.
4. Ibid., 65.
5. Ibid., 54-5, 57-9.
6. W. J. Bausch, *Ministry* (Mystic, Conn. 1982), 53, 60.
7. See *Catholic Encyclopaedia*, viii (New York 1910), 748-9.
8. L. Civardi, *A Manual of Catholic Action*, trans. C. C. Martindale (London 1935), 2, 5, 6-9, 16-18, 21-34.
9. Ibid., 19.
10. See León Ó Broin, *Frank Duff: A Biography* (Dublin 1982), 33, 49.
11. See E. M. Hogan, 'Decolonisation or Liberation—A Study of African Independence' (1977), 10-12 (S.M.A. Archives, Cork).
12. The author arrived at this estimate after consultations with some of those directly involved in recruitment of graduates, with missionary bishops and priests, and also after studying statistics garnered from missionary publications.

13. See Hickey, op. cit., 87-93, 147-60.
14. See Ó Broin, op. cit., 49, 58; cf. pp. 69ff.
15. Edwina Gateley, *Psalms of a Laywoman* (Chicago/Los Angeles 1981), ii, 85.
16. Ibid., 90-1.
17. Ibid., 91, 95.
18. Hugh Brady, 'History of Viatores Christi' (1978), 1 (Viatores Christi Office, Harcourt Terrace, Dublin).
19. Ibid., 2.
20. Ibid., 4.
21. Viatores Christi, *Annual Report, 1986,* 54.
22. *Lumen gentium* (henceforth *L.G.*), 31.
23. *Apostolicum actuositatem* (henceforth *A.A.*) (Decree on the Apostolate of Lay People), 26 (in *Vatican Council Documents,* ed. Austin Flannery (Dublin 1975), 790-1); see also *L.G.*, 30.
24. E. J. Kilmartin, 'Lay Participation in the Apostolate of the Hierarchy' in J. H. Provost (ed.), *Official Ministry in a New Age* (Washington D.C. 1981), 89. See also *L.G.*, 31; *A.A.*, 2.
25. Such charisms, it must be understood, are not mere replications of those current in the Early Church, but are proper to each church in its unique historical setting (see T. F. O'Meara, *Theology of Ministry* (New York 1983), 209).
26. *L.G.*, 33; cf. Kilmartin, op. cit., 89.
27. *Ad gentes*, 41.
28. See Gateley, op. cit., 102.
29. Quoted in Leonard Doohan, *The Lay-Centered Church: Theology and Spirituality* (Minneapolis 1984), 13-14.
30. *L.G.*, 32.
31. Goal is an agency founded in 1977 by John O'Shea, a sports journalist, to bring primary health care to developing countries and emergency relief to regions hit by disaster.
32. The Irish Missionary Union was established in 1970 with a view to coordinating missionary endeavour; see p. 172 below.
33. This figure includes missionaries from the Protestant churches.
34. Richard Quinn, *The Missionary Factor in Irish Aid Overseas* (Dublin 1980), 31.
35. See Colm Regan (ed.), *Ireland in an Unequal World* (CONGOOD, Dublin 1984), 66.
36. E. M. Hogan, *Catholic Missionaries and Liberia: A Study of Christian Enterprise in West Africa, 1842-1950* (Cork 1981), 80-115.
37. See James McCaslin, *The Spirituality of Our Founders* (Society of St Columban, Dublin 1986), appx 4, 'Columbans Who Died Violently', 225.
38. Quinn, op. cit., 43ff.
39. Among the more prominent theologians were Juan Luis Segundo, Gustavo Gutiérrez, Leonardo Boff and Jon Sobrino. The Latin American Conference of Bishops made a signal contribution at its meeting at Medellin (1968) and again at Puebla (1979).

40. Donal Dorr, *Option for the Poor* (Dublin 1983); Donal Dorr, *Spirituality and Justice* (Dublin 1984); Brendan Lovett, *Life Before Death: Inculturating Hope* (Phillippines 1986); Peader Kirby, *Lessons in Liberation* (Dublin 1981); Seán MacDonagh, *To Care for the Earth* (Dublin 1987); James O'Halloran, *Living Cells* (Dublin 1984); James O'Halloran, *Pastoral Planning* (Dublin 1986); James O'Halloran, *Go Not Gently* (Dublin 1985); S. J. Healy and Brigid Reynolds, *Social Analysis in the Light of the Gospel* (Dublin 1983); S. J. Healy and Brigid Reynolds, *Ireland Today Reflecting in the Light of the Gospel* (Dublin 1985).

41. Robin Challis, *Sowing the Seeds: The History of Gorta* (Dublin 1986), 12,14-21, 25-33.

42. Ibid., 14ff.

43. Regan, op. cit., 62, 65, 87, 90.

44. See *Bishops of Ireland on Development* (Catholic Communications Institute of Ireland, Dublin, 2 Feb. 1973); cf. *Trócaire 10th Anniversary International Seminar: Report* (Dublin, June 1983), 11-16; Eamonn Casey, 'What We Have Learned', ibid., 1.

Chapter 12: Communicating the Message: The Role of the Missionary Magazine (pp. 145-158)

1. Some of the material in this chapter has already appeared in E. M. Hogan, 'The Motivation of the Modern Irish Missionary Movement, 1912-39', *Journal of Religion in Africa*, x, 3 (1979), 157-73.

2. Response to questionnaire (dated 20 Sept. 1976) circulated among institutes which published magazines and journals at this period. The circulation of the *Irish Catholic* in 1900 was approximately 7,500 copies per issue and well exceeded that of the English-based *Universe* and *Catholic Times*. At a time when linotype and the rotary press were in their infancy this was considered a large figure (see 'Letter to Author' from the manager of the *Irish Catholic*, 3 Mar. 1973).

3. M. J. Phelan, 'The Destiny of the Irish Race', *Far East* (henceforth *F.E.*), Mar. 1919; see *African Missionary* (henceforth *A.M.*), May–June 1917, 10; ibid., May–June 1920, 17; *Missionary Record of the Holy Ghost* (henceforth *M.R.*), May 1919; *F.E.*, Apr., 1918, 4; ibid., Jan. 1918, 3.

4. *F.E.*, July 1919, 3.

5. *Missionary Annals* (henceforth *M.A.*), Oct. 1921, 2; see *A.M.*, July–Aug. 1921; *M.A.*, Sept. 1920, 4; ibid., Feb. 1922, 22; *F.E.*, Dec. 1921, 185.

6. *M.A.*, Nov. 1921, 9.

7. *F.E.*, Dec. 1921, 185.

8. See e.g. *M.A.*, Mar. 1923, 42; *F.E.*, Nov. 1922, 2; *M.A.*, Aug. 1923, 145; ibid., June 1923, 102 *inter al.*

9. *A.M.*, May–June 1917, 5-6.

10. Ibid.; see also ibid., May–June 1919, 9; ibid., Sept.–Oct. 1919, 20; *M.R.*, Jan. 1920, 1; *M.A.*, Apr. 1921, 1; *F.E.*, Nov. 1918, 1-2.

11. See e.g. F. A. Forbes, 'Marching Song of the African Missions', *A.M.*, Nov.–Dec. 1918, 5.
12. Ibid., Jan. 1920, 2.
13. *M.A.*, July 1921, 3.
14. *A.M.*, July–Sept. 1914, 7.
15. Ibid., Jan.–Feb. 1922, 130.
16. Ibid., May–June 1922, 169.
17. See e.g. ibid., Apr.–June 1914, 3; J. F. Murphy 'Irish Missionaries', ibid., Mar.–Apr. 1917; ibid., May–June 1917; 'Native Clergy in Africa', ibid., Nov.–Dec. 1917 (repr. from *Catholic Missions* (New York), Sept. 1917); M. Collins, 'Ireland's Second Spring', ibid., Mar.–Apr. 1920, 18-19; *M.A.*, Apr. 1921, 3 ibid., June 1920, 153; *F.E.*, Jan. 1918, 1; ibid., Sept. 1918, 2; ibid., Jan. 1920, 1; ibid., Apr. 1921, 49; *A.M.*, 1924, 122; ibid., Nov.–Dec. 1923, 115.
18. *A.M.*, Apr.–June 1914; ibid., Jan.–Mar. 1914, 1; *M.R.*, May 1919, 1-2, 5; *M.A.*, Sept. 1921, 1-2; *F.E.*, Apr. 1918; ibid., July 1919, 3.
19. The early medieval movement was the product of a Church largely monastic in structure and spirit. Irish monks went into exile in order to practise a higher form of asceticism. (See Tomás Ó Fiaich, 'The Beginnings of Christianity ' in T. W. Moody and F. X. Martin (ed.), *The Course of Irish History* (Cork 1967), 74)
20. *A.M.*, Apr.–June 1914, 3.
21. Ibid., Jan.–Feb. 1917, 13; *M.A.*, Sept. 1920, 1; ibid., Oct. 1920, 4; ibid., Feb. 1920, 15; see also ibid., Aug. 1924, 145; *F.E.*, July 1918, 4; ibid., Aug. 1927, 162.
22. *M.A.*, Aug. 1924, 145.
23. Ibid., Dec. 1920, 13.
24. *F.E.*, Aug. 1927, 162.
25. 'Home Notes', *M.A.*, Feb. 1920, 14.
26. *Lumen gentium*, 14-16.
27. *A.M.*, Jan.–Feb. 1917, 13. See also J. F. Murphy, 'Irish Missionaries', ibid., Mar.–Apr. 1917; *M.A.*, Aug. 1920, 1-2; ibid., Mar. 1920.
28. *M.A.*, May 1921, 1; ibid., June 1923, 102; *F.E.*, May 1922, 66.
29. *A.M.*, Mar.–Apr. 1923, 35.
30. Ibid., Jan.–Feb. 1917, 13; cf. ibid., Mar.–Apr. 1917; *M.A.*, Sept. 1924, 162; *F.E.*, Spring 1921, 49; see also *A.M.*, July–Aug. 1922, 183.
31. *A.M.*, July–Sept. 1914, 7; cf. ibid., May–June 1920, 17; *M.A.*, Dec. 1920, 10; ibid., July 1921, 3; *A.M.*, Mar.–Apr. 1922, 141.
32. *A.M.*, Oct.–Dec. 1914, 227.
33. Ibid., 10ff.
34. *M.A.*, June 1922, 133.
35. *A.M.*, May–June 1915, 6.
36. Ibid., Nov.–Dec. 1915, 6.
37. *F.E.*, Aug. 1918, 1; see ibid., Feb. 1919, 3.

38. 'Why Africa?', *A.M.*, Oct.–Dec. 1914, 7; ibid., Sept.–Oct. 1915, 5ff; ibid., Sept.–Oct. 1916, 4-5; ibid., July–Aug. 1921, 67; *M.A.*, June 1921, 7; *A.M.*, Jan.–Feb. 1923, 18.
39. 'Africa's Native Clergy', *A.M.*, July–Aug. 1917, 2-5; 'Native Priests', ibid., 11; 'The Real Value of the Catechist', ibid., July–Aug. 1918, 7-8; 'The Native Catechist', ibid., July–Aug. 1919, 13; 'A Native Clergy for Africa', ibid., Jan.–Feb. 1921, 2; 'Mgr Broderick Interviewed', ibid., Mar.–Apr. 1921, 25; 'The Catechists', *M.A.*, Feb. 1920, 1; Joseph Shanahan, 'How the Native Catechist Helps', ibid., June 1921, 7; Joseph Shanahan, 'First Native Seminary in Southern Nigeria', ibid., Nov. 1924, 203.
40. *A.M.*, May–June 1919, 13.
41. 'Mgr Broderick Interviewed', ibid., Mar.–Apr. 1921, 25.
42. Ibid.

Chapter 13: Style and Structure of the Irish Missionary Movement (pp. 159-173)
1. Seán Farragher, 'Account of the Early Days' (n.d.) (A.I.P., Box 2, f. 3).
2. F. Devoucoux to A. Planque, 27 Apr. 1878 (S.M.A. Generalate Archives, Rome, 14/1, 32222).
3. Melchior de Marion Bresillac, *Souvenirs de Douze Ans de Mission* (Rome 1986), 484.
4. Ibid., 495.
5. E. M. Hogan, 'The Congregation of the Holy Ghost and the Evolution of the Modern Irish Missionary Movement', *Catholic Historical Review*, lxx, 1 (1984), 2n.
6. Ibid.
7. Ibid.
8. Later, after he became better informed, he was to change his views on the colonial clergy.
9. See pp. 41-3 above.
10. William Barrett, *The Red Lacquered Gate: The Biography of Bishop Galvin, Co-Founder of the Columban Fathers* (New York 1967), 75.
11. E. M. Hogan, *Catholic Missionaries and Liberia: A Study of Christian Enterprise in West Africa, 1842-1950* (Cork 1981), 32.
12. In the early years of the century the average tour of duty for Irish missionaries was five years. After the Second World War this was commonly reduced to three years.
13. Hogan, op. cit., 31, 222 (n. 84).
14. See Joseph McGlade, 'The Missions: Africa and the Orient' in Corish, *Ir. Catholicism*, v (Dublin 1967), 29-30; cf. D. Lujo Schorer, *Statistica Circumscriptionum Ecclesiasticarum* (Rome 1958); *Report from Irish Missionary Union* (Dublin, July–Sept. 1987); additional figures supplied to author by Sedos (Rome), Fr Paul Chatigné (Paris), Fr Jan Gooren (Holland) and by the Pontifical Aid Societies of Belgium, Germany and Holland.

The author has found it impossible to locate comprehensive statistics despite approaches to the Congregation for the Evangelisation of Peoples and to Sedos. However, the following figures give a clear indication of the statistical trend.

Priests deployed in Africa and Asia in 1957: France 3,069; Belgium 2,630; Holland 2,119; Ireland 1,403; Italy 1,400; Germany 734; Spain 437.

Sisters deployed in Africa in 1957: Germany 2,570; France 1,901; Belgium 1,896; Ireland 1,589; Italy 924; Holland 348; Spain 368.

Priests, sisters and brothers deployed in Third World countries in 1970: France 8,890; Holland 4,923; Ireland 7,120; Belgium 5,520; Germany 6,610.

Priests, sisters and brothers deployed in Third World countries in 1985: France 7,140; Holland 3,650; Ireland 5,225; Belgium 3,843; Germany 5,427.

15. See Diarmuid Ó Laoghaire, 'Irish Spirituality in Modern Times' in Michael Maher (ed.), *Irish Spirituality* (Dublin 1985), 124ff.
16. Lamin Sanneh, *West African Christianity: The Religious Impact* (New York 1983), 68.
17. Elizabeth Isichei, *Varieties of Christian Experience in Nigeria* (London 1982), 191ff.
18. Hogan, op. cit., 30-41.
19. Ibid., 37.
20. Ibid.
21. Ibid., 222.
22. The details of this incident were obtained from interviews with several Irish missionaries who worked in Nigeria during the 1930s.
23. Hogan, op. cit., 42-3, 172-3.
24. C. M. Cooke, 'Irish Diocesan Priests in Southern Nigeria, 1920-42' (M.A. thesis, University College, Cork, 1971), 175; Very Rev. Fr Peter O'Reilly (Superior General) to author, 24 May 1973.

Chapter 14: Epilogue: Towards the Future (pp. 173-192)

1. *Evangelii nuntiandi* (henceforth *E.N.*), 52.
2. From the time of its formation in 1622 Propaganda Fide had sought to render the right of patronage (previously enjoyed by the Portuguese and Spanish monarchies) obsolete by nominating its own vicars apostolic whenever jurisdictions became vacant, or by creating new jurisdictions directly under its supervision. Ultimately the success of Propaganda's efforts rested on the formation of indigenous clergy who in time would provide the local ecclesiastical leadership. The great religious orders which were to continue to dominate the missionary movement into the second half of the nineteenth century (also the first of the exclusively missionary societies, the Paris Foreign Missions Society) subscribed in theory to the idea of a native clergy, but in practice did little to make it a reality, often arguing that the time was inopportune or that the idea was impractical. Proponents of the

idea recognised behind these excuses the influences of racial prejudice and a conservatism based on fear and selfishness. Despite the best efforts of Propaganda, attitudes were to change only very gradually. In Africa, one of the major missionary theatres, it was well into the twentieth century before a substantial cadre of indigenous clergy was created and the goal of an indigenous episcopate could be realised. (See E. M. Hogan, 'The Views of Mgr de Marion Bresillac on Mission' in 'Report of the Charism–Mission–Spirituality Commission of the Society of African Missions' (MS in S.M.A. Generalate Archives, Rome))

3. See *Maximum illud*, 1919, in Raymond Hickey (ed.), *Modern Missionary Documents and Africa* (Dublin 1982), 30.
4. *Fidei donum* in Hickey, op, cit., 118.
5. *Ad gentes* (henceforth *A.G.*), 2.
6. Ibid., 6.
7. *Lumen gentium* (henceforth *L.G.*), 23.
8. See John Power, *Mission Theology Today* (New York 1971), 56.
9. *A.G.*, 20.
10. Anthony Bellagamba, 'The Missionary Movement of the Churches of the South', *African Christian Studies* (Nairobi) (Dec. 1987), 81-110.
11. It is true that the Franciscan Missionaries of Mary was founded in India in 1877. However, it would be wrong to categorise this foundation as 'indigenous' or inspired by a local church. The foundress and those who formed the nucleus of the institute were former sisters of the Society of Marie Reparatrice, almost all Europeans.
12. Yves Congar and Karl Rahner in the earlier stages and in later years Henri de Lubac, Jean Danielou, Josef Ratzinger *inter alia*.
13. *L.G.*, 9, 10.
14. Ibid., 5.
15. Ibid., 1; see Power, op. cit., 17-32; quotation on p. 28.
16. *L.G.*, 1.
17. *Gaudium et spes* (henceforth *G.S.*), 1.
18. *L.G.*, 16-18.
19. *Nostra aestate* (1965), 2.
20. Ibid.
21. *G.S.*, 2.
22. *L.G.*, 3.
23. *A.G.*, 2.
24. Ibid., 3.
25. Ibid., 8, 9.
26. Ibid., 3, 9.
27. Ibid., 12.
28. Ibid., 7.
29. Ibid., 5.
30. Ibid., 12.

31. Ibid., 22.
32. Ibid., 5.
33. Ibid., 6.
34. Ibid.
35. Ibid.
36. The influence exercised by bishops from missionary regions on the deliberations of the synod was to be more considerable than that exercised on the Council. Missionary bishops had indeed helped to shape the Conciliar statements on missions; however, in most cases interventions were made on an individual basis. Vatican II's decrees constituting regional episcopal conferences created a framework for greater co-ordination among missionary bishops in their approach to theological and pastoral questions. This was soon to bear fruit. The Second General Conference of Latin American Bishops at Medellin (Columbia) in 1968 brought Vatican II's theology of development and liberation onto a new plane and did much to set the agenda of the synod on that topic. No less influential at the synod was the contribution of the Episcopal Conference of African Bishops which submitted a substantial report on the work of evangelisation in their continent. This addressed a variety of topics including human development and liberation, dialogue with non-Christian religions, inculturation and primary evangelisation—topics which all featured in *Evangelii nuntiandi* and which bear the imprint of the African report.
37. The term 'missionary' was used to describe the nature of the Church, but also to describe an aspect of that nature (e.g. missionary enterprise).
38. *E.N.*, 18.
39. Ibid.
40. Ibid., 20.
41. Ibid., 17.
42. Ibid., 15.
43. Ibid., 24.
44. *A.G.*, 6.
45. *E.N.*, 52.
46. Bede McGregor, 'Commentary on *Evangelii nuntiandi*', *Doctrine and Life*, Special Issue (Mar.–Apr. 1977), 82.
47. *E.N.*, 35.
48. Ibid., 37.
49. See McGregor, op. cit., 72.
50. *E.N.*, 29.
51. See Bishops' Council for Research and Development, 'Irish Priests and Religious, Personnel Projection, 1986-96' (Maynooth 1987).
52. See the following: Editorial, *Intercom* (Catholic Communications Institute of Ireland, Dublin), May 1987, 3; 'Vocations in Ireland' (Reports of the Bishops' Council for Research and Development, Maynooth 1986 and 1987); John Weafer and Ann Breslin, 'Irish Catholic Clergy and Religious, 1970-81'

(Research and Development, Maynooth 1982); Austin Flannery, 'Religious and Dwindling Numbers', *Religious Life Review,* xxvi (Mar.–Apr. 1988) 'Reports on Irish Missionary Personnel' (Irish Missionary Union, Dublin); 'Irish Priests and Religious, Personnel Projection, 1986-96, op. cit.

53. Those going overseas under the aegis of the Viatores Christi, V.M.M., V.S.O and I.M.U. The term missionary may also be applied to those inspired by strong religious motivation who are sponsored by the non-denominational agencies.

54. Testimony to the good health of the lay movement is the fact that in 1984 180 unsolicited inquiries were made to the I.M.U. The extent to which this was related to the recession remains to be tested but it is unlikely that the recession was a major factor since the majority of applicants were actually in employment.

55. See Raymond Hostie, *The Life and Death of Religious Orders,* trans. from the French (Washington D.C. 1983); L. Cada et al., *Reshaping the Coming Age of Religious Life* (New York 1979); Jeremiah Newman, 'Vocations in Ireland, 1966', *Christus Rex,* xxi, 2 (1966); D. Ó Murchú, *The Seed Must Die* (Dublin 1980); cf. M. Corbett and D. Ó Murchú, 'From Large to Small Community: Reflections on Two Workshops', *Religious Life Review,* xxvii (May–June 1988), 122-8; Austin Flannery, 'Religious and Dwindling Numbers', ibid., xxvi (Mar.–Apr. 1988), 91-6; cf. J. A. Weafer, 'Change and Continuity in Irish Religion, 1974-84', *Doctrine and Life,* xxxvi (Dec. 1986), 507-17; Ann Breslin and John Weafer, *Religious Beliefs, Practice and Moral Attitudes: A Comparison of Two Surveys, 1974-84* (Bishops' Council for Research and Development, Maynooth 1985); *Intercom,* May 1987; T. Hanna, 'The Catholic Youth—An Endangered Species', *The Furrow,* xxxviii (1987).

56. Austin Flannery, 'Religious and Dwindling Numbers', *Religious Life Review,* xxvi (May–June 1988), 95-6.

57. Donal Neary, 'Vocations to Priesthood and Religious Life', *Intercom,* May 1987, 8.

58. Jeremiah Newman, 'Vocations in Ireland, 1966', *Christus Rex,* xxi, 2 (1966).

59. J. A. Weafer, 'Change and Continuity in Irish Religion, 1974-84', *Doctrine and Life,* xxvi (1986), 507; see also J. A. Weafer, 'Vocations: A Review of National and International Trends', *The Furrow,* xxxix (1988), 508.

Select Bibliography

Introductory Note

Detailed bibliographical references are to be found in the notes to each chapter. Here it is intended only to present a selection of the more important sources. The modern Irish missionary movement is as yet poorly documented, for reasons already discussed in the Introduction to this book (see pp. 7-8 above). Moreover, the documentation, such as it is, has been uneven, tending to concentrate on certain missionary agencies and personalities to the neglect of others no less important. Nor has the perspective always been sufficiently critical. Some excellent published and unpublished studies are available on selective topics. But the value of much of the material and, most notably, the extensive magazine material and many of the missionary biographies has been limited by a desire to create an inspirational literature. As to primary source material, there is little uniformity in the quality of the various archival holdings. Some are well organised; others are virtually inaccessible. The very multiplicity of these holdings and their uncertain standard of organisation, together with the scarcity of 'serious' primary studies, poses immense problems to the production of a general survey such as is attempted in this book. The author sought to overcome these difficulties by in many cases consulting the archivists (or librarians) of the various missionary institutes and agencies directly on specific questions relating to his subject. Nonetheless, primary source material was also procured through personal consultation of archives and libraries in Ireland and overseas over a period of some sixteen years.

(A) REPOSITORIES PROVIDING PRIMARY SOURCE MATERIAL
(Records, Reports, Statistical Information, Memoirs, Correspondence)

Agency for Personal Service Overseas (APSO), Fitzwilliam Square, Dublin

All Hallows College, Drumcondra, Dublin

Assumption Sisters, Ballynahinch, Co. Down

Congregation of the Holy Ghost: Archives of the Irish Province, Richmond Avenue South, Dublin (A.I.P.)

Convent of Mercy, Lower Baggot Street, Dublin

Convent of St Louis, Monaghan

Concern, Upper Camden Street, Dublin

Dominican Convent, Cabra, Dublin

Franciscan Missionary Sisters for Africa, Dundalk, Co. Louth

Gorta, Herbert Street, Dublin

Irish Christian Brothers, Booterstown, Co. Dublin

Loreto Sisters, Rathfarnham, Dublin

Marist Provincial Office, Sacred Heart College, Johannesburg, South Africa

Medical Mission Sisters, Philadelphia (8400 Pine Road, Pa. 1911)

Medical Missionaries of Mary, Drogheda, Co. Louth

Medical Missionary Society, University College, Cork (Chaplain's Office, U.C.C.)

Mill Hill Missionaries, St Joseph's College, Mill Hill, London

Missionary Sisters of St Columban: Archives, Magheramore, Co. Wicklow (A.M.S.C.)

Missionary Sisters of the Holy Rosary, Blackrock, Co. Dublin

Nazareth House, Hammersmith Road, London

Patrician Brothers: Generalate Office, Tullow, Co. Carlow

Presentation Brothers, Mount St Joseph, Cork

Presentation Sisters, Douglas Street, Cork (Office for the Cause of Nano Nagle)

Propaganda Fide: Archives of the Sacred Congregation for the Evangelisation of Peoples, Via de Propaganda, Rome

St Columban's Missionary Society: Central Research Service, Dalgan Park, Navan, Co. Meath; Central History Archive, ibid.; Columban Central Raheny Archive, Dublin

St Mary's Dominican Priory, Tallaght, Co. Dublin

St Patrick's Missionary Society, Kiltegan

Sisters of Our Lady of Apostles, Cork

Society of African Missions: Generalate Archives, Via della Nocetta, Rome; Irish Provincial Archives, Blackrock, Cork

Trócaire: The Catholic Agency for World Development, Booterstown Avenue, Co. Dublin

Viatores Christi, Harcourt Terrace, Dublin

Vincentian Community, Provincial House, Cabra Road, Dublin

Volunteer Missionary Movement, Grace Park Road, Dublin

(B) MANUSCRIPT SOURCES

Association for the Propagation of the Faith, Minute Book of the Standing Committee, Dublin (Archives of Pontifical Aid Societies, Lower Rathmines Road, Dublin)

Blowick, John, 'Blowick's Account of the Early Days' (c. 1921-23) (Columban Central Raheny Archive, vol. i, 48)

Bolster, Angela, 'Expansion of Congregation of Sisters of Mercy' (Chapter 24 of 'Documentary Study for the Canonisation Process of Catherine McAuley', Rome 1985)

Brady, Hugh, 'History of Viatores Christi' (1978) (Viatores Christi Office, Harcourt Terrace, Dublin)

'Bulletin of the Irish Province' (A.I.P.)

Byrne, Joseph, 'A Review of the History and Development of the Irish Province of the C.S.Sp.' (A.I.P.)

Farragher, Seán, 'Account of the Early Days' (n.d.) (A.I.P., Box 2, f. 3)

Foley, Jeremiah, 'Medical Aid to the Missions' (text of a lecture delivered to a medical conference in Rome, 1949; MS in possession of Maurice Foley, Glasheen Road, Cork)

Gantly, Patrick, 'History of the Society of African Missions, 1856-1900' (MS in preparation for publication, S.M.A. Generalate Archives, Rome)

Medical Missionary Society, Annual Reports and Council Minute Books (Chaplain's Office, University College, Cork)

O'Neill, Michael, '1916 and All That' (Columban Central History Archive, Dalgan Park, Navan, Co. Meath, code 1916, vol. i, 17)

'Presentation Sisters' Medical Work in South India' (n.d.) (Presentation Convent, Douglas Street, Cork)

'Prospectus for a College' (All Hallows College, Dublin, Archive, 38/2, K²)

Questionnaire circulated in 1973 by the author among all institutes of sisters (located in Ireland) known to have been involved in missionary work before 1900. Thirty-two replies were received. The purpose of the questionnaire was to discover the extent of Irish involvement in non-Christian missions during the nineteenth century.

(C) PRINTED SOURCES

Africa (Journal of St Patrick's Missionary Society, Kiltegan) (1939-)

The African Missionary (Journal of the Society of African Missions, Irish Province) (1914-)

Annals of the Association for the Propagation of the Faith (Paris/Dublin 1838-1930) (subsequently entitled *Missions Catholiques / Pagan Missions*)

Barrett, William, *The Red Lacquered Gate: The Biography of Bishop Galvin, Co-Founder of the Columban Fathers* (New York 1967)

Bellagamba, Anthony, 'The Missionary Movement of the Churches of the South', *African Christian Studies* (Nairobi) (Dec. 1987), 81-110

Bishops of Ireland, *Bishops of Ireland on Development* (Catholic Communications Institute of Ireland, Dublin, 2 Feb. 1973)

Boucher, M., 'Ex Glande Quercus: Bishop Griffith at the Cape', *Historia*, ii, 4 (Dec. 1966), 245-55

Brain, J. B. (ed.), *The Cape Diary of Bishop Patrick Raymond Griffith for the years 1837-39* (Cape Town 1988)

Brown, W. E., *The Catholic Church in South Africa* (London 1960)

Burton, Katherine, *According to the Pattern* (The Story of Dr Agnes McLaren and the Society of Catholic Medical Missionaries) (Toronto 1946)

Callan, Patrick, 'Ambivalence towards the Saxon Shilling:The Attitudes of the Catholic Church in Ireland towards Enlistment during the First World War', *Archivium Hibernicum*, xli (1986), 99-111

Canning, A. M., 'South America' in P. J. Corish (ed.), *A History of Irish Catholicism*, vi (Dublin 1971)

Capuchin Annual (1955), 254-376

Carty, Xavier, *Irish Missionaries* (Dublin 1970)

A Centenary Tribute to the Founder of the Holy Rosary Sisters (Dublin 1971)

Challis, Robin, *Sowing the Seeds: The History of Gorta* (Dublin 1986)

The Christian Brothers Education Record (Dublin 1892)

Colmcille, Mother Mary, *First the Blade: History of the I.B.V.M. (Loreto) in India, 1841-1962* (Calcutta 1986)

Condon, Kevin, *The Missionary College of All Hallows, 1842-91* (Dublin 1986)

Cooke, Colm M., 'Irish Diocesan Priests in Southern Nigeria, 1920-42' (M.A. thesis, University College, Cork, 1971)

——*Mary Charles Walker: The Nun of Calabar* (Dublin 1980)

——'The Modern Irish Missionary Movement', *Archivium Hibernicum,* xxxv (1980), 234-46

Doyle, Bernard Francis, 'South Africa' in P. J. Corish (ed.), *A History of Irish Catholicism,* vi (Dublin 1971)

Ensign (Journal of the Pontifical Missionary Union, Dublin)

The Far East (Journal of the Missionary Society of St Columban) (1918-)

Farragher, Seán P., *Père Leman, Educator and Missionary, 1826-80* (Dublin 1988)

Finnegan, Francis, 'Irish Missionaries in Bengal', *I.E.R.,* 5th ser., xcix (1963), 159ff

Fischer, Edward, *Maybe a Second Spring: The Story of the Missionary Sisters of St Columban in China* (New York 1983)

Fraser, J. M., 'Prospects of the Catholic Church in China', *I.E.R.,* 4th ser., xxx (1911), 277ff

Gateley, Edwina, *Psalms of a Laywoman,* ii (Chicago/Los Angeles 1981)

Gavan Duffy, Thomas, 'An Irish Missionary Episode', *I.E.R.,* 5th ser., xvii (1921), 465ff

Hally, Cyril, 'A Hundred Years of Irish Missionary Effort', *The Furrow,* xxii (1971), 327-49

Hickey, Raymond (ed.), *Modern Missionary Documents and Africa* (Dublin 1982)

Hogan, Edmund M., 'African Conversion to Roman Catholicism', *African Ecclesial Review,* xxiv, 2 (Apr. 1982), 71-80

——*Catholic Missionaries and Liberia: A Study of Christian Enterprise in West Africa, 1842-1950* (Cork 1981)

——'The Congregation of the Holy Ghost and the Evolution of the Modern Irish Missionary Movement', *Catholic Historical Review,* lxx, 1 (1984), 1-14

——'The Modern Irish Missionary Movement', *Ireland Today,* no. 1026 (Mar 1986), 7-10

——'The Motivation of the Modern Irish Missionary Movement, 1912-39', *Journal of Religion in Africa,* x, 3 (1979), 157-73

——'The Society of African Missions in Ireland, 1877-1916' (M.A. thesis, University College, Cork, 1973)

Irish Catholic Directory (1839-1909)

Irish Missionary Union Brochure (Dublin 1972)

Jedin, Hubert, et al. (ed.), *History of the Church,* vii-x (London 1981)

Jordan, J. P., *Bishop Shanahan of Southern Nigeria* (Dublin 1949; 2nd ed., 1971)

Joyful Mother of Children (Biography of Mother Frances Mary Teresa Ball) (Dublin 1961)

Keaney, Marian, *They Brought the Good News: Modern Irish Missionaries* (Dublin 1980)

Keenan, Desmond J., *The Catholic Church in Nineteenth-Century Ireland* (Dublin 1983)

Kelly, Patrick, 'A Man of Ideas', *Far East,* Oct. 1972, 8-9

Kielt, J. A., 'The Maynooth Mission to China', *I.E.R.*, 5th ser., cvi (1966), 193-204

Koren, Henry, *The Spiritans* (Pittsburgh 1958)

Louis, Sr M., *Love is the Answer* (Biography of Mother Kevin, foundress of the Franciscan Missionary Sisters for Africa) (Dublin 1964)

McCarthy, E. J., 'Catholic Medical Missions', *Far East*, Feb. 1918, 9-12

McCaslin, James, *The Spirituality of Our Founders* (Society of St Columban, Dublin 1986)

McGinley, Monica M., 'Mother Anna Dengel, M.D.—A Pioneer Medical Missionary', *Worldmission* (1980), 27-31

McGlade, Joseph, 'The Missions: Africa and the Orient' in P. J. Corish (ed.), *A History of Irish Catholicism*, v (Dublin 1967)

McGregor, Bede, 'Commentary on *Evangelii nuntiandi*', *Doctrine and Life*, Special Issue (Mar.–Apr. 1977), 53-97

The Medical Missionaries of Mary (Journal of the Medical Missionaries of Mary) Jubilee Edition, xlix, 2 (1987)

Meehan, Denis, 'Maynooth and the Missions', *I.E.R.*, 5th ser., lxvi (1945), 224-37

Metzler, Josef, 'Die Missionen in Sûdafrica und auf den Ostafrikanischen Inseln', *Sacrae Congregationis de Propaganda Fide Memoria Rerum*, iii, 1, ed. Josef Metzler (Rome 1973)

Missionary Annals (Journal of the Congregation of the Holy Ghost—first appeared under the title *Missionary Record of the Holy Ghost* in 1919)

'The Modern Irish Missionary Movement', *Herder Correspondence*, iv (1967), 204-13

Notes et Documents Relatifs à la Vie et à l'Oeuvre du Vénérable F. M. P. Libermann, iii (Paris 1933)

Ó Broin, León *Frank Duff: A Biography* (Dublin 1982)

O'Donnell, T. J., 'Centenary of All Hallows College', *Studies*, xxxi (1942), 430ff

O'Haire, James, *Recollections of Twelve Years' Residence as a Missionary Priest in the Western District of the Cape of Good Hope* (Dublin c. 1877)

Pigott, Jeremiah, 'Maynooth, 1910-17, and the 1914 Concursus', *Far East*, Oct. 1972, 5-7

Purcell, Mary, *The Story of the Vincentians* (Dublin 1973)

——*To Africa With Love: The Biography of Mother Mary Martin* (Dublin 1987)

Quinn, Richard, *The Missionary Factor in Irish Aid Overseas* (Dublin 1980)

Regan, Colm (ed.), *Ireland in an Unequal World* (Dublin 1984)

Russell, Henry J., *Ireland's Nuns in Africa* (Irish News Ltd, Belfast n.d.)

Summers, Sarah, 'Women Energising Women', *The Medical Missionaries of Mary*, xlix, 2 (1987), 58-61

Tidings (Journal of the Sisters of Our Lady of Apostles), Centenary Issue (Cork 1976)

Towey, John, *Irish De La Salle Brothers in Christian Education* (Dublin 1980)

Trócaire, *10th Anniversary International Seminar: Report* (Dublin, June 1983)

Walker, R. F., 'The Centenary of the Holy Ghost Fathers in Ireland, 1860-1960', *Pagan Missions*, Spring 1960, 18ff

Walsh, T. J., *Nano Nagle and the Presentation Sisters* (Cork 1959; repr. Kildare 1980)

Weafer, John A., 'Change and Continuity in Irish Religion, 1974-84', *Doctrine and Life*, xxxvi (Dec. 1986), 507-17

Index